FIVE GREAT PLAYS
FROM THE FRENCH THEATER

THE CID—Corneille based his illustrious drama on the exploits of Spain's most popular hero. In vigorous, exalted verse he tells a storm-swept tale of love and honor contending for victory.

PHAEDRA—The title role in Racine's treatment of Euripides' theme has become the PIÈCE DE RÉSISTANCE of French tragediennes. The play is a remarkable exploration of the passion-obsessed mind.

THE INTELLECTUAL LADIES—In Molière's final masterpiece, one of the world's great playwrights attacks pedantry and preciosity with high comedy.

THE GAME OF LOVE AND CHANCE—Marivaux' charming and witty comedy, written in 1730, still delights French audiences.

THE BARBER OF SEVILLE—Uninhibited comedy, robust intrigue, and vivid characterization mark this work by the redoubtable satirist Beaumarchais.

BANTAM WORLD DRAMA

JOHN GASSNER

*Late Sterling Professor of
Dramatic Literature
Yale University*

GENERAL EDITOR,
The Library of World Drama

CLASSICAL FRENCH DRAMA

EDITED AND
TRANSLATED BY
WALLACE FOWLIE
DUKE UNIVERSITY

BANTAM BOOKS
TORONTO · NEW YORK · LONDON

CLASSICAL FRENCH DRAMA
Bantam Classic edition published April 1962
2nd printing ...... January 1968

CAUTION: *All rights reserved. These plays in their printed form are designed for the reading public only. All dramatic, motion picture, radio, television and other rights in them are fully protected by copyright in the United States of America, the British Empire, including the Dominion of Canada, and all other countries of the Copyright Union. No performance, professional or amateur, nor any broadcast, nor any public reading or recitation may be given without written permission in advance.*

All professional inquiries in the U.S.A. and Canada should be addressed to Bantam Books, Inc., 271 Madison Avenue, New York, N.Y. 10016.
Copyright, 1962, by Bantam Books, Inc.
This book may not be reproduced in whole or in part, by mimeograph or any other means, without permission.

Published simultaneously in the United States and Canada

Bantam Books are published by Bantam Books, Inc., a subsidiary of Grosset & Dunlap, Inc. Its trade-mark, consisting of the words "Bantam Books" and the portrayal of a bantam, is registered in the United States Patent Office and in other countries. Marca Registrada. Bantam Books, Inc., 271 Madison Avenue, New York, N.Y. 10016.

PRINTED IN THE UNITED STATES OF AMERICA

Contents

FRENCH "CLASSICISM" by John Gassner	1
Foreword by Wallace Fowlie	7
THE CID by Pierre Corneille	9
PHAEDRA by Jean Racine	69
THE INTELLECTUAL LADIES by Molière	125
THE GAME OF LOVE AND CHANCE by Pierre Marivaux	169
THE BARBER OF SEVILLE by Pierre-Augustin Beaumarchais	217
Selected Bibliography	276

French "Classicism"

BY

JOHN GASSNER

Shakespeare had been dead twenty years when the French theater acquired its first masterpiece, Corneille's *Le Cid*, in 1636 or early in January 1637, as recent scholarship would have it. Although medieval drama had ended in France by 1548, when the performance of the Mysteries and Miracles, the customary biblical and saint plays, was prohibited by law, the French theater arrived at greatness *after,* not during, the Renaissance. But once launched on its distinguished career, it produced a succession of masterworks for nearly sixty years, almost twice the life-span of the Elizabethan dramatic period. Moreover, France continued to produce noteworthy plays, though only in the field of comedy, for nearly another century. The last comic masterpieces, Beaumarchais' *Le Barbier de Séville* and *Le Mariage de Figaro,* appeared in 1775 and 1784, one year before the American and five years before the French Revolution, respectively. When this first great period of the French theater, the classic and the pseudo-classic, started, the monarchy was well on its way toward achieving supremacy as the palladium of law, order, and reason. When the period ended with the social dynamite of *The Marriage of Figaro,* which it took less wit to write than to get past the censorship, the monarchy of the Bourbons, the *ancien régime,* was bankrupt and ready for demolition.

I

It would be difficult to exaggerate the significance of the classic French drama in the history of the European theater; one way to estimate its importance is to note the many efforts that were made to assimilate French classicism in other lands or to reject its influence not only in foreign lands, but in France itself. It took one artistic revolution, in the last third of the eighteenth century, to overcome this influence in Germany; and it took another, in the first third of the nineteenth, to overcome it in France.

As for the masterpieces of French classicism themselves, it is fortunately not at all a question of their having been banished from the stage. In the case of the chief tragic poets, Pierre Corneille (1606–1684) and Jean Racine (1639–1699), their "influence" may have vanished, but the life in their masterpieces has remained remarkably undiminished. The best of their plays, especially those in the present collection, continue to absorb and excite the French public. In the case of the comedies, there is even less reason to suspect a decline of interest. The theatrical genius of Molière is a preservative against time's erosion of all but his least characteristic writings. The liveliness of Marivaux' graceful encounters with the affections and the affectations is as apparent today in good *Comédie Française* productions as it must have been in the eighteenth century. And it would be difficult to convince a civilized reader that Beaumarchais' satiric humor can ever suffer eclipse with and even without benefit of Mozart's and Rossini's music.*

Only in English have the masterpieces of Louis XIV's reign and of the eighteenth century encountered difficulties. These have been mainly problems of translation, aggravated in the case of the tragedies by their formal discursiveness. The comedies have had only moderate and widely spaced success on the English-speaking stage, while no successes at all outside the academic world have been registered in the case of the tragedies. It would seem that this discouraging situation is at last being modified. A distinguished version of *The Misanthrope* by the poet Richard Wilbur was recently staged in New York, though only on a small "off-Broadway" stage and with modest success. A production of *Tartuffe* in 1950, at the Lyric Hammersmith in London, fared well, as did a Theatre Guild production in the 1930's of *The School for Husbands* in an adaptation by the poet Arthur Guiterman and the producer Lawrence Langner. More recently, Jacques Barzun's version of Beaumarchais' comic masterpiece under the title of *Figaro's Marriage* has earned praise for conveying the vivacity of the original. But a great deal more effort will have to be made before the work of Corneille and Racine becomes sufficiently accessible to the American public, and one such effort is the publication of the present collection of translations

---

* Mozart's opera, *The Marriage of Figaro*, and Rossini's *The Barber of Seville*.

plainly designed to make access to both the comedies and tragedies easier.

II

It may be best to approach the plays without assuming any obligation to understand neo-classical theory, which Corneille himself did not particularly fathom when he gave the French theater its first masterpiece. It would only impede the general reader if instead of reading for interest and pleasure, he were made to feel that he had to first acquaint himself with the principles of seventeenth century criticism and participate in literary battles fought long ago. Is the reader stirred by the youthful drama of love and honor contained in *The Cid?* Does the glorious paradox of high tragedy impinge on him as he reads the *Phèdre?* Is he paradoxically troubled and uplifted by this drama of inexorable passion and fatality? Do the comedies of Molière, Marivaux, and Beaumarchais entertain him, and at the same time quicken his spirit, as do the distinguished high comedies written in our own language?

Only one question may be considered at once, if only to dispose of it. Are there any impediments to immediate appreciation in the plays themselves exclusive of the problems of translation? In the case of the comedies, there are none. Molière and Beaumarchais communicate with us directly, and so can Marivaux unless we are indifferent to well-spoken sensibility and are constrained to frown rather than laugh at the heroes and heroines of a mannered aristocracy. Impediments do, however, challenge the English reader when he turns to classic French drama. In the tragedies and tragi-comedies of Corneille and Racine there is often considerable formalism in the dialogue, and it is made especially apparent by the strict syllabic versification of the rhymed hexameter couplets. The more or less elegant characters, moreover, observe the formalities of refined society, and they often discourse at great length and with much precision in the midst of grave situations and fateful crises. All this makes the characters too self-conscious for honest feeling, we think, when we bring to the play habits of reading and playgoing formed in an age of casual realistic writing. But it is well to remember that the formal manners of an age or a people are an essential part of reality, and its formalities and social restraints are likely to be an expression of emotion as well as a defense against it. The writers of

French tragedy, moreover, deal with uncommon rather than common characters. The protagonists have a position to maintain and perhaps a mask to wear that may have become indistinguishable from the face and that they would gladly tear off if only they could. The result is genuine dramatic tension, and their very punctilio and worrying about propriety may be an aspect of their tragic condition.

As for the unities of time, place, and action in the plays, they are not as conducive to artificiality as has sometimes been imagined. The rules of the unities may have been launched with pedantry and maintained with censoriousness—not unchallenged, be it said, in their own time. But whatever restraints they may have imposed on the romantic expansiveness of later generations, the unities did make for concentration. A crisis of principle in Corneille or an emotional crisis in Racine receives its full measure of dramatic realization. It is noteworthy that when Ibsen developed social drama and Strindberg psychological tragedy they went out of their way to attain a similar concentration of experience and argument. Neoclassical "rules" were not held in reverence by Ibsen and Strindberg, and there were no pressures on the twin-founders of the modern drama to observe them, yet they returned to the unities. The former's *Ghosts* and the latter's *Miss Julie* would have outraged arbiters of taste in the seventeenth and eighteenth centuries who laid great stress on "propriety," but the plays would have seemed as classical in structure as any reasonable critic could have desired. Compared with them, in fact, *The Cid,* with its welter of action in a single day that makes it surely one of the busiest since time began, would seem "romantic" rather than "classical."

From this observation, moreover, it is but a step to the conclusion that there was more "freedom" in French classicism than is often realized. Undoubtedly its theoretical requirements were unsuited to the romantic and realistic genius of English and American literature. Undoubtedly, too, neoclassical theory served as a straitjacket for Corneille's dramatic talent in a number of plays; but he managed to evade the "rules" in *The Cid* and to adapt them to his needs in certain other plays and in his critical writing. It is also to be noted that *The Cid,* with its eventfulness, retained its popularity despite the criticism of the official literary circle. Like any other public, the French public was never successfully weaned from its partiality for the exciting action which was

FRENCH "CLASSICISM"

abundantly available to it in the comedies and spectacles of the period. It is doubtful that any genuine dramatist actually lost his appetite for excitement while retaining possession of his talent for the theater. Even Racine, who worked so well within the "rules," managed to whip up a good deal of excitement. His last tragedy, *Athalie,* was written for performance by the pupils of a religious boarding school, the Maison de St.-Cyr, maintained by Louis XIV's pious mistress, Madame de Maintenon. Yet it is as vigorous a work as any tragedian has created without losing himself in melodrama or overextending himself in a spectacular chronicle.

Excitement did not vanish from good French tragedies written during the vogue of classical or quasi-classical prescriptions. If the excitement is not always easy to locate, the reason is that it became *internal.* It shifted from the surface of plot to the inner person who usually had to struggle with principle in Corneille's work or with passion in Racine's; Corneille produced "moral" and Racine "psychological" drama. The external formalism of the plays needs no apology whenever it is associated with poetic and dramatic values. But the formalism can be seriously misleading if it causes us to ignore the essential enrichment and, I venture to say, modernization of the drama by *interior* conflict.

That prince of modern sophisticates, the late Jean Giraudoux, was surely mistaking the shadow for the substance when he declared in the 1920's that "There is not a sentiment in Racine that is not a literary sentiment." A great deal of evidence has been accumulated in Racine scholarship since then to contradict him. The very assumption that classic art is impersonal and that the classical writer never put himself into his work is questionable. It is questionable even when the author conceals himself behind the mask of comedy, as did Molière. Molière the man appears in Alceste, the comic hero of *The Misanthrope,* with considerable transparency, and Molière's comedies of jealousy contain a substantial ingredient of personal discomfiture. How much of Racine himself appears not only in the heroes of his tragedies but in his heroines is a pertinent question. Racine, it can be surmised if not indeed shown,[*] plunged into the very recesses of felt passion. But there is hardly any need for biographical investigation to reject the view that Racine was merely a gifted

---

[*] As in recent books by René Jasinski and Charles Mauron, *Vers la vrai Racine* and *L'Inconscient sans l'oeuvre et la vie de Racine,* respectively.

artificer. His plays are all the evidence one needs to realize he was concerned with the complexities of the inner self not only as an instinctive psychologist but as a moralist for whom the sinfulness of human nature was a personal experience as well as an article of faith.

It has been aptly said indeed that this member of a strict religious sect (which he abandoned for a while but to which he returned after severe disappointments in the courtly world) was inclined to portray "fair women full of Attic grace but lacking the grace of God." His heroine Phaedra is obviously one of these. Like other great tragedians, Racine was concerned with the state of man's soul. Corneille was also concerned with it, but noted mostly the soul's capacity for stoic endurance, high resolve, and noble decision. It is no wonder that he proposed to add "admiration" to the elements of "pity" and "fear" Aristotle considered essential to our experience of tragedy. But Racine noted "tragic flaws" in his characters that are flaws in human nature itself.

Much more can be said about an "existentialist" vein in Corneille's work and about a "tragedy of reason" or of "rationality meeting its opposite" in Racine's. Nevertheless, we must not overlook the poetic beauty and theatrical effectiveness, including the effective intrigue and rhetoric, of the plays we admire for their depth. Even the gratifications offered by the great tragic poets are first and last dramatic and esthetic. And it is not exclusively the tragic or near-tragic drama that speaks for the theatrical period that starts in the reign of Louis XIII and ends in that of Louis XVI. The period teemed with comedies not only by the playwrights represented in the present volume but by other observant and deft humorists, such as the less well known Regnard, Le Sage, and Destouches. Molière's encounters with folly and pretense, here represented by *Les Femmes savantes*, combine satiric correction with comic delight, Marivaux' comedy of sentiment glitters, and Beaumarchais' comedy of intrigue and mischief abounds in tart entertainment. Professor Fowlie's volume of French plays introduces us to a total theater of pleasure as well as pain, and of bright surfaces as well as sombre depths.

Foreword

The five French plays from the seventeenth and eighteenth centuries chosen for this collection are the works of five playwrights who have an international reputation in the history of the theater, and who at the same time are representative of a rigorously French style and tone. The selections are key texts from the viewpoint of French literary history and examples of plays which have been successful with several generations of theatergoers in France.

Each language has its own particular quality and power, and each national theater has its own conventions. A translation, no matter how many liberties are taken, cannot possibly recapture poetic style or very specific theatrical and linguistic traits. The principle followed in preparing these translations has been faithfulness to the original text rather than adaptation. Only in the case of the Molière play have a few passages been slightly shortened in order to provide a more suitable acting version of the text.

The five plays represent five genres, or five types of play: a tragicomedy in *Le Cid,* a tragedy in *Phèdre,* a high comedy in *Les Femmes savantes,* a comedy of love in *Le Jeu de l'Amour et du Hasard,* and a comedy of intrigue in *Le Barbier de Séville.* Each text is preceded by a brief historical-critical introduction which attempts to describe the importance of the play in the history of the French theater, the literary position of the playwright, and the general meaning of the play.

The conventions of tragic style and poetry are such that tragedy loses more in translation than comedy. It may well be that Corneille and Racine cannot be put into another language and provide anything comparable to the theatrical experience of performances in French. Comedy has more recognizable conventions and more universal traditions, and therefore seems to suffer less in translation than tragedy.

The Cid
(LE CID)
1636

❦

A TRAGICOMEDY IN FIVE ACTS
BY
PIERRE CORNEILLE

❦

translated by WALLACE FOWLIE

Pierre Corneille
(1606–1684)

In recent years there has been a renewed critical interest in the tragedies of Corneille, an appreciative re-evaluation of his dramatic art. And yet the general theatergoing public has never given his plays the support and the enthusiasm they have given to Racine and Molière. The strong moralizing accent of his work accounts to some degree for his position among the classical playwrights. His poetry is vigorous but tends toward the bombastic. His language seems today somewhat archaic and oratorical, but he was a master of the alexandrine verse. His poetic style has clarity and precision and a firm sense of rhythm. The poetry of his best tragedies, *Le Cid, Horace, Cinna, Polyeucte,* is a poetry of action, an intellectual language projecting the feelings and dilemmas of the characters.

Corneille's biography is sober and uneventful. He was a Norman, born in Rouen, in 1606. There he was educated by the Jesuits, who gave him a solid training in Latin and the humanities and who introduced him to the theater in school productions. He was a sincerely pious man throughout his life and devoted to his large family. His last years were disturbed by disappointment at the public's waning interest in his work, and by jealousy over the fame of his younger rival Racine.

The principle of the Cornelian form of tragedy is truth, resemblance to life, or, as it is sometimes called, verisimilitude. Although the three unities of Greek tragedy were not fully established in France when Corneille wrote *Le Cid* in 1636, he did subscribe to them. However, the unities of time, place, and action were not always easy for him to observe. Only in the work of Racine do they seem to be the natural laws of tragedy, observed in order to reach in the art a maximum verisimilitude.

The theater of Corneille ignores the trappings of melodrama which were used in the plays of his predecessors. He does have complications, but they are of a moral order. The moral problem in his play may be extraordinary, but it is always human and believable. He follows the precept of Aristotle in electing almost always an historical subject, and therefore one which, in large part, is true to fact. *Le Cid*, for example, had an immediate poetic source, but it had also a basis in history.

The type of human nature which Corneille depicts is highly intelligent and willful. Repeatedly he uses as protagonists clear-thinking, passionate individuals who are almost fanatical in their exaltation. His theory of love is close to that of Descartes. Love, to Corneille, is the desire for the good, and it is based upon knowledge of the good. One falls in love because of the perfection that is visible in the beloved. This formula applies to the love of Chimene and Rodrigue. Even in persecuting Rodrigue, Chimene believes she has the right and the duty to love him.

If esteem is the determining factor in love, as it seems to be in Corneille, then the lover acts, not because of love, but because of honor and duty, because of his *gloire*. The lovers are more worthy of love after making an effort of will which may threaten the very existence of love. Thus Rodrigue, in killing the father of Chimene, and Chimene, in demanding the death of Rodrigue, are examples of the supreme triumph of will. Cornelian heroism is always the exaltation of will which is looked upon as a free faculty of man. The very structure of the tragedy is based upon this freedom and power of will. The hero and the heroine, Rodrigue and Chimene, are equal in their strength of will. Their opposition to one another is evenly balanced, as if the play were a carefully calculated mathematical, as well as a moral, problem.

Every aspect of the play's structure reiterates this psychology of will. It is in the form of the Cornelian dialogue, both the long eloquent speeches or *tirades* which are convincingly reasoned arguments, and the brief elliptical answers where arguments and ideas are reduced to maxims, and where the language is harsh and tense.

The immediate source of *Le Cid* was a long Spanish drama of 1618: *Las Mocedades del Cid*, by Guillén de Castro. One of the principal episodes of this Spanish work was converted into the French *tragi-comédie*. In extracting *Le Cid* from *Las Mocedades del Cid*, Corneille was guided by the laws of classical tragedy, the three unities, and by his desire to reduce the extravagances, the coarseness, and the surprising changes of fortune which characterized the *tragi-comédie* of his day.

In this type of play, a series of events which threaten to become tragic are resolved in a happy ending. To Corneille, the event itself is not as interesting as the sentiment arising from it. Hence, the violent events—the death of the Count, the battle with the Moors, and the duel between Rodrigue and Don Sanche—do not take place on stage. The real action of *Le Cid* is the struggle between love and filial piety.

The formula which Corneille worked out fixed the basic form of French tragedy. *Le Cid* is a character study, a demonstration in which human beings are engaged in spiritual or psychological conflict. The interest in the play is not in the historical background, the melodramatic events of Spanish history, but in the psychological truths and stresses which arise from the play's action.

Despite the popular success of *Le Cid* in 1636 and 1637, there was considerable critical objection to the play. Cardinal Richelieu forced the newly organized Académie Française (1637) to pass judgment on it. Their report, *Les Sentiments sur Le Cid,* was a work of critical narrowness and prejudice, but in no way did it discourage the public from enjoying the play. *Le Cid* has remained steadfastly in the classical repertory as one of the most stirring plays on the theme of youthful passion and honor. Charles Péguy once called it *the* poem on honor: "Honor loved with love, and love honored with honor."

The Cid

CHARACTERS

Don Ferdinand, King of Castille
The Infanta, his daughter
Don Diegue, father of Don Rodrigue
Count Gomes, father of Chimene
Don Rodrigue, in love with Chimene
Don Sanche, in love with Chimene
Don Arias, noble
Don Alonso, noble
Chimene
Leonor, confidante of the Infanta
Elvire, confidante of Chimene
A Page

Scene: Seville. The King's palace, Chimene's house, a street in Seville.

ACT I

Scene 1. *Chimene and Elvire.*

Chimene. Are you telling me the truth, Elvire?
Have you kept back any of my father's words?

Elvire. I am still under the spell of those words.
He respects Rodrigue as much as you love him,
and if I am not mistaken in my reading of his heart,
he will command you to accept Rodrigue's love.

Chimene. Please tell me once again
what makes you feel he approves of my choice.
Tell me once more what hope I may cherish.
You cannot repeat such joyous news too often.
Keep promising, to the passion of our love,
the sweet privilege of its being revealed.
What did he say about the intrigue

in which Don Sanche and Don Rodrigue have involved you?
Did you not show too clearly the choice I have made
between my two suitors?

ELVIRE. No, I described your heart as indifferent,
neither raising nor quelling the hope of either one,
looking upon them neither severely nor with favor,
and waiting your father's order to choose a husband.
He loved your respect. His words and countenance
gave instant testimony to it.
And since you want me to repeat the story,
this is what he said, in haste, about you and about them:
"She is dutiful. Both men are worthy of her.
Both come from a noble lineage that is strong and sure,
both young, but with eyes that reveal
the dazzling virtue of their brave ancestors.
Every expression on Rodrigue's face
displays the true image of a courageous man.
His family is so endowed with warriors
that they seem to have been born with laurel leaves.
The valor of his father, who was without peer in his day,
was looked upon as miraculous.
His prowess is now engraved in the creases of his brow,
marking for us the sign of his past deeds.
What the father accomplished I look for in the son,
and if my daughter loves him, she pleases me thereby."
He was late for the council when I saw him
and had to cut short his speech,
but in those few words I can tell
he is not hesitating between your two suitors.
The King has to choose a tutor for his son,
and your father is the obvious choice for this honor.
There is no doubt, for his exceptional valor
allows no rival to be feared.
His lofty exploits have no parallel,
and for so well-deserved a hope there is no competition.
Don Rodrigue has convinced his father
to make this proposal at the end of the council.
You may be sure he will choose the right moment,
and all your desires will soon be realized.

CHIMENE. Yet my soul is troubled.
It refuses this joy and is bewildered.

One moment may give different masks to the same fate,
and in my great happiness I fear a great reversal.

ELVIRE. This fear of yours will end in good fortune.

CHIMENE. Come with me while we await the outcome.

SCENE 2. *Infanta, Leonor, Page.*

INFANTA. Page, go find Chimene and tell her
that today she has delayed her visit too long,
and that my love for her complains of her absence.

(*Exit* PAGE.)

LEONOR. Your Highness, each day the same desire compels you.
Each day she comes to you and I hear you ask
how far her love for Rodrigue has developed.

INFANTA. It is not without motive. I have almost forced her
to welcome the arrows which wound her.
She loves Rodrigue and it was I who gave him to her.
Thanks to me he overcame her scorn.
Since I created the love which binds these lovers,
I am eager to see an end to their torment.

LEONOR. But your Highness, this happy outcome
stirs excessive sorrow in you.
Does this love which crowns them with joy,
transform your heart to sadness?
Does the great interest you have in them
make you wretched when they are happy?
But I presume too much and am indiscreet.

INFANTA. My sadness grows stronger when it is secret.
Listen now to the struggle I have waged.
Let me tell you of the attacks made on my virtue.
Love is a tyrant who spares no one.
I am in love with this knight, with this lover
I have given away.

LEONOR. You are in love!

INFANTA. If you put your hand
on my heart, you would see how it beats at the name
of its conqueror.

LEONOR. I apologize
if I seem disrespectful in censuring this love.
How can a princess forget her birth

and allow her heart to love a simple knight?
What would the King say? And Castille?
Have you forgotten whose daughter you are?

INFANTA. I remember so well that I would take my life
before stooping to belie my rank.
I could answer that in a well-born soul
merit alone has the right to incite love;
and that if my passion sought an excuse,
a hundred famous examples might serve as precedents.
I will not go where my honor may be endangered.
The flaring of my senses will not affect my
  courage;
and I still tell myself that being the daughter
  of a king,
no man save a monarch is worthy of my name.
When I saw that my heart could not protect itself,
I gave what I did not dare take.
Rather than myself, I led Chimene into the bonds of love.
I ignited their flame in order to extinguish mine.
Do not be amazed if my troubled soul
now waits impatiently for their marriage.
Today my peace of mind depends on it.
If love lives on hope, it dies with the death of
  hope.
It is a fire that goes out when there is nothing left
  to feed it.
Despite the trial of my sad adventure,
when Chimene has taken Rodrigue as husband,
my hope will be dead, my torment over.
But meanwhile the anguish of my suffering continues.
Until that marriage, I will love Rodrigue.
I am doing all I can to lose him though I cannot bear
  losing him.
This is the pattern of my secret sorrow.
It is hopelessly clear that love is forcing me
to long for the man I must avoid.
My mind is split in two.
My courage is strong, but my heart is in flames.
This marriage is my death: I both want it and
  fear it.
All I can hope for is an imperfect joy.
My honor and my love have such power

that I will die with this marriage, and die if
   there is no marriage.

LEONOR. Your Highness, there is nothing for
   me to say,
except that I join you in your lament.
If I blamed you once, I now pity you.
But since your honor resists the charm and the power
of so sweet and painful a grief,
repulses the attack and rejects the allure,
it will restore peace to your bewildered mind.
Place all your hope in it and in the passage of time.
Place your hope in God whose justice
will not allow your honor to suffer too long.

INFANTA. My sweetest hope is to lose hope.
(PAGE *enters*.)

PAGE. At your Highness' order, Chimene is here.

INFANTA. Go speak to her outside.

LEONOR. Do you wish to be alone with your thoughts?

INFANTA. No, but I need a few minutes
in which to recover my composure.
Then I will join you.   (LEONOR *and* PAGE *leave*.)
               O God, whose help I need,
Put an end to the suffering that has hold of me.
Grant me rest and preserve my honor.
I seek happiness in the happiness of someone else.
This marriage has meaning for all three of us.
Make it come about more swiftly or make my soul
   stronger.
If these two are joined in the bonds of marriage,
then my bonds will be broken and my torment over.
Chimene is waiting. I must go to her
and let her words lessen my pain.

SCENE 3. *The Count, Don Diegue.*

COUNT. So it is you who win, and the King's favor,
in making you tutor to the Prince of Castille,
raises you to a rank which was due me.

DIEGUE. This mark of honor he bestows on my family
proves to all he is just and willing
to reward past services.

COUNT. Whatever their power may be, kings are human like all of us
and may make a mistake like other men.
This choice demonstrates to all courtiers
that kings give small recompenses for present services.

DIEGUE. Let's have no more words about this choice which so upsets you.
Favor may have caused it as much as merit.
But we owe to his divine right the respect
of questioning nothing when it is the will of a king.
To the honor he has paid me, add one more.
Let us join in a sacred bond my house and yours.
You have but one daughter, and I one son.
Their marriage will make us something more than friends.
Grant us this grace and accept my son as yours.

COUNT. Your handsome son should aim higher now.
The new brilliance of his honor
must swell his heart with further vanity.
Exercise your honor, Diegue, and teach the prince.
Show him how a province must be ruled,
how the people must tremble under his law,
how the good must be filled with love and the wicked with terror.
Join to these the virtues of a captain.
Show him how he must toughen himself in work
and surpass everyone else in soldiery,
how he must spend days and nights on horseback,
sleep in his armor, storm a wall,
and win a battle by his own prowess.
Be his model and make him perfect,
explaining your lessons to him by accomplishments.

DIEGUE. To learn in this way, by examples,
he will merely read the story of my life.
There, in a long series of noble actions,
he will see how nations are conquered,
how a city square is attacked and an army organized,
and how one's fame is built on great exploits.

COUNT. Living examples have a better effect.
A prince ill learns his duty from books.
What did your many years accomplish

THE CID

which one of my days cannot equal?
If you were valiant once, I am valiant today,
and my arm is the strongest support of the kingdom.
Granada and Aragon tremble at the flash of my sword,
my name is a rampart for all of Castille.
If I were not here, you would soon be under other laws
and your enemies would be your kings.
To heighten my honor, each day and each moment
piles laurels on laurels, and victory on victory.
At my side, the prince, in battle, would
test his courage under the shadow of my arm.
He would learn how to conquer by watching me,
and to give swift answer to his noble spirit,
he would see . . .

DIEGUE. I know this. You serve your king well.
I have seen you fight and command under me.
When age sent its icy coldness through my veins,
your exceptional valor took over my place.
To cut short these unnecessary words,
you are today what I was in earlier years.
Yet you see that in this rivalry
the monarch does establish a difference between us.

COUNT. All that I deserved, you have won.

DIEGUE. The man who triumphed over you deserved it.

COUNT. He who can train the prince is the worthier man.

DIEGUE. But to be refused is not a good sign.

COUNT. The old courtier in you won this by intrigue.

DIEGUE. My only spokesman was the fame of my past deeds.

COUNT. Let us be clear: the King pays honor to your age.

DIEGUE. If so, the King measures it by my courage.

COUNT. And thereby this honor should have come to me.

DIEGUE. He who did not get it did not deserve it.

COUNT. Did not deserve it? You mean me?

DIEGUE. You.

COUNT. Your impudence
and your presumption deserve this.
(*He gives him a slap.*)

PIERRE CORNEILLE

DIEGUE (*drawing his sword*).
Come, take my life after such an insult.
I am the first of my family to blush with shame.

  COUNT. And what do you plan to do in your impotence?

  DIEGUE. Oh God, my weakened strength is of no use now.

  COUNT. Your sword is mine, but you would be too vain
if my hand took this shameful trophy.
Adieu. In spite of envy, let the prince
read, for his lesson, the story of your life.
This just punishment for your insolent words
will not become a small episode for his amusement.

SCENE 4. *Don Diegue.*

  DIEGUE. My years are my enemy!
Have I lived this long only to know such infamy?
Has my hair turned white in the labor of battles
to see all my laurels wither in one day?
My arm, once acclaimed by all Spain,
my arm which saved the empire countless times,
and so often supported the throne of its king
now betrays my quarrel and leaves me helpless.
Now the memory of my honored life is cruel
and the labor of so many days is wiped out in one day.
A new honor comes and destroys my happiness.
A high precipice from which my name is hurled down!
Must I see this count triumph over my honor,
and die unavenged or live in shame?
Let the count now be the governor of my prince:
such a rank is not permitted a dishonored man.
The daring insult from his jealous pride
has made me unworthy, in spite of the King's choice.
You, once glorious instrument of my battles,
now useless ornament for a body grown cold,
sword that was once feared, but which in this offense
served me as a decoration, not as a defense,
leave me, the least of men,
and pass into better hands for my revenge.

THE CID

Scene 5. *Don Diegue, Don Rodrigue.*

DIEGUE. Rodrigue, have you courage?

RODRIGUE. Any man save my father
could test it at this moment.

DIEGUE. Righteous anger!
Your noble feeling is sweet to my pain.
I recognize my blood in your fine wrath.
My youth lives again in your swift zeal.
My son who are my blood, will you make amends for my shame?
Will you avenge me?

RODRIGUE. For what?

DIEGUE. For so harsh an insult
that it bears a mortal blow to the honor of us both:
for a hand that struck my face! The wretch would have died,
but my age tricked my high-minded desire;
this sword which my arm can no longer support,
I hand over to you for vengeance and punishment.
Test your courage against a proud man's.
Such an outrage is settled only with blood.
Die or kill. Moreover—I must not mislead you—
I am giving you as adversary a much-feared man.
I have seen him, covered with blood and dust,
bring terror to an entire army.
I have seen a hundred squadrons routed by his strength,
and—to tell you one more thing about him—
more than being a brave soldier and a great captain,
this man is . . .

RODRIGUE. In God's name, tell me.

DIEGUE. The father of Chimene.

RODRIGUE. The . . .

DIEGUE. Don't try to answer. I know your love.
But an infamous man is not worthy to live.
The dearer the offender, the greater is the offense.
Well, you know the insult and you hold the instrument of vengeance.
I will say nothing further. Avenge me and avenge yourself.

Show that the son is worthy of his father.
Bowed down with the woes of destiny,
I must withdraw, but you, rush with speed to vengeance.

Scene 6. *Don Rodrigue.*

RODRIGUE. My heart is pierced with this word,
as unexpected as it is mortal,
I stand unable to move,
wretched avenger in a just cause,
sad victim of unjust rigor,
and my soul yields to this killing blow.
So close to seeing my love rewarded!
Oh God! what a strange plight!
In this insult, my father is offended,
and the offender, the father of Chimene.

A bitter fight is being waged in me
where my love takes sides against my honor.
I have to avenge a father and lose my betrothed.
One incites my anger, and the other holds back my arm.
My sad choice is to betray my love
or live in infamy.
Either way my suffering is endless.
Oh God! what strange punishment!
Must I leave this insult unpunished?
Must I punish the father of Chimene?

My father or my betrothed, my honor or my love.
Harsh constraint or pleasing tyranny.
Either my joy is over or my honor stained.
One makes me wretched, and the other unworthy of
  life.
Cherished and cruel hope of a noble soul
which is at the same time in love.
Worthy enemy of my greatest happiness,
sword which creates my pain,
were you given me to avenge my honor,
were you given me to lose my Chimene?

It is better to die.
I owe my life to my betrothed as well as to my father.
By avenging myself, I will earn her hate and wrath;

not avenging myself, I will earn his scorn.
To my sweetest hope, one makes me unfaithful,
and the other makes me unworthy of her.
My pain grows as I yearn to cure it.
Everything increases my suffering.
Come, Rodrigue, since I must die,
at least let me die without offending Chimene.

Die without obtaining satisfaction!
Seek a death so fatal to my honor!
Allow Spain to ascribe to my memory
the refusal to defend the honor of my house!
Respect a love whose collapse
my dazed mind knows is certain!
I must stop thinking of that enticing image
which only increases my suffering.
Come! At least I will save my honor,
since in either outcome I will lose Chimene.
Yes, my mind was deceived.
I owe all to my father before my betrothed.
Whether I die in combat or die from sorrow,
I will shed my blood as pure as I received it.
I have delayed too long
and must rush to vengeance.
I am ashamed of having hesitated this much.
Let my suffering be over,
since today my father is insulted,
even if the offender is the father of Chimene.

ACT II

Scene 1. *Don Arias, the Count.*

COUNT. I acknowledge it. My anger was too strong
and over one word it mounted to violence.
But since it is done, the deed cannot be repaired.

ARIAS. Let your great courage bend to the King's will.
He has an interest in this affair, and his irritation
will go against you with all the weight of his authority.
You have no valid defense.
The rank of the offended man and the magnitude of the offense
demand duties and submissions
which exceed ordinary reparations.

COUNT. At his will, the King may dispose of my life.

ARIAS. An excess of anger follows hard on your mistake.
The King still loves you. Appease his wrath.
He said: "I wish it thus." Will you disobey?

COUNT. But considering all the esteem in which I am held,
a slight disobedience is not so great a crime.
And however great it is, my services today
are more than enough to efface it.

ARIAS. However illustrious and important the service be,
a king is never indebted to his subject.
You deceive yourself, for you must know
that who serves his king well, does only his duty.
You will bring disaster if you persist in your belief.

COUNT. I will believe you after the test.

ARIAS. You should fear the power of a king.

COUNT. A single day does not wipe out a man like myself.
Let him in all his greatness prepare for my punishment.
The entire state will perish if I perish.

ARIAS. So, you fear sovereign power so little . . .

COUNT. A scepter which would drop from his hand without me?
My life has too much value for him.
If my head fell, his crown would follow.

THE CID

ARIAS. Let reason soothe your spirits.
Listen to good advice.

COUNT. My decision is made.

ARIAS. What shall I say then? I have to bring him word.

COUNT. That I will in no way consent to my shame.

ARIAS. But remember that kings are absolute.

COUNT. The die is cast. There is no need for further talk.

ARIAS. I take leave then, since I cannot change your mind.
With all your laurels, you should still fear divine
wrath.

COUNT. I will wait without fear.

ARIAS. But not without result.

COUNT. In that case Diegue will have satisfaction.

(DON ARIAS *goes out*.)

He who has no fear of death has no fear of threats.
My courage is stronger than the harshest disgrace.
I can be forced to live without happiness
but I cannot be forced to live without honor.

SCENE 2. *The Count, Rodrigue.*

RODRIGUE. A word with you, Count.

COUNT. Speak.

RODRIGUE. Dispel my doubts.
Do you know Don Diegue?

COUNT. Yes.

RODRIGUE. Listen carefully.
Did you know that my father was the virtue,
the valor and the power of his time? Did you know that?

COUNT. Perhaps I did.

RODRIGUE. Do you know that the ardor
in my eyes comes from him? Do you know that?

COUNT. It is not my concern.

RODRIGUE. It will be your concern a few paces from here.

COUNT. Presumption of youth!

RODRIGUE. Don't let emotion color your words.
It is true I am young, but in the well-born,
valor does not wait for age.

COUNT. What vanity puts you in my class?
You have never carried arms into battle.

RODRIGUE. Men like me need no second test to show their valor.
Their trial stroke is also their master stroke.

COUNT. Do you know who I am?

RODRIGUE. Yes. Any other man
at the sound of your name would tremble with fear.
The victory wreaths that have crowned your head
would seem to bear the sign of my defeat.
I am rashly attacking a man who has always conquered.
But my courage will give me great strength.
Nothing is impossible for a son avenging his father.
You are unconquered but not invincible.

COUNT. That very courage which shows forth in your words,
I have seen in your eyes day after day,
and believing I had found in you the honor of Castille,
I was pleased to think of you as a future son.
I know of your love and I am gratified to see
all of its power yield to the power of duty.
Your passion has not weakened your noble ardor,
and your virtue justifies my esteem.
In wanting a perfect warrior for a son,
I was not wrong in choosing you.
But now my pity is involved in what I feel for you.
I admire your courage and I pity your youth.
Do not attempt a trial duel that would be fatal.
Spare me an uneven fight.
No honor would accompany such a victory.
In winning without danger, a man triumphs without glory.
All would know you were defeated without effort,
and I would be left with sorrow for your death.

RODRIGUE. Such unworthy pity follows fast on your boldness.
So, the man who takes my honor fears taking my life?

COUNT. Leave this place.

RODRIGUE. Let's go together without more talk.

COUNT. Are you tired of living?

RODRIGUE. Are you afraid of dying?

COUNT. So be it! Do your duty. The son degenerates
who for one moment survives the honor of his father.

THE CID

Scene 3. *Infanta, Chimene, Leonor.*

INFANTA. Chimene, your suffering will lessen,
and your strength will overcome this blow.
Peace will return after this slight storm.
If your joy is covered now by a few clouds,
you will lose nothing by having it delayed.

CHIMENE. There is no more hope in my vexed and outraged heart.
So swift a storm upsetting a smooth sea
brings the sign of certain catastrophe.
I cannot doubt it, and I am perishing in the harbor.
I loved, I was loved, and our fathers had consented.
I was telling you this joyous news
at the fatal moment of their quarrel.
That wretched story, as soon as it was told to you,
violated my sweet expectations.
Oh! accursed ambition and hateful wrath
whose tyranny sways the noblest men!
This honor so pitiless to my dearest desires
will cost me the tears and sighs of a lifetime.

INFANTA. You have no reason to fear anything from this quarrel.
It sprang up in a moment, and it will be over in a moment.
It has caused too much uproar not to be put down,
and already the King plans to pacify them.
And you know that I, who am sensitive to your affliction,
will do the impossible to eradicate its source.

CHIMENE. Compromises will have no effect at this point.
Such mortal insults are not forgiven.
It is futile to use force and prudence.
If the evil is cured, it will only be in appearance.
The hate which is preserved by the heart within
feeds passion that is hidden, but all the more ardent for that.

INFANTA. The holy bond which will join Rodrigue and Chimene
will disperse the hate between the enemy fathers,
and we shall soon see your stronger love
stifle this discord in a happy marriage.

CHIMENE. I long for this more than I hope for it.
Don Diegue is too proud and I know my father.
The tears I want to hold back are beginning to flow.
The past is my torment and the future my fear.

INFANTA. What do you fear? The impotence of an old man?

CHIMENE. Rodrigue is courageous.

INFANTA. He is too young.

CHIMENE. Such men are valiant in their first duel.

INFANTA. There is no need to fear for him.
He is too much in love to will your displeasure,
and two words from you will arrest his anger.

CHIMENE. If he does not obey me, what suffering lies ahead?
And if he obeys, what will they say of him?
How can he, of such birth, bear such an outrage?
If he accepts or resists the love which binds us,
I shall be either ashamed of his respect
or bewildered by his refusal.

INFANTA. You have a noble soul, and although it is deeply distressed,
it will not allow a base thought.
If I made this perfect lover my prisoner
until the day of reconciliation,
and thus prevented any sign of his courage,
would your loving spirit take offense?

CHIMENE. If you do this, my worry is over.

SCENE 4. *Infanta, Chimene, Leonor, Page.*

INFANTA. Page, seek out Rodrigue and bring him here.

PAGE. The Count Gomes and he . . .

CHIMENE. Oh! it is too late!

INFANTA. Speak!

PAGE. . . . left the palace together.

CHIMENE. Alone?

PAGE. Alone! They were arguing in a low voice.

CHIMENE. They are already fighting, and it's useless to speak further.
Your Highness, forgive them for this haste.

THE CID

Scene 5. *Infanta, Leonor.*

INFANTA. A new conflict rises up in my mind.
I am sorry for her suffering, and I still love Rodrigue.
There is no peace in my mind, for my love is rekindled.
What separates Rodrigue from Chimene
brings back to life my hope and my pain.
Their estrangement grieves me
and creates a secret pleasure in my bewitched mind.

LEONOR. Does the lofty virtue of your soul
give over this quickly to an unworthy love?

INFANTA. Do not call it unworthy; within me
it is now a strong triumphant law.
Pay it respect since it is dear to me.
My virtue fights it, but I hope in spite of myself.
My ill-protected heart, full of so mad a hope,
flies to the lover whom Chimene has lost.

LEONOR. Are you allowing your honorable courage to collapse,
and is reason losing its sway over you?

INFANTA. Reason speaks with little effect
when the heart is reached by such spell-binding poison!
When the sick man loves his sickness,
he will not allow any remedy to be administered.

LEONOR. Your hope has changed you and your sickness is sweet,
but Rodrigue is unworthy of you.

INFANTA. I know it too well. But if my virtue yields,
learn how love soothes a heart it possesses.
If this one time Rodrigue is victor,
if this great warrior falls under his valor,
I may esteem him, I may love him without shame.
If he wins over the Count, what will he not do?
I can imagine that at his most inconspicuous feats,
entire kingdoms will submit to his law.
My flattering love already persuades me
that I see him seated on the throne of Granada,
with the subjugated Moors trembling as they kneel,
with Aragon welcoming the new conqueror,
and Portugal submitting, and all his noble days
bearing beyond the seas his great mission,

and the blood of Africa watering his laurels.
Everything that is said of famous warriors,
I expect of Rodrigue after this victory,
and out of his love I will make a cause for my own
  honor.

Leonor. Your Highness, see how far you have led him
from a duel which perhaps will not take place.

Infanta. Rodrigue is insulted. The Count is the offender.
They have gone off together. What more is needed?

Leonor. Well, if you insist, let them have their fight,
but will Rodrigue go as far as you have imagined?

Infanta. You are right! I have lost my mind.
You can see the disasters my love creates.
Come with me and help me with your words.
Do not leave me in my bewildered state.

Scene 6. *The King, Don Arias, Don Sanche.*

King. So, the Count is that vain and that unreasonable!
Does he still believe his crime can be pardoned?

Arias. I spoke to him at some length in your name.
I did my best, Sire, with no result.

King. Can it be that a presumptuous subject
has so little respect and so little desire to please me?
He insults Don Diegue and scorns his king!
Before my court he lays down the law.
He is a brave warrior and a great captain,
but I have the means to quell such a proud spirit.
Were he valor itself and the god of war,
he will see what it means to disobey.
Despite all that such violence deserved,
I had decided first to treat him gently.
But since he goes so far, arrest him today
whether he makes resistance or not.

Sanche. A little time, perhaps, would temper his rebellion.
He was caught still angry from his quarrel.
In the heat of a first impulse, Sire,
so noble a heart submits with difficulty.
He understands he is wrong, but his pride
will not allow him to confess his guilt at once.

King. Be silent, Don Sanche, and know
that to take his side is criminal.

THE CID

SANCHE. I obey and I will be silent, but I entreat you, Sire, one further word in his defense.

KING. What can you say?

SANCHE. That a spirit accustomed to great deeds
cannot bend to submission.
Every form of submission will be shameful.
Only this act did the Count resist.
He found in this duty too much harshness,
and would obey you if he had less heart.
Command that his arm, so strengthened in battle,
repair this insult with the point of his sword.
He will give satisfaction, Sire.

KING. Your respect for me diminishes, but I pardon your age,
and excuse the ardor of your youthful courage.
A king whose prudence has a better goal
is a better steward of his subjects' blood.
I watch over my people; my care protects them,
just as the head needs the members which serve it.
So your reason is not reason for me.
You speak as a soldier; I must act as a king.
Despite what you say and what he believes,
the Count in obeying me cannot lose his honor.
Moreover this insult affects me. He dishonored
the man whom I had made governor of my son.
To attack my choice is to attack me,
and to belittle my sovereign power.
But no more of this. Ten vessels of our old enemy
have been sighted raising their flags.
They have dared approach the mouth of the river.

ARIAS. The Moors know you by the strength of your army,
and, conquered so often, have lost the courage
to risk themselves against so great a conqueror.

KING. Yet they will never regard without jealousy
my scepter ruling Andalusia.
This noble country which they owned too long
is always looked upon with envy.
This is the one reason that has forced me for ten years
to place the throne of Castille in Seville,
in order to see them at closer range, and, with a swifter order
overturn at once whatever they undertook.

ARIAS. At the expense of their best leaders
they know your presence assures your victory.
You have nothing to fear.

KING. And nothing to neglect.
Overconfidence attracts danger.
You know what a simple thing it is
for the rising tide to bring them here.
Yet I would be wrong, since the information is uncertain,
to spread panic in the hearts of my people.
The terror which a useless alarm would produce
would disturb the city too much tonight.
Double the guard at the walls and the harbor.
That is enough for now.

SCENE 7. *The King, Don Sanche, Don Alonso.*

ALONSO. Sire, the Count is dead.
Don Diegue, through his son, has been avenged.

KING. As soon as I learned of this affront, I foresaw the vengeance,
and I tried at once to prevent calamity.

ALONSO. Chimene is bringing her grief into your presence.
Tearfully she comes to plead for justice.

KING. Although I share in her affliction,
the Count fully deserved
this penalty for his rashness.
Yet however justified his punishment,
I cannot without regret lose such a captain.
After a long service to his country,
after the countless wounds he received for me,
whatever resentment his pride imposes on me,
his loss weakens us and his death grieves us.

SCENE 8. *The King, Diegue, Chimene, Sanche, Arias, Alonso.*

CHIMENE. Sire! Give me justice!
DIEGUE. Sire, listen to me!
CHIMENE. I kneel before you.
DIEGUE. I bow at your feet.
CHIMENE. I ask for justice.
DIEGUE. Heed my defense.

CHIMENE. Punish the insolence and rashness of this youth.
He has slain the support of your scepter.
He has killed my father.

DIEGUE.　　　　　　　He has avenged his own father.

CHIMENE. A king owes justice to his subjects.

DIEGUE. For a just vengeance there can be no punishment.

KING. Rise up, both of you, and speak more deliberately.
Chimene, I share in your sorrow.
My own heart weeps with yours.
(*To* DON DIEGUE.)
You will speak afterward. Do not interrupt her complaint.

CHIMENE. Sire, my father is dead. My eyes saw his blood
gush forth from his side.
It was that life-blood which preserved your ramparts
and so often won battles for you.
His blood is still angered
at being shed for someone other than yourself.
In the midst of danger, war itself could not spill his blood.
Rodrigue in your court has covered the earth with it.
Without strength or color I ran to the spot
and found him lifeless. Pardon my grief,
Sire, my voice fails me in this fatal story.
Let my tears and sobbing tell you the rest.

KING. Take courage, my child, and know that today
your king will replace your father.

CHIMENE. Sire, too great an honor follows on my woe.
I repeat, I found him lifeless.
His side was opened, and to move me even more,
his blood inscribed my duty on the dust:
or rather, his valor, reduced to such a state,
spoke to me through his wound and urged me to action.
To be heard by the most just of kings,
it borrowed my voice from that grievous opening.
Sire, do not allow such license
to reign before your very eyes.
Do not allow the bravest of your subjects
to be exposed to a rash attack,
or a proud youth to triumph with impunity over such a man's honor,

bathe in his blood and defy his memory.
The death of so valiant a soldier as he who has just been
  taken away
weakens the will to serve you if he is not avenged.
My father, Sire, is dead, and I want vengeance
more for your own interests than for my consolation.
You are the loser in this death of a man of his rank.
Avenge it by another. One death for one death.
Slay him, not for me, but for your crown,
for your highness, for your person.
I repeat, Sire, sacrifice for the good of the state
the man whom so lofty an assault has inflated with pride.

KING. Give answer, Don Diegue.

DIEGUE.   A man is to be envied
when, on losing his strength, he also loses his life,
and when, at the end of his career, a long life
has prepared his noble spirit for a calamitous fate.
My labors in the past had brought me honors.
Victory once followed me wherever I went,
but today, because I have lived too long,
I was unable to avenge an insult.
The Count, in your court, almost before your eyes,
did what had never been done
by combat, siege, or ambush,
neither by Aragon nor Granada,
neither by your enemies nor those envious of me.
He was jealous of your choice and proud of the advantage
which the impotency of my years gave to him.
Sire, my hair, which has turned white under your armor,
my blood, often spilled in your service,
this arm, which was once dreaded by your enemies,
would have descended, covered with shame, into the tomb,
if I had not brought forth a son worthy of me,
worthy of his country and worthy of his king.
He lent me his strength and killed the Count.
He gave me back my honor and effaced my shame.
If showing courage and anger,
if avenging an insult, deserve punishment,
the wrath of the tempest should fall on me.
Whether you name the cause of our contention a crime or not,
Sire, I am the head and he is but the arm.
Chimene laments that Rodrigue killed her father, but

THE CID

he would never have done it, if I had been able to.
Slay rather this head which old age will soon cut down,
and save for yourself the arm which can serve.
Satisfy Chimene by shedding my blood.
I will not resist. I consent to my penalty.
Rather than complaining over so rigorous a decree,
dying without dishonor, I shall die without regret.

KING. The affair is important and the positions well considered.
It should be deliberated in open council.
Don Sanche, take Chimene back to her house.
Don Diegue will have as a prison my court and his word.
Find Rodrigue. I will mete out justice.

CHIMENE. O King, it is just that a murderer die.

KING. Take some rest, my child, and quiet your grief.

CHIMENE. To order me to rest is to increase my grief.

ACT III

Scene 1. *Rodrigue, Elvire.*

ELVIRE. Rodrigue, what are you doing? Why are you here?

RODRIGUE. To carry out the sad ending of my fate.

ELVIRE. How can you have the boldness and the pride
to appear in this house which you have made a place
of mourning?
Have you come to defy the body of the Count?
Didn't you kill him?

RODRIGUE. His life was my shame.
My honor demanded that deed from my hand.

ELVIRE. But a murderer does not seek refuge
in the house of death.

RODRIGUE. I know. I come to give myself up to my judge.
Don't look at me with such surprise.
I am here for my death—after giving death.
My judge is my love, my judge is Chimene.
I deserve death because I deserve her hatred.
And I have come to receive, as a sovereign good,
the decree from her lips and the sword from her hands.

ELVIRE. It is better to leave her alone and avoid her violence.
Don't stay to witness her first outburst.
Leave and don't expose yourself
to the fresh impulse of her anger.

RODRIGUE. No! I have pained her.
Let her anger be boundless for my punishment.
I will avoid a hundred deaths which await me
if by dying sooner I can redouble it.

ELVIRE. Chimene, all in tears, is in the palace,
and she will return with an escort.
Go, Rodrigue, I beg you. I will be blamed.
What will they say if you are here?
Do you want some slanderer, as a final blow,
to accuse her of seeing the assassin of her father?
She is returning. I can see her now.
At least hide, for the sake of her honor.

Scene 2. *Don Sanche, Chimene, Elvire.*

SANCHE. Yes, my Lady, you must have the blood of the murderer.
Your anger is just and your tears justified.
I will not attempt with my words
to soften your anger or bring you consolation.
But if I am able to serve you,
use my sword to punish the guilty man.
Use my love to avenge this death.
My arm will be strong when it is directed by you.

CHIMENE. What woe there is for me!

SANCHE. Let me serve you.

CHIMENE. I would offend the King who has promised justice.

SANCHE. The justice of the law moves slowly
and often the crime is forgotten in the passing of years.
Time in its slowness brings forth too much weeping.
Permit a knight to avenge you by a duel.
It is a surer way and swifter for punishment.

CHIMENE. That is for the last recourse. If I have to come to it,
and if you still feel pity for my plight,
I will then give you leave to avenge me.

SANCHE. It is the one happiness I yearn for.
Since you give me hope, I take my leave now.

Scene 3. *Chimene, Elvire.*

CHIMENE. At last I am freed from the court
and do not have to hide my grief.
I can sigh without restraint
and open up to you my heart and my woe.
My father is dead, Elvire, and the first sword
held by Rodrigue in duel, cut off his life.
Let all my tears flow!
Half of my life put the other half into the grave,
and forces me to avenge after this fatal deed
my father's death on the life of Rodrigue.

ELVIRE. You must take some rest.

CHIMENE.   "Rest" is a strange word
in the midst of such calamity.
How will my sorrow ever end
if I cannot hate the hand which caused it?
And what can I hope for—save endless pain
if I prosecute for a crime and love the criminal?

ELVIRE. He deprives you of a father, and you still love him?

CHIMENE. Love is not strong enough, Elvire, I worship him!
My passion contends with my anger.
Within my enemy I find my lover,
and I know that despite all my wrath,
Rodrigue is still fighting my father in my heart.
He attacks him, bears down, withdraws, defends himself.
He is strong, then weak, then triumphant.
But in this harsh combat of anger and passion,
he tears my heart without dividing my soul.
Yet despite the power of love over me,
I do not hesitate over the way of duty.
I have followed the obligations of honor.
Rodrigue is precious to me, and I am aggrieved in his interest.
My heart takes his side, but that does not count.
I know what I am and that my father is dead.

ELVIRE. Do you intend to prosecute him?

CHIMENE.   That unreal word!
I must prosecute him.
I must demand his head and fear obtaining it.
My death will follow his, and I must punish him.

ELVIRE. Give up this tragic plan.
Don't put yourself under so harsh a law.

CHIMENE. But my father died, almost in my arms.
Am I deaf to his blood crying for vengeance?
My heart, shamefully held by the spell of love,
believes that I owe him only useless tears.
Shall I allow a seductive love
to stifle my honor under cowardly silence?

ELVIRE. You will be excused
if you show less wrath for the man you love,
for so loved a suitor. You have done enough.
You have seen the King. Do not insist on more.
Do not persist in this strange mood.

THE CID

CHIMENE. My honor is at stake. I must be avenged.
However strong the desire of my love,
a noble spirit cannot make a shameful excuse.

ELVIRE. But you love Rodrigue. He cannot offend you.

CHIMENE. I know that.

ELVIRE. Well then, what do you plan to do?

CHIMENE. To preserve my honor and end my sorrow,
I will prosecute, have him slain, and die after him.

SCENE 4. *Rodrigue, Chimene, Elvire.*

RODRIGUE. There is no need to prosecute.
You will have the honor of ending my life.

CHIMENE. Where are we, Elvire? Who is this?
Is Rodrigue here? Is Rodrigue in my house?

RODRIGUE. Do not spare my blood. There is no obstacle now
to my death and to your vengeance.

CHIMENE. God!

RODRIGUE. Listen to me.

CHIMENE. I cannot!

RODRIGUE. For one moment.

CHIMENE. Go, let me die.

RODRIGUE. I will be brief.
And then you can answer with this sword.

CHIMENE. It is still wet with my father's blood.

RODRIGUE. Chimene!

CHIMENE. Take it out of my sight.
It reproaches me for your crime and your life.

RODRIGUE. Look at it then and let it arouse your hate,
and bring on your anger and hasten my punishment.

CHIMENE. It is tainted with my blood.

RODRIGUE. Plunge it into mine,
and it will lose the color of yours.

CHIMENE. What cruel fate is this that in one day
kills the father by the sword and his child by the
sight of the sword!
Take it away from here. I cannot bear it.
You want me to listen and you cause my death.

RODRIGUE. I will obey. I still long
to see my life end by your hand.
Do not expect from my love
any cowardly repentance for a good deed.
Your father's irreparable insult
dishonored my father and shamed me.
You know the effect of such a gesture on a noble spirit.
I was involved in this affront and I sought out the man.
I came to him, and avenged my honor and my father.
I would do it again if there were need.
At first my love fought on your behalf
against my father and myself.
You can judge of its power: even in that offense
I hesitated before taking vengeance.
Faced with displeasing you or suffering an affront,
I thought I was too quick to take the sword
and blamed myself for too much violence.
Your beauty would have been the victor,
had I not been convinced
that a man without honor was unworthy of you,
that despite the place I had in your heart,
you would hate me dishonored;
listening to your love and obeying its voice
would desecrate the choice of your love.
Let me say it again, although it is painful,
let me say it until I breathe my last breath:
I have offended you—but I had to
in order to wipe out my shame and deserve you.
But now that I have satisfied my father and my honor,
I come to satisfy you.
I am here in order to offer my life.
I did what was my obligation, and now this is my present duty.
I know that the death of a father hardens you against
  my crime,
and I will not rob you of a victim.
Sacrifice courageously to the blood he lost
the man whose honor was in shedding it.

CHIMENE. Rodrigue, it is true. Even if I am your enemy,
I cannot blame you for escaping infamy.
However strong my outburst of grief,
I do not accuse you and I weep for sorrow.
I know what honor, after such outrage,

THE CID

demands of a noble heart.
You did your duty as a knight,
and in doing it, you taught me mine.
Your fateful valor instructs me in its victory.
It avenged your father and preserved your honor.
The same pride is before me, and, for my grief,
I must preserve my honor and avenge my father.
My love for you is my despair.
If some other cause had taken my father from me,
I would have found in the joy of seeing you
the one solace I could have hoped for.
I would have found a cure to my grief
when your loving hand dried my tears.
Now I have to destroy you after losing him.
This quelling of my love is due my honor.
And this frightful duty, whose demand is my death,
forces me to strive toward your death.
Do not expect from my love
any cowardly sentiments. In the cause of your punishment,
though our love pleads in your favor,
my soul must equal yours in nobleness.
In offending me, you became worthy of me.
In asking for your death, I will be worthy of you.

RODRIGUE. Don't put off any longer what your honor claims.
It wants my life and I give it to you.
Sacrifice it to your noble purpose.
The blow will be as welcome to me as the decree.
If after my crime you wait upon slow justice,
you will delay your honor as well as my punishment.
I will die in happiness if it is by your hand.

CHIMENE. I am your adversary. I am not your executioner.
If you offer me your hand, is it for me to take?
I have to attack your life but you have to defend it.
I must get it from someone other than from you.
I am to prosecute you but not punish you.

RODRIGUE. Whatever our love plead in my favor,
your soul must equal mine in nobleness.
To borrow someone else in order to avenge a father
is no solution, my Chimene.
My hand alone avenged my father,
your hand alone should avenge yours.

CHIMENE. Why do you insist on this cruel point?
You were avenged without help and yet you offer me help!
I will follow your example. My courage is too great
to allow my honor to be shared with you.
My father and my honor will owe nothing
to the force of your love and your despair.

RODRIGUE. Oh! the hardness of this honor! Can I do nothing
to win this grace from you?
In the name of a dead father, in the name of our love,
punish me through vengeance or at least through pity.
Your wretched lover will be less grieved
in dying by your hand than in living with your shame.

CHIMENE. I do not hate you.

RODRIGUE. You should.

CHIMENE. I cannot.

RODRIGUE. Have you such little fear of blame and slander?
When my crime is learned and your love still endures,
what will not envy and falsehood proclaim?
Force them to silence and without further speech,
preserve your fame by causing me to die.

CHIMENE. It will be more manifest if you live.
I want the voice of the blackest envy
to raise to heaven my honor and to pity my grief,
knowing that I love you and still prosecute you.
Leave me. You stand before me
as the man I love and whom I must destroy.
Conceal your departure under the shadow of night.
If you are seen leaving here, my honor may be imperiled.
The one chance for slander
is to learn that here I allowed your presence.
Do not give it cause to attack my virtue.

RODRIGUE. Let me die!

CHIMENE. Go!

RODRIGUE. To what are you resigned?

CHIMENE. Despite my love, which thwarts my anger,
I will do all I can to avenge my father.
And yet in the face of so cruel a duty,
my one wish is to have no power.

RODRIGUE. Miracle of love!

CHIMENE. No greater distress is possible.

THE CID

RODRIGUE. Our fathers will cost us countless woes.

CHIMENE. Rodrigue, who would have believed
that our happiness which was so close could fail?

RODRIGUE. Chimene, who would have said
that so close to the harbor, against all appearances,
so swift a storm would have broken all hope?

CHIMENE. Leave now. I wish to hear no more.

RODRIGUE. Farewell. I will pursue a dying life
until your prosecution takes it from me.

CHIMENE. If I succeed in that, I pledge my word
not to live an hour after your death.
Farewell. Go now and take care no one sees you.

ELVIRE. However great our trials, heaven . . .

CHIMENE. Trouble me no further. Leave me to myself.
For my tears I need silence and the night.

SCENE 5. *Don Diegue.*

DIEGUE. A perfect happiness is impossible to know.
Our happiest moments are tinged with sadness.
A few worries in every event always
disturb the purity of our satisfaction.
In the midst of happiness my soul is troubled:
I am surrounded with joy and yet tremble with fear.
I have seen the corpse of the man who insulted me,
and yet I cannot find the hand which avenged me.
I have uselessly exerted myself
in looking throughout the city—despite my age.
The meager strength my years have left me
is wasted vainly in seeking the victor.
Everywhere throughout this dark night
I thought I was embracing him but it was a shadow.
And my love, tricked by this deceptive ghost,
engenders suspicions which redouble my fears.
I can find no signs of his flight.
I fear the friends and consorts of the dead count.
Their numbers terrify my mind.
Either Rodrigue is dead or languishing in prison.
God in heaven! Is my sight again deceived,
or is this at last my one hope?
Yes, it is he, there is no doubt. My prayers are answered,
my fears are over and my worry ended.

SCENE 6. *Don Diegue, Don Rodrigue.*

DIEGUE. Rodrigue, at last heaven sends you to me!

RODRIGUE. Alas!

DIEGUE. Do not mingle your sighs with my joy.
Let me catch my breath before praising you.
My valor has no reason to disown you.
You emulated it and your famed daring
means the heroes of my race live again in you.
You are their descendant and you come from me.
Your first thrust of the sword equals all of mine.
Ardently your virile youth
reaches my fame in this great test.
Support of my old age, height of my happiness,
touch this white hair which you have honored,
kiss this cheek and you will see the spot
where the insult was stamped, wiped out by your courage.

RODRIGUE. The honor was due you. I could do nothing less,
since I had come from you and was raised by you.
I consider myself privileged and my heart is content
that my first combat pleases the author of my days.
But in your pleasure, do not be jealous
if I dare in my turn to seek satisfaction.
Allow my despair now freely to burst forth.
For too long have your words tricked it.
I am not sorry I served you,
but give me back the happiness this combat stole.
My arm, to avenge you, raised against my love,
took away my soul in that honorable fight.
Say nothing more to me. For your sake, I have lost everything.
What I owed you, I have paid back generously.

DIEGUE. Raise higher than this the fruit of your victory.
I gave you life and you have given back honor to me.
And because honor is dearer to me than life,
I owe you all the more in return.
But you must expel from your noble heart all weakness.
We have only one honor. There are many mistresses.
Love is but a pleasure, honor is a duty.

RODRIGUE. What are you saying to me?

DIEGUE. What you must know.

RODRIGUE. My offended honor is taking vengeance on me,
and you dare urge me to the shame of infidelity!
It is the same infamy and is equally attached
to the warrior without courage and the perfidious lover.
Do not mock my fidelity.
Let me be noble without being a perjurer.
My bonds are too strong to be broken thus.
Even without hope, my faith still binds me,
and unable to leave Chimene or to possess her,
the death I am seeking is my sweetest torment.

DIEGUE. There is no time left to seek your death.
Your prince and your country need you.
The boats that were feared, already at the river,
are planning to surprise the city and pillage all about.
The Moors are on us. The tide and the night
will bring them noiselessly in one hour to our walls.
Disorder reigns in the court, and the people are alarmed.
All you hear are shouts and all you see are tears.
In this public disaster luck granted
my finding at my door five hundred friends,
who, knowing of my insult, and prompted by the same zeal,
came to offer themselves to avenge my quarrel.
You anticipated them. But their valor
can be better used against the African army.
March at their head where honor places you.
Their noble company wants you as their leader.
Go and withstand the attack of our old enemies.
If you wish to die, you will find there a worthy death.
Seize this chance, since it is offered you.
Your king will hereby owe his safety to your sacrifice.
But I would rather you return with palm leaves on your head.
Do not limit your honor to avenging an affront.
Bear it farther. Let your valor force
our monarch to a pardon and Chimene to silence.
If you love her, know that to return victorious
is the one way of again winning her heart.
But time is too precious to be lost in words.
Let me interrupt you here and send you off.
Come, I will show you the way, and you will show your king
that what he loses in the Count, he recovers in you.

ACT IV

Scene 1. *Chimene, Elvire.*

CHIMENE. Isn't this a mere rumor? Are you sure, Elvire?

ELVIRE. You would never believe how he is admired by all;
how all, with one voice, raise to heaven
the glorious deeds of this young hero.
The Moors, to their shame, scattered before him.
Their landing was swift, their flight was swifter.
Three hours of combat gave to our warriors
full victory and two kings as prisoners.
Our leader's valor found no obstacle.

CHIMENE. Did Rodrigue's hand perform those miracles?

ELVIRE. The two kings are the prize of his great effort.
It was his hand which conquered and took them.

CHIMENE. From whom have you learned this bewildering news?

ELVIRE. From the people who shout his praise everywhere.
They call him the author of their joy,
their guardian angel and their liberator.

CHIMENE. How does the King look upon such valor?

ELVIRE. Rodrigue has not yet dared to appear in his presence.
But Don Diegue, elated, in the name of his son
has presented him with the two crowned captives in chains,
and has asked of our noble prince that, as a favor,
he receive the man who saved the country.

CHIMENE. Is he wounded?

ELVIRE. There is no report of that.
Your color changes. Try to recover your feelings.

CHIMENE. I must try to recover my weakened anger.
Through worry for him, must I forget myself?
He is praised and acclaimed, and my heart consents.
My honor is mute and my duty powerless.
Silence, my love, let my anger come forth!
He may have conquered two kings, but he killed my father.
This dress of black where I can see my grief
is the first result of his valor,
and no matter what is said elsewhere of his great heart,
here every object speaks to me of his crime.

THE CID

You who give strength to my anger,
veils, crepe and dress, ornaments of woe,
pomp which his first victory enjoins on me,
sustain my honor against my passion;
and when my love is too powerful,
speak to my mind of my sad duty.
Fear nothing as you attack a triumphant man.

ELVIRE. Calm your feelings, here is the Infanta.

SCENE 2. *Infanta, Chimene, Leonor, Elvire.*

INFANTA. I do not come here to console you;
I come to mingle my sighs with your tears.

CHIMENE. Rather should you participate in the common joy
and delight in the fortune that heaven sends you.
No one but me has the right to lament.
The peril out of which Rodrigue has drawn us,
and the safety of the people which his valor has preserved,
allow only me to shed tears on this day.
He has saved the city and served his king.
His warrior's arm was fatal only to me.

INFANTA. It is true, Chimene, he has performed miracles.

CHIMENE. When this painful report reached my ears,
I heard him loudly called
as brave in war as he is unfortunate in love.

INFANTA. But why should this public acclaim be painful to you?
He possessed your soul and lived by your laws.
If you praise his valor, you will honor your own choice.

CHIMENE. Everyone else can praise him with justice.
But for me his praise is a new torment.
By raising him so high, you embitter my pain.
I see what I am destroying when I see what he is worth.
This is cruel vexation for the mind of a lover.
The more I learn of his valor, the more my passion grows.
Yet my duty is still the stronger,
and in spite of my love, it will seek his death.

INFANTA. You were highly esteemed yesterday for this duty.
The struggle you waged was so noble,
so worthy of a great heart, that every courtier
admired your courage and pitied your love.
Will you accept now the counsel of a faithful friend?

CHIMENE. I would be criminal not to obey you.

INFANTA. What was lawful yesterday is no longer today.
Rodrigue now is our one support.
He is the hope and the love of a jubilant people,
the prop of Castille and the terror of the Moors.
Even the King subscribes to the truth
that your father lives again in him,
and, to explain matters briefly,
in his death you pursue the destruction of us all.
To avenge a father is it permissible
to give over one's country to the enemy?
Is your prosecution fair to us?
Do we have any part in this crime?
You are not obliged to marry
the man whom a dead father obliged you to accuse.
Let me help remove this desire from your heart.
Obliterate your love but leave us his life.

CHIMENE. It is not for me to have such kindness.
The duty that embitters me is not limited.
Although my love is still involved with this conqueror,
even if the people worship him and the King flatters him,
even if he is surrounded by valiant warriors,
I will go under the cypress trees to crush his laurels.

INFANTA. It is a noble thing, when to avenge a father
our duty attacks so beloved a person,
but it is more noble and of the highest worth
to give up for the public good the interests of family.
Believe me, it is enough that you extinguish your love.
He will be punished enough if he is no longer in your heart.
Let the prosperity of the nation impose this law on you:
Besides, what can the King grant you now?

CHIMENE. He can refuse me, but I will not be silent.

INFANTA. Dear Chimene, reflect carefully on what you should do.
Adieu. You must reach your decision in solitude.

CHIMENE. After this death of my father, I have no choice.

SCENE 3. *The King, Diegue, Arias, Rodrigue, Sanche.*

KING. Noble heir of an illustrious family
which was always the glory and support of Castille,
race with so many ancestors famous for their valor,

THE CID

whom you matched in your trial valor,
my power is too limited to reward you.
It is less than the merit you have shown.
The country, made safe from so fierce an enemy,
my scepter, firmly placed in my hand by yours,
the Moors, defeated before I could give
orders to repulse their attack—
these are not exploits which leave your king
the means or the hope of paying his debt to you.
But your two captive kings have spoken your reward.
Both of them called you their Cid in my presence.
Since in their language Cid is the equal of Lord,
I will not begrudge you this honorable title.
Henceforth you are the Cid: may all obstacles collapse before this name!
May it fill Granada and Toledo with fear,
and may it show to all who live under my law
what you mean to me and what I owe to you!

RODRIGUE. Sire, will your Majesty spare my shame!
It values too highly a meager service,
and forces me to blush before so great a king
at deserving so poorly the honor I have received.
I know that to the welfare of your empire I owe
the blood coursing in my veins and the air I breathe,
and even if I lost them for so worthy an object,
I would merely be carrying out the duty of a subject.

KING. All those who are bound by this duty to my service
do not satisfy their obligations with the same courage,
and when valor does not attempt the impossible,
it does not produce such extraordinary results.
Allow this praise, then, and tell me
at greater length the real tale of your victory.

RODRIGUE. Sire, you learned that in the press of this danger,
which cast over the entire city a deep fright,
a group of friends meeting at my father's house
pleaded with my heart which was still confused . . .
But Sire, you must pardon my boldness
if I dared to use it without your authority.
The danger was coming close. Their brigade was ready.
If I had come to the court, I was risking my life,
and if I had to lose my life, it was more pleasing for me
to die when I was fighting for you.

KING. I pardon the violence with which you avenged your
   insult.
The State you defended speaks in your defense.
Henceforth Chimene's plea will not be considered.
I will listen to her and console her. That is all.
Continue.

RODRIGUE.   Under my direction these men advanced,
and showed on their faces a virile confidence.
We were five hundred at first, but with a swift reinforcement,
we were three thousand when we reached the harbor;
and seeing us march, with determination in our faces,
the most terrified recovered their courage.
On arriving, I hid two-thirds of the men
in the bottom of the boats which we found there.
The rest, whose numbers increased hourly,
remained close by, devoured by impatience,
and lay on the ground, where they kept silence,
and spent a part of a magnificent night.
At my command, the guard did likewise,
and staying out of sight, they helped my stratagem.
Then I boldly pretended I had received from you
the order I announced and gave to all.

   That obscure light which falls from the stars
at last showed us, with the tide, thirty ships.
The wave swelled under them, and in a joint effort
the Moors and the sea entered the harbor.
We let them pass. Everything semed quiet to them.
Not a soldier at the harbor, not a soldier at the city walls.
Our deep silence deceived them
and they no longer doubted they had caught us.
Fearlessly they approached, anchored, disembarked,
and rushed into the hands waiting for them.
We rose up then, and all together
uttered a thousand war cries which reached the heavens.
More of our men answered these cries from their ships.
We appeared in arms. The Moors were thrown into rout.
Terror seized them while they were still landing.
Before the fighting began, they knew they had lost.
They were bent on pillaging and they encountered battle.
We attacked by water and by land,
and caused rivers of their blood to flow
before one of them could resist.

THE CID

But soon, in spite of us, their princes rallied them,
their courage came back and their terror fled.
The shame of dying without combat
stopped their confusion and reanimated their valor.
Against us they firmly drew their scimitars
and made a horrible mingling of our blood with theirs.
The land, the river, their ships, the harbor
were the sites of slaughter where death reigned.

    Countless acts and courageous deeds
were not even visible under the cover of darkness,
where each man, the only witness of his own thrusts,
could not see whom fortune was favoring.
I went everywhere encouraging our men,
making some move ahead, lending support to others,
placing those who joined with us, urging them on,
and I did not know the result until daybreak.
At last its light showed our advantage.
The Moors saw their defeat and then lost courage
when they saw reinforcements come to our help.
The hope of victory turned into the fear of death.
They reached their ships and cut the cables.
With terrible shrieks resounding everywhere,
they retreated in an uproar, without considering
whether their kings could retreat with them.
Their terror was too strong for them to heed this duty.
The incoming tide had brought them, and the ebb tide took them away
while their kings, in combat with us,
and a few of their men, wounded by our swords,
fought valiantly and sold their lives dearly.
In vain I urged them to surrender,
but they held their scimitars and refused to listen.
Then seeing all their men fall at their feet
and aware they were fighting in vain,
they asked for the leader. I came forward and they surrendered.
I sent both of them to you at the same time.
And the fighting stopped because there were no more fighters.
    It was thus that in serving you . . .

SCENE 4. *The King, Diegue, Rodrigue, Arias, Alonso, Sanche.*

ALONSO. Sire, Chimene is here asking for justice.
KING. I am sorry to hear this. Her duty is now oppressive.
(*To* RODRIGUE.)
Leave. There is no need to force her to see you.
Rather than thanking you, I am sending you away.
But before you leave, come here, let me embrace you.
(*Exit* RODRIGUE.)
DIEGUE. Chimene prosecutes him and yet wants to save him.
KING. I was told she loves him and I will now test her.
(*To* DIEGUE.)
Show more sadness on your face.

SCENE 5. *The King, Diegue, Arias, Sanche, Alonso, Chimene, Elvire.*

KING. You can rest now,
Chimene, because the outcome satisfies your request.
If Rodrigue won over our enemies,
he died in our presence from the wounds he received.
Offer thanks to Heaven who has avenged you.
(*To* DIEGUE.)
See her face, how it changes color.
DIEGUE. She is fainting, Sire, and from perfect love.
See all the signs in her swoon.
Her grief has betrayed the secrets of her soul.
We can no longer doubt her love.
CHIMENE. You say Rodrigue is dead?
KING. No, he lives,
and bears for you an unchanging love.
Quiet your grief which we aroused.
CHIMENE. Sire, it is possible to faint from joy as well as from sorrow.
Excess of happiness is able to weaken us,
and when it surprises the soul, it overcomes the senses.
KING. Do you want us to believe the impossible on your behalf?
Your grief, Chimene, was too visible.
CHIMENE. Sire, then add this climax to my woe,
and call my fainting the result of my grief.

THE CID

A just anger had overcome my feelings.
His death had taken away the object of my prosecution.
If he dies from wounds received for the good of his country,
my vengeance is lost and my plans betrayed.
Such a noble end is offensive to my cause.
I am asking for his death, but not a glorious death,
not one which elevates him so high in acclaim,
not on a bed of honor, but on a scaffold.
Let him die for my father, and not for his country.
Let his name be sullied and his memory tarnished.
To die for one's country is not a sad fate.
That noble death is immortality.

Therefore I am glad for his victory, and I am unashamed.
It assures the State and gives me back my victim.
He is noble now and famous among all warriors.
He is the leader, crowned, not with flowers but with laurel,
and, to say in one word what I think of him: he is
worthy of being sacrificed to the shade of my father.

Alas! the vain hope I indulged in!
Rodrigue has nothing to fear from me.
What power could my tears, that are scorned, have against him?
Your whole empire is a place of refuge for him.
He will be given every freedom under your rule.
He triumphs over me as he did over his enemies.
In their spilled blood strangled justice
serves as a new trophy for the conqueror's crime.
We increase the pomp, and scorn for the law
makes us follow his chariot between two kings.

KING. My daughter, your outburst is too violent.
When justice is meted out, everything has to be weighed.
Your father was killed, but he was the aggressor.
Justice itself commands me to use leniency.
Before you accuse my judgment,
consult your heart. Rodrigue is its master,
and your love secretly gives thanks to your king,
whose favor protects your lover.

CHIMENE. Not my lover! My enemy! He's the object of my anger,
the author of my woes! the assassin of my father!
You give so little heed to my just prosecution
that you think you favor me by not listening to me!

Since you refuse my grief any justice,
Sire, allow me to have recourse to weapons.
That is the manner in which I must be avenged.
I ask all your warriors for his head.
Let one of them bring it to me, and I am his conquest.
Let the combat begin, Sire, and when it is over,
if Rodrigue is punished, I will marry the conqueror.
Allow this to be published under the seal of your authority.

King. This custom, long ago established here,
under the pretense of punishing an unjust assault,
weakens the State with the loss of good fighters.
Often the deplorable outcome of this abuse
crushes the innocent and defends the guilty.
I exempt Rodrigue from it. He is too valuable
to expose to the blows of a capricious fate;
and whatever crime his magnanimous heart did commit,
the Moors took away in their flight.

Diegue. Sire, for him alone are you reversing a law
observed by your court many times?
What will your people believe, what will envy say,
if under your protection he runs no risk
and makes this a pretext not to appear
where men of honor seek a noble death?
Such favors would sully his honor.
Let him taste, without blushing, the fruits of his victory.
He punished the Count's rashness;
he did it as a brave man and must maintain it.

King. Since you wish it, I will grant him leave.
But a thousand would take the place of one conquered warrior,
and the prize which Chimene has promised the conqueror
would make of all my warriors his enemies.
To set him alone against all would be unjust.
Let him go into the lists only once.
Choose the man you wish, Chimene, and choose well.
But after this one combat, ask for nothing more.

Diegue. Do not excuse thereby those who might be terrified.
Leave the lists opened. No one will enter
after Rodrigue's revelation today.
Who has enough courage to attack him?
Who would risk his life against such an adversary?

THE CID

SANCHE. Open the lists and you will find the assailant.
I am this rash man—or better, I am this valiant man.
Grant this grace to my ardor, Chimene.
You will remember your promise.

KING. Chimene, will you put your cause into his hands?

CHIMENE. I gave my promise, Sire.

KING.   Be ready tomorrow.

DIEGUE. No, Sire, let there be no delay.
A courageous man is always ready.

KING. Can he fight again so soon after the battle?

DIEGUE. He has taken rest by telling you all that happened.

KING. At least for one or two hours I insist that he rest.
But for fear lest such a combat become an example,
and to testify to all that regretfully I allow
this bloody proceeding which never had my favor,
he will not have the presence of myself or of my court.
(To ARIAS.*)*
Only you will judge the valor of the fighters.
See to it that both behave as honorable men,
and when the fight is over, bring the victor to me.
Whoever he be, his effort will earn the same prize.
I myself will present him to Chimene,
and he will receive her troth as a reward.

CHIMENE. Sire, how can you impose on me so hard a ruling!

KING. You complain, but your love, rather than confessing your complaint,
will accept it without compulsion if Rodrigue is victor.
Stop complaining about so sweet a decree.
Whichever it is of the two, I will make your husband.

ACT V

Scene 1. *Chimene, Rodrigue.*

CHIMENE. Rodrigue! You dare show yourself here in daytime!
You jeopardize my honor. Leave at once, I beg you.

RODRIGUE. I am going to die, Chimene, and I come to you here,
before the mortal deed, to bid you my last farewell.
The unchanging love which binds me under your law
will not accept my death unless I pay you homage with it.

CHIMENE. You are going to die!

RODRIGUE. I am hastening to those happy moments
which will give my life over to your resentment.

CHIMENE. You are going to die! Is Don Sanche so terrible
that he instills fear in your invincible heart?
Who has made you so weak, or who has made him so strong?
Rodrigue, about to fight, thinks he is already dead!
The man who had no fear of the Moors or of my father,
is going to fight Don Sanche, and gives up hope!
So, in time of need, your courage collapses?

RODRIGUE. I am going to my punishment and not to a duel.
Since you want my death, my faithful love
relieves me of any desire to defend my life.
My heart is the same, but my arms are useless
when they would preserve what does not please you.
Last night would also have been mortal for me,
if I had fought solely for myself.
But in defending my king, his people and my land,
I would have been traitor had I fought badly.
My spirit does not have enough hate of life
to wish to die by faithlessness.
Now that only I am concerned,
you ask for my death and I accept your decree.
Your resentment has chosen the hand of a warrior
(I was not worthy of dying by your hand):
I will not ward off the sword thrusts of this man.
I owe respect to the one who fights for you,
and since it is your honor that is being defended,

THE CID

I will uncover my chest before him
and worship in his your hand which will slay me.

CHIMENE. If the just violence of a sad duty
which forces me in spite of myself to prosecute your valor,
prescribes for your love so hard a law
that it makes you defenseless before the man who fights for me,
do not forget in this blindness
that your honor is at stake as well as your life,
and that despite the glory Rodrigue knew alive,
when he is dead, he will be looked upon as vanquished.
Your honor is dearer to you than I am,
since it plunged your hands into my father's blood,
and made you renounce, in spite of your passion,
the secret hope of possessing me.
Yet you esteem this so lightly
that without fighting back you ask to be vanquished.
What inconsistency is debasing your honor?
Why did you lose it, or why did you once have it?
Are you honorable only in your will to insult me?
Have you no courage except to offend me?
Did you treat my father with such harshness
so that after defeating him, you could allow a conqueror?
Give up wishing to die. Let me prosecute you
while you defend your honor, even if you have no desire to live.

RODRIGUE. After the death of the Count and the defeat of the Moors,
does my honor need any more exploits?
It can now scorn the need of self-defense.
It is known that my courage will undertake anything,
that my valor is strong and that nothing is precious to me
under Heaven after my honor.
No, believe what you wish, in this combat
Rodrigue may die without harming his honor,
without being accused of lacking courage,
without being defeated, without allowing a victor.
People will say: "He loved Chimene.
He had no desire to live and deserve her hate.
He yielded to the rigor of that fate
which forced Chimene to seek his death.
She demanded his head, and had he refused,
his generous heart would have committed a crime.

In avenging his honor, he lost his love,
in avenging his beloved, he lost his life,
preferring, more than the hope which had ruled his soul,
his honor to Chimene and Chimene to his life."
Thus, in this combat you will see my death
increase my honor rather than diminish it.
And this honor will follow my willful death
which in no other way could have satisfied you.

CHIMENE. Since your life and your honor are too weak
to keep you from rushing into death,
even if I loved you, Rodrigue,
defend yourself now as revenge, to keep me from Don Sanche.
Fight to release me from a condition
which gives me over to the object of my aversion.
Must I say more? think of your own defense
in order to force my duty, and impose silence on me.
If you feel your heart still in love with me,
come out victorious from a combat of which Chimene is the prize.
Farewell. These last words cover me with shame.

RODRIGUE. Does the enemy exist whom I could not defeat?
Appear before me: Navarese, Moors, and Castillans,
and all valorous men whom Spain has raised.
Join together and form an army
to fight a single man aroused as I am.
Join all your efforts to defeat so sweet a hope.
You would be too few to reach success.

SCENE 2. *Infanta.*

INFANTA. Respect for my birth, shall I heed you again
who make a crime of my love?
Shall I listen to you, love, whose sweet power
makes my prayers revolt against this proud tyrant?
Poor princess, to which of the two
must you be obedient?
Rodrigue, your valor makes you worthy of my name,
but though you are valiant, you are not the son of a king.

Pitiless fate whose rigor separates
my honor from my desire!
Can it be said that the choice of so rare a virtue
costs my passion such deep sorrow?

What sighs must my heart
be prepared to utter
if it is never able from so long a torment
to extinguish my love or accept my lover!

I have too many scruples and my reason is amazed
at my scorn for such a worthy choice.
Although my birth gives me to monarchs alone,
I will live honorably, Rodrigue, under your law.
Since you conquered two kings,
could you lack a crown?
Does not the great title of Cid which you have just won
show clearly over whom you should reign?

He is worthy of me, but he belongs to Chimene.
The gift I made is now my undoing.
The death of a father has put so little hate between them
that the duty to her family prosecutes him regretfully.
I must hope for no result
of his crime or of my suffering,
since, to punish me, fate has allowed
love to continue even between two enemies.

SCENE 3. *Infanta, Leonor.*

INFANTA. Why do you come, Leonor?

LEONOR.   To rejoice, your Highness,
over the peace which your soul has found at last.

INFANTA. How could such peace come into my endless pain?

LEONORE. If love lives on hope, and dies with it,
Rodrigue can no longer charm your courage.
You know the fight in which Chimene engages him.
Since either he will die or become her husband,
your hope is over, and your mind is cured.

INFANTA. How far it is from being that!

LEANOR.   What do you hope for?

INFANTA. Rather what hope would you forbid me?
If Rodrigue fights under these conditions,
I have many means to change the result.
Love is the author of my cruel suffering
and love teaches wiles to the minds of lovers.

LEONOR. What would your power be, since a dead father
could not arouse discord in their minds?
For Chimene easily shows by her conduct
that hate does not direct her prosecution.
She was granted a combat and for her fighter
she just now accepted the first one to offer himself.
She had no recourse to those noble men
who have become famous in their great exploits.
Don Sanche is all she has and he deserves her choice,
because he is fighting for the first time.
In this duel she prefers this lack of experience.
As he is without fame, she is without fear.
The ease of all this must show you
that she is seeking a combat which will fulfill her duty,
give Rodrigue an easy victory,
and permit her to appear appeased.

INFANTA. I have seen this, and yet my heart,
as much as Chimene's, worships this conqueror.
How can I be resigned?

LEONOR. You must remember your birth.
Heaven owes you a king, and you are in love with a
 subject!

INFANTA. My passion has changed its object.
I am not in love with Rodrigue, a mere noble.
My feelings give him another name.
I love the author of those marvelous deeds.
I love the valiant Cid, the master of two kings.
Yet I will overcome my feelings, not through fear of
 censure,
but to refrain from tormenting so beautiful a love;
and when, to suit my purpose, he is crowned,
I will not take back what I gave away.
Since his victory in such a battle is certain,
I will once again give him to Chimene.
And you who know the real suffering of my heart,
will watch me accomplish what I began.

SCENE 4. *Chimene, Elvire.*

CHIMENE. Elvire, can you see my suffering and my plight?
Nothing can be hoped for and everything is to be feared.
My heart forms no prayer that is acceptable.

THE CID

Each of my desires brings a quick repentance.
Two rivals for my hand are in combat,
and the happier outcome will cost me tears.
Whatever fate commands on my behalf,
my father is unavenged or my lover is dead.

ELVIRE. In either way you will be consoled.
Either you have Rodrigue or you are avenged.
And whatever fate decides for you,
it will glorify your honor and give you a husband.

CHIMENE. He will be the object of my hate or my anger.
The murderer of Rodrigue or my father's murderer!
In either case, I will have a husband
stained with blood I have cherished.
My soul rebels against both solutions.
More than death I fear the end of my quarrel.
Vengeance and love, bewildering me,
have no consolation at this high price.
May the prime mover of my outrageous fate
end this combat without a victor,
without making one of them a conqueror or a defeated man!

ELVIRE. That would be too harsh an outcome.
The combat will be a new suffering for you
if it obliges you to ask again for justice,
to live with your worthy resentment,
and continue to seek the death of your lover.
It is better that his unusual valor
impose silence on you as it crowns his brow,
that the law of the duel stifle your sighs
and that the King force you to follow your desire.

CHIMENE. When he is victor, do you think I will surrender?
My duty is too strong and my loss too great.
The law of the duel and the will of the King
are not enough to make the law for me.
He can overcome Don Sanche with very little effort,
but not so easily the honor of Chimene.
And whatever a monarch has promised the victor,
my honor will make for me a thousand enemies more.

ELVIRE. Take care lest Heaven, to punish this strange pride,
allow you to be avenged at the end.
Why persist in refusing the joy
of maintaining an honorable silence?
What does your duty expect, and what does it hope for?

Will the death of your lover give you back your father?
Is one calamity so insignificant for you
that you need loss after loss and grief after grief?
Come now! In the obstinate caprice of your mind
you do not deserve the lover you are destined to have.
Heaven in justified anger may well
leave you Don Sanche for a husband after Rodrigue's death.

CHIMENE. Elvire, I have endured enough suffering.
Do not increase it with this fatal augury.
If I can, I will avoid both men.
If I can't, my prayers are for Rodrigue in this duel.
Not that a mad passion inclines me toward him,
but if he were defeated, I would belong to Don Sanche.
This fear gives rise to my desire.
(DON SANCHE *enters.*)
It is he, Elvire, all is over!

SCENE 5. *Don Sanche, Chimene, Elvire.*

SANCHE. Since I have to lay this sword at your feet . . .
CHIMENE. Still covered with Rodrigue's blood?
Traitor, how can you come into my presence
after taking the life of the man I loved?
Now I can speak of love, there is no need to hide it.
My father is appeased, there is no more constraint.
The same sword assured my honor,
thrust my soul into despair and released my love.

SANCHE. With a more calm mind . . .
CHIMENE. You still dare to speak,
and you are the hated slayer of a hero whom I love!
You killed him treacherously. So valiant a warrior
could not have succumbed to such an adversary.
Hope for nothing from me. You did not serve me.
You took life itself away when you thought
  you were avenging me.

SANCHE. Your false impression—if only you would listen . . .
CHIMENE. Do you want me to listen to you boast of his death,
to hear calmly the insolence with which
you depict his woe, my crime, and your bravery?

THE CID

SCENE 6. *The King, Diegue, Arias, Sanche, Alonso, Chimene, Elvire.*

CHIMENE. Sire, there is no need now to conceal from you
what all my efforts were not able to hide.
I was in love. You knew this. But to avenge my father,
I was willing to proscribe my beloved.
Your Majesty, Sire, could see
how I subordinated my love to duty.
Now Rodrigue is dead, and his death has changed me
from an implacable enemy into an afflicted lover.
I owed this vengeance to the man who gave me life,
and now I owe these tears to my love.
Don Sanche destroyed me by taking my defense,
and I am the reward for the arm that destroyed me.
Sire, if pity can move a king,
I beg you to revoke so harsh a law.
As a prize for a victory in which I lost the man I loved,
I leave him my fortune. And I pray he leave me to myself.
In some sacred cloister let me weep without pause,
to the end of my life, for my father and for Rodrigue.

DIEGUE. She is still in love, Sire, and does not believe it a crime
to confess in words so legitimate a love.
Chimene, learn that Rodrigue is not dead.
Don Sanche was defeated and made a false report.

SANCHE. Sire, she was deceived, in spite of my efforts, by too much ardor.
I had left the fight in order to tell her of the outcome.
The noble warrior who charms her heart
said when he disarmed me, "Have no fear.
I would rather leave the victory uncertain
than take your life which was risked for Chimene.
But since my duty calls me to the King,
go tell her for me of our combat,
and take her your sword in the name of the victor."
Sire, I went to Chimene. The sword deceived her.
On seeing me, she thought I was the victor,
and her anger at once betrayed her love
with such transport and impatience
that I could not make myself heard.

Although defeated, I look upon myself as fortunate,
and despite the anxiety of my own love,
losing infinitely much, I welcome my defeat
which ensures the noble outcome of so perfect a love.

KING. My daughter, you must not be ashamed of this pure love,
nor look for ways of disavowing it.
A praiseworthy shame should have no power over you.
Your honor is redeemed and your duty is discharged.
Your father is at peace, and you are avenged
by placing Rodrigue in danger so many times.
You see that Heaven decrees a different end.
Having done so much for your father, do something now for yourself.
Do not rebel against my command
which gives you a husband you have loved so dearly.

SCENE 7. *The King, Diegue, Arias, Rodrigue, Alonso, Sanche, Infanta, Chimene, Leonor, Elvire.*

INFANTA. Dry your tears, Chimene, and gladly receive
from the hands of your princess this noble conqueror.

RODRIGUE. Do not be offended, Sire, if in your presence
my loving respect bends my knees before her.
I am not here, Chimene, to demand my conquest.
I have come again to offer you my life.
My love will not exploit for myself
the law of combat or the will of the King.
If all that has been done is too little for a father,
tell me in what way you will be satisfied.
Must I fight a thousand more rivals,
extend my labors to the two extremes of the earth,
attack a camp singlehanded, rout an army,
exceed the fame of legendary heroes?
If my crime can thus be pardoned,
I will undertake and carry out any deed.
But if your proud honor is still unbending,
and will not be appeased without the death of the criminal,
do not arm the power of a man against me.
My head is here before you. Avenge yourself with
   your own hand.
Your hand alone has the right to overcome me.

THE CID

Take this vengeance which no one else can.
But then let my death be sufficient for the punishment.
Do not banish me from your memory.
And since my death preserves your honor,
preserve my memory as you take your revenge,
and say at times as you pity my fate,
"If he had not loved me, he would not be dead."

CHIMENE. Stand up, Rodrigue. Let me speak, Sire.
I have said too much, to deny my words.
Rodrigue has a strength I cannot despise.
When a king commands, he should be obeyed.
But to whatever you have condemned me,
can you before your very eyes allow this marriage?
And even if you wish from me this dutiful effort,
can the justice of your kingship permit it?
If Rodrigue becomes so necessary to the state,
must I be the reward for what he does for you?
Must I give myself up to the eternal reproach
of having bathed my hands in the blood of my father?

KING. Often enough, time has justified
what once seemed criminal.
Rodrigue won you. You belong to him.
But although his valor conquered you today,
I would have to be an enemy of your honor
to give him now the reward of his victory.
A deferred marriage will not infringe upon a law
which promises him your faith without heed to time.
Take a year, if you wish, to dry your tears.
In the meantime, Rodrigue, you must take up arms.
After conquering the Moors on our shores,
upsetting their plans and repulsing their efforts,
go wage war on them in their own land,
command my army and pillage their cities.
They will tremble with fear at your name of Cid.
They have called you lord and will want you for a king.
But be faithful to her in all your great deeds.
Come back from there, if that is granted, still more worthy of her.
Have yourself so esteemed by your exploits
that it will be an honor then for her to marry you.

RODRIGUE. In order to marry Chimene and serve you,

I will carry out every command you give.
Whatever I have to endure in my separation from her,
Sire, to be able to hope is my great happiness.

KING. Take hope in your courage and in my promise.
And since you already possess the heart of your beloved,
to triumph over a point of honor which is against you,
rely on time and valor and on your king.

Phaedra
(PHÈDRE)
1677

A TRAGEDY IN FIVE ACTS
BY
JEAN RACINE

translated by WALLACE FOWLIE

Jean Racine
(1639–1699)

Racine was educated at Jansenist schools, especially at Port-Royal, where he lived between the ages of fifteen and eighteen. The Jansenists stressed, in addition to the Bible and theology, the study of Greek. They were Catholic priests, followers of Jansenius, who emphasized, in their moral teaching, a severe concept of man's sinful nature. Jansenism, which undoubtedly explains some of Racine's psychology, has come to designate a belief in the fundamental corruption of human nature, or at least in its weakness, its impotency. The picture it gives of man as victim of his instincts and passions is in accord with the characterizations of many of Racine's heroines.

As a young playwright in Paris, where he met Boileau and Molière, Racine broke with Port-Royal. His first success was *Andromaque,* in 1667. *Phèdre* was written and produced ten years later, in 1677, and by then his enemies formed such a strong opposition to the play that Racine left the theater and became reconciled with his former teachers at Port-Royal. For Madame de Maintenon's school at Saint-Cyr, he wrote two Biblical plays, *Esther* and *Athalie.*

The achievement of Racine as dramatist is due in part to his theory of tragic action and to his penetration as psychologist, but it is also in part due to his poetic gifts, to the elegance of his expression, to the beauty of his style. Racine's particular triumph is in the fusion he performed between meaning and music, between tragic sentiment and the pure sound of his alexandrine line. He was familiar with the style of the *précieux,* and there are elements of preciosity throughout his tragedies. But on the whole he rejected superfluous ornaments and excluded unusual words from his vocabulary. When the occasion called for it, Racine could write lines as vibrantly eloquent as those of Corneille. French poetry was not to know again such human poignancy and such stylistic simplicity and dramatic meaning as Racine, at his best, represented until the publication of Baudelaire's poetry in the nineteenth century.

Racine did not bring any new formulas to the art of tragedy. The unities presented no difficulties for him. This is made clear in his various *préfaces*. If Corneille solved the conflict between will and passion by the triumph of will, Racine solved it in the triumph of passion. The leading characters in Corneille are men, whereas the leading characters in Racine are women. *Phèdre*, like all of his tragedies, begins when the dramatic action is well advanced, when the end is not far off. The action takes place on an inner level. If a violent act—such as the appearance of the sea monster and the death of Hippolytus in *Phèdre*—does take place, it is not shown, but narrated.

Phaedra is the great example in the theater of Racine of a woman driven by passion and all the conflicting emotions of modesty, hope, shame, remorse, jealousy, repentance. In the psychological sense, the role is the richest in the entire classical repertory. Phaedra passes through four or five momentous phases of suffering. At first, she hides her passion and wishes to die. When she believes Theseus is dead, she acknowledges her passion. On his return, she allows the greater crime of calumny to be committed. Repentant at the end, she makes a public confession and takes her life.

Based principally on the tragedy of Euripides, Racine's *Phèdre* has preserved the atmosphere of terrifying and supernatural legends without ever sacrificing the universal human truth of the story. The passion of Phaedra is so intense and so thwarted that she becomes the persecutor and the enemy of the man she loves. Love and hate are, in the dramaturgy of Racine, strong sentiments which are difficult to dissociate or separate. The idealistic chivalric love which dominates the plays of Corneille is replaced in Racine by a possessive and brutal type of love. Racinian love is the negation of the freedom which can be seen in the psychology of Corneille's heroes and heroines.

Racine constantly doubts the power of man's reason and intelligence to aid in the solution of a moral or psychological dilemma. Here he recalls a Jansenistic suspicion that the heart of man is easily duped by itself. *Les Maximes* of La Rochefoucauld testified at the same time in the seventeenth century to man's fundamental dishonesty with himself. The Greek sense of faith which was often a force exterior to the protagonist is transposed by Racine to an inner passion, to a personal malady which incites remorse and scorn of self.

Phaedra speaks of her guilt being so strong that she tries to escape from daylight.

If Racine emphasizes the subject of love in his tragedies, it is because love is the blindest of all passions, the one most deliberately pointed toward self-destruction. Such a theme as ambition, for example, would have to by definition maintain a greater lucidity and self-esteem. The whole meaning of tragedy is revived and explored by Racine in his treatment of love.

The tragic is irremediable for this poet. Catastrophe is omnipresent from the very beginning of the play. It is a necessity for Phaedra. It is a part of her very nature. In every century the literary art of tragedy is the picture of man confronting a superior force which defeats him. In this sense, *Le Cid* is not a tragedy, but *Phèdre* is. Even for the Greeks, fate is not in the power of the gods; it is beyond them. It is a force that cannot be named. It is not identical with the scientific determinism of the nineteenth century, nor is it exactly comparable to the Jansenist predestination of the seventeenth century. It seems to be in Racine, and especially in *Phèdre*, an inner psychological determinism, a state of the heart in which the drama unfolds. In its implacable aspect it resembles the rigors of Jansenist theology. The protagonist of Racine is a victim to whom no choice is offered. Phaedra can find no way out of the labyrinth of her passion. And yet there are two possible explanations of the catastrophe in *Phèdre:* a human explanation in terms of passion, and a divine explanation in terms of Venus and Neptune.

Phaedra

CHARACTERS

THESEUS, son of Aegeus, King of Athens
PHAEDRA, wife of Theseus, daughter of Minos and Pasiphaë
HIPPOLYTUS, son of Theseus and Antiope, Queen of the Amazons
ARICIA, princess of the royal blood of Athens
THERAMENES, tutor of Hippolytus
OENONE, nurse and confidante of Phaedra
ISMENE, confidante of Aricia
PANOPE, lady-in-waiting to Phaedra
GUARDS

Scene: Troezen, a city of the Peloponnesus.

ACT I

SCENE 1. *Hippolytus, Theramenes.*

HIPPOLYTUS. I have made up my mind, Theramenes.
I am leaving this place; I am leaving beautiful Troezen.
My idleness shames me
because of the deadly doubt filling my heart.
Separated from my father for more than six months,
I know nothing of his fate.
I do not even know the place where he hides.

THERAMENES. My lord, where will you go to look for him?
To placate your justified fear,
I have already crossed the two seas Corinth separates.
I have asked about Theseus of the people on those shores
where the Acheron disappears into Hades.
I have visited Elis, and leaving Taenarus behind me,
I went as far as the sea into which Icarus fell.

N.B. An index of proper names follows the translation.

With what new hope and in what happy land
do you expect to discover the trace of his passing?
And who can tell whether the King your father
wants the mystery of his absence to be known?
and whether, when with you we fear for his life,
that hero, at peace and concealing a new love,
is not waiting until his deceived mistress . . .

HIPPOLYTUS. Stop, Theramenes, and show respect for Theseus.
He has left all his youthful errors behind him
and is not detained now by any unworthy obstacle.
By her prayers Phaedra changed his fatal inconstancy
and for a long time has feared no rival.
I will be doing my duty if I look for him,
and I shall get away from Troezen which I no longer want to see.

THERAMENES. My lord, for how long have you feared the presence
of this peaceful town you loved as a boy,
and which I have seen you prefer
to the noise and pomp of Athens and the court?
What danger, or rather, what sorrow, sends you away?

HIPPOLYTUS. The time of happiness is over. Everything has changed
since the gods sent to these shores
the daughter of Minos and Pasiphaë.

THERAMENES. I understand. I know the cause of your suffering.
Phaedra makes you suffer and humiliates you.
She is a hostile stepmother who, when she saw you,
tried to send you into exile.
But her hatred, once fixed on you,
has disappeared or has diminished.
And what dangers can this dying woman,
who wants to die, make you endure?
Phaedra, struck down by a sickness she will not name,
tired of herself and the daylight around her,
cannot construct any plots against you.

HIPPOLYTUS. Her vain enmity is not what I fear.
Hippolytus is fleeing another enemy.
Let me confess it. I am fleeing Aricia,
the last fatal descendant of a house conspiring against us.

PHAEDRA

THERAMENES. Are you, also, my lord, persecuting her?
Never did the gentle sister of the Pallantides
participate in the plots of her treacherous brothers!
How can you hate her innocent charms?

HIPPOLYTUS. If I hated her, I would not flee her.

THERAMENES. My lord, may I try to explain your flight?
Is it possible you have ceased being proud Hippolytus,
the implacable enemy of the laws of love
and of the yoke which Theseus wore so often?
Does Venus, whom your pride scorned for so long a time,
want at last to justify Theseus?
And placing you in company with other mortals,
has she forced you to light incense on her altars?
Are you in love, my lord?

HIPPOLYTUS. You are bold to ask this question.
You who have known my heart since the beginning of my life,
can you ask me to disavow shamefully
the sentiments of so proud and scornful a heart?
My pride which amazes you was fed me
with my mother's milk and her Amazon pride.
When I reached an older age
I approved of all I learned about myself.
Serving me then with sincere zeal,
you told me the story of my father.
You know how my soul, attentive to your voice,
gloried in the tales of his noble exploits
when you portrayed him as an intrepid hero
consoling men for the absence of Hercules,
killing monsters and pursuing brigands:
Procrustus, Cercyon, Sirron, and Sinnis,
and scattering the bones of the giant of Epidaurus,
and saving Crete with the blood of the Minotaur.
But when you told me the less glorious deeds,
his promise of marriage offered in a hundred places—
Helen stolen from her parents in Sparta,
Salamis comforting the tears of Periboea,
and others whose names he has forgotten,
overconfident hearts whom his passion deceived,
Ariadne telling her story of injustice to the rocks,
Phaedra, brought to Athens for a legitimate cause—
as I listened embarrassed to those stories,
you remember how I urged you to shorten them,

happy if I could efface from memory
the unworthy half of so noble a life!
Can it be that now I, in my turn, am bound?
Can it be that now the gods have humiliated me?
I am more to be scorned in my cowardly sighs
because so many honors were the excuse for Theseus.
I have destroyed no monsters
and have therefore no right to weaken as he did.
Even if my pride could be softened,
should I have chosen Aricia for my conqueror?
Can't my bewildered senses remember any longer
the eternal obstacle which separates us?
My father disapproves of her, and a severe decree
forbids that her brothers should ever have nephews.
He fears an offspring from such a guilty line,
and wishes to bury their name with their sister.
He claims she is under his control until death,
and never will the marriage fire be lighted.
Can I espouse her rights against an angry father?
Shall I be the example of a presumptuous action,
and in this mad love, will my youth . . .

THERAMENES. My lord, once your fate is inscribed,
Heaven can take no account of your reasonings.
Theseus opened your eyes in wishing to close them,
and his hate, exciting a rebellious passion,
gives to his enemy a new grace.
But why be afraid of a chaste love?
If it is sweet to you, why not taste it?
Will you always be restrained by scruples?
Do you fear losing your way in following Hercules?
Think of the strong wills which Venus has overcome.
Where would you be, you who fight Venus,
If Antiope, opposing her laws,
had not desired Theseus with modest ardor?
Why pretend with these proud words?
Confess it and all will change. For several days now
you have seemed a proud and solitary figure, rarely
driving a chariot along the shore,
or, learned in that art invented by Neptune,
bending to a halter an untamed horse.
The forests resound less often now with our cries.
Your eyes have grown heavy with some inner torment.

PHAEDRA

There is no more doubt of it. You are in love and
  you are suffering.
You are perishing from a malady you conceal.
Has beautiful Aricia cast a spell over you?

  HIPPOLYTUS. I am leaving, Theramenes, to search for my father.

  THERAMENES. Will you not see Phaedra before going, my lord?

  HIPPOLYTUS. It is my intention. You may inform her.
I will see her, for my duty demands this.
  (OENONE *enters.*)
What new woe has upset her faithful Oenone?

SCENE 2. *Hippolytus, Oenone, Theramenes.*

  OENONE. Alas, my lord, what sorrow is equal to mine?
The Queen is approaching the end of her fate.
In vain I have been keeping watch over her day and night.
In my arms she is dying from a malady she hides from me.
An endless disorder reigns in her mind.
The suffering of her mind allows her no rest.
She wants to see the daylight, and her deep grief
insists that I send everyone away.
She is coming . . .

  HIPPOLYTUS.   I understand. I will leave her alone.
My presence would be displeasing to her.

SCENE 3. *Phaedra, Oenone.*

  PHAEDRA. Let us go no farther. Stay here, Oenone.
I cannot stand up. My strength has gone.
My eyes are dazzled by the daylight I see
and my trembling knees are giving way.
Alas! (*She sits down.*)

  OENONE. Would that our tears might appease the gods!

  PHAEDRA. These useless ornaments and these veils are heavy on me.
Some irksome hand, by weaving these knots,
has tied my hair tight over my head.
Everything pains and harms me, and conspires to harm me.

  OENONE. Your wishes are destroyed as soon as they are expressed!

You yourself, condemning your unjust plans,
urged us just now to dress and prepare you.
You yourself, remembering your earlier strength,
wanted to appear and behold again the light of day.
But as soon as you see it, you turn to hide
as if you hate the very light you came to see.

PHAEDRA. O Sun, noble and shining author of a wretched family,
whose daughter my mother boasted of being,
and who perhaps now blushes at seeing my shame,
I am here to see you for the last time.

OENONE. Will you never renounce this cruel desire?
Am I to see you renouncing life
and making the funereal preparation of your death?

PHAEDRA. Why am I not sitting in the shadow of the forests?
When shall I follow with my eyes
through the dust of the roads, a chariot racing
along the course?

OENONE. What did you say?

PHAEDRA. I am a fool. Where am I and what did I say?
To what extremes did my desires and my mind wander?
I have lost my mind. The gods have deprived me of it.
Oenone, shame is written over my face.
You can see too clearly my shameful grief,
and my eyes, in spite of myself, are filling with tears.

OENONE. If you must blush, let it be from that silence
which still embitters the violence of your woe.
Rebellious to our attention and deaf to our speech,
will you without feeling let your days end?
What madness limits them in the midst of their course?
What witchcraft or what poison has dried up their source?
Three times have shadows darkened the sky
since sleep entered your eyes.
And three times has day dispelled the blackness of night
since your body has languished without food.
By what terrifying plan are you being tempted?
What right have you to attack your own life?
You offend the gods who are authors of that life.
You fail your husband to whom you are joined in pledge.
And finally you fail your wretched children

PHAEDRA

whom you place under a rigorous yoke.
Remember that a single day will take their mother away
and give hope to the son of the foreign woman,
to that implacable enemy of your family,
the son who was carried in the womb of an Amazon,
Hippolytus . . .

PHAEDRA.   Stop!

OENONE.   My reproach moves you!

PHAEDRA. Wretched woman, what name did you utter?

OENONE. How justified is your anger!
I am glad to see you startled by that fatal name.
You must live and not allow a Scythian's son,
as he crushes your children under his hateful authority,
to command the noblest offspring of Greece and of the gods.
Do not delay. Each moment may be mortal.
Bring back now some of your impaired strength
while your life, on the point of being extinguished,
may still endure in its flame and be rekindled.

PHAEDRA. I have too far prolonged its guilty length.

OENONE. What kind of remorse torments you?
What crime has brought about such bewilderment?
Have your hands been soiled by innocent blood?

PHAEDRA. Thanks to heaven my hands are not criminal.
Would that my heart were as innocent as they are!

OENONE. What terrible project have you conceived
that your heart is so anguished by it?

PHAEDRA. I have said enough to you. Spare me the rest.
I wish to die in order not to make so cruel a confession.

OENONE. Die and maintain your inhuman silence.
But look for someone else to close your eyes.
Although you are left with so little inner light,
my soul will descend to the dead first.
Many easy ways lead there,
and my grief will choose the shortest.
Cruel mistress, when did my devotion ever betray you?
Remember that when you were born, my arms received you.
I left everything for you, my country and my children.
Is this the reward for my faithfulness?

PHAEDRA. What can you hope for by thus forcing me?
If I break my silence, horror will seize you.

OENONE. What could you say that would be worse
than the horror of seeing you die before my eyes?

PHAEDRA. When you learn of my crime and the fate crushing me,
I shall not die any less, and I shall die more guilty.

OENONE. For the sake of the tears I have shed for you,
here, at your faltering legs which I embrace,
free my mind from this fatal doubt.

PHAEDRA. Since you must know it, stand up.

OENONE. Speak! I am listening.

PHAEDRA. What can I tell her? Where can I begin?

OENONE. Stop offending me by this vain terror.

PHAEDRA. The hatred of Venus and her fatal anger
caused a perverted love to grow in my mother.

OENONE. You must forget that. Hide that memory
in unbroken silence throughout all the future.

PHAEDRA. My sister Ariadne, wounded by a strange love,
died at the rock where she was left.

OENONE. Why are you saying this? What mortal torment
urges you today to speak against all your family?

PHAEDRA. It is the will of Venus that of all my family
I shall die the last and the most wretched.

OENONE. Are you in love?

PHAEDRA. I feel all the furies of love.

OENONE. For whom?

PHAEDRA. You are going to hear the extreme of all horrors.
I love . . . At his fatal name I shudder and tremble.
I love . . .

OENONE. What man?

PHAEDRA. You know the son of the Amazon woman,
the prince I persecuted for so long?

OENONE. Hippolytus? All gods of heaven!

PHAEDRA. It was you who named him.

OENONE. My blood is congealed in all my veins.
The despair of this crime! The accursed race!
The unhappy voyage! Why did you have to come
to the shore of this dangerous land?

PHAEDRA

PHAEDRA. My suffering comes from farther back. Scarcely was I bound
by the marriage law to the son of Aegeus,
my peace of mind and happiness seeming secure,
than Athens showed my proud enemy.
When I saw him I blushed and turned pale.
I grew troubled and anguished.
I was unable to see and unable to speak.
My body was either cold or on fire.
I recognized Venus and her fearful passion,
and the fatal torment of a family she persecutes.
I believed I could turn this aside by faithful prayers.
I built a temple in her name and adorned it.
Every hour I offered victims
and sought in their pierced flanks to recover my mind.
It was a powerless remedy for an incurable love.
Vainly I burned incense on the altars.
While my lips implored the name of the goddess,
I was worshipping Hippolytus. And seeing him constantly,
even at the foot of the altars where I made sacrifices,
I offered up everything to him I dared not name.
Wherever I went, I avoided him,
but I would see him in the features of his father.
At last I revolted against myself.
I stirred up my anger in order to persecute him.
In order to banish the enemy I idolized,
I pretended to show the meanness of an unjust stepmother.
I urged his exile and my endless cries
wrenched him away from the arms of his father.
Then I breathed, Oenone, and after his absence,
my days were less troubled and passed innocently.
Submissive to my husband, and hiding my torment,
I took care of the children of his unhappy marriage.
My fate made all this useless.
When Theseus himself brought me to Troezen,
I came upon the enemy I had sent away.
And the wound of love opened again.
It is no longer fire hidden in my veins.
It is Venus beating down on her prey with all her strength.
My crime now justly terrifies me.
I despise my life and my horrible love.
By dying I wanted to protect my honor,
and blot out from the day so black a flame.

I was unable to bear your tears and your questions.
So I have told you all, and I have no regret for this,
provided you will respect my death
and will not afflict me with unjust reproaches.
Do not try to recall
the remnants of a life which is ready to die.

Scene 4. *Phaedra, Oenone, Panope.*

PANOPE. I tried to conceal the sad news from you,
but I am forced to disclose it now.
Death has taken your invincible husband.
Only you are ignorant of this disaster.

PHAEDRA. Panope, what you are saying?

PANOPE.   I say you are deceived,
and there is no point in asking heaven for Theseus' return.
From vessels now in the harbor,
Hippolytus, his son, has just learned of his death.
Athens is divided over the choice of a master.
Some give their vote to your son the prince,
and others, forgetful of the laws of the state,
dare give their votes to the son of the foreign woman.
It is even rumored that a bold plot
plans to place on the throne Aricia and the blood
of the Pallantides.
I had to warn you of this peril.
Even Hippolytus is making plans to leave for Athens,
and it is feared that if he appears in this unforeseen turmoil,
the fickle part of the populace will rally around him.

OENONE. That's enough, Panope. The Queen has heard you
and will not neglect this important warning.

Scene 5. *Phaedra, Oenone.*

OENONE. My lady, I had given up urging you to live,
and already I had planned to follow you to the tomb.
I had no more desire to turn you away from it.
But this unexpected catastrophe forces other obligations on you.
Your position has changed and taken on a new meaning.
The King is dead, my lady, and you must take his place.
His death leaves you a son to whom you owe everything.

PHAEDRA

If you die, he will be a slave; if you live, he will
 be a king.
Who will be a support for him in this affliction?
There will be no one to dry his tears,
and his innocent cries, heard on high by the gods,
will work hardship on his mother and anger her ancestors.
You must live. You have nothing with which to reproach
 yourself.
Your love has become an ordinary love.
In his death Theseus has dissolved the complications
which made of your passion a fearful crime.
Hippolytus is less to be feared by you now.
You can see him without feeling guilty.
If he is convinced of your hate,
he may lead the revolt against you!
You must remove the error and bend his heart.
He is the king of this happy land. Troezen is his lot.
But he knows that the law gives to your son
the proud ramparts which Minerva has built.
Both of you have a natural enemy.
You should unite in order to oppose Aricia.

PHAEDRA. I agree and I yield to your advice.
I will live, if I can move back into life,
and if the love for my son at this moment of mourning,
can bring life to my weak spirit.

ACT II

Scene 1. *Aricia, Ismene.*

ARICIA. You say Hippolytus wants to see me here?
He is looking for me and wants to make his farewell?
Do you speak truthfully, Ismene? Or are you mistaken?

ISMENE. This is the first reaction to the death of Theseus.
You must be ready, my lady, to see from all sides
people flocking to you who were rejected by Theseus.
You are now the mistress of your fate
and you may soon see all of Greece at your feet.

ARICIA. Are you sure, Ismene, it is not an ill-founded rumor?
Am I through being a slave? Have I no more enemies?

ISMENE. No, my lady, the gods no longer oppose you.
Theseus has joined the shades of your brothers.

ARICIA. Is it known what accident ended his life?

ISMENE. Unbelievable stories are circulating about his death.
It is said he was the ravisher of a new mistress *Persefne*
and was drowned in the sea because of his infidelity.
It was even said—and this circulated widely—
that he descended into hell with Pirithous
where he saw the Cocytus and its dark banks,
and appeared as a living man before the spirits of the dead;
but that he could not get out from that wretched place
and cross back over those shores which are never
  crossed twice.

ARICIA. Am I to believe that a mortal, before his last hour,
can penetrate the deep dwelling of the dead?
What magic drew him to those fearful shores?

ISMENE. Theseus is dead, my lady, and you alone doubt this.
Athens is afraid. Troezen has learned of it
and has already recognized Hippolytus as its king.
Phaedra, in his palace, is trembling for her son
and asking advice of her worried friends.

ARICIA. Do you believe that Hippolytus, more humane toward me
than his father was, will lighten my slavery?
Do you think he will pity my affliction?

ISMENE.   I do, my lady!

PHAEDRA

ARICIA. But do you know the coldness of Hippolytus?
What meager hope makes you think he will pity me
and respect in me alone a sex he scorns?
For some time he has been avoiding us
and seeking places where we are not.

ISMENE. I know what is said about his lack of feeling,
but I have seen this proud Hippolytus in your presence,
and as I watched him, the reports about his inhumanity
increased my curiosity.
His appearance did not correspond to these rumors.
As soon as you looked at him, he seemed upset.
His eyes, trying in vain to avoid looking,
full of yearning, could not leave you.
The name of lover offends his pride perhaps,
but he has the eyes of a lover, if he has not the language.

ARICIA. Dear Ismene, my heart listens avidly
to your words which doubtless have no basis.
You who know me, is it believable
that the sad plaything of a pitiless fate,
a heart like mine, fed on bitterness and tears,
could know love and its mad grief?
Descendant of a king and a noble family,
I alone escaped the fury of the war.
I lost, in the flower of their youth,
six brothers . . . They were the hope of a famous lineage!
The sword cut them down, and the wet earth
sorrowfully drank the blood of Erechtheus' nephews.
Since their death, you know of the severe law
which forbids the Greeks to pity me.
It is feared that the rash flame of the sister
will one day reanimate the ashes of her brothers.
But you also know how scornfully
I watched the worry of the suspicious conqueror.
You know my long opposition to love
and my gratitude to unjust Theseus
whose rigorous law happily supported my scorn.
My eyes at that time had not seen his son.
It is not that, shamefully bewitched by my eyes,
I love in him his beauty and his esteemed grace,
gifts by which nature has honored him,
which he himself repudiates or seems to ignore.
I love and esteem in him the noblest riches,

the virtues of his father, and not the weaknesses.
Let me confess it, I love the noble pride
which has never bent under the yoke of passion.
Vainly was Phaedra honored by the sighs of Theseus.
I am prouder than she, and I flee the easy glory
of winning an homage offered to a hundred others,
and entering a heart which has opened to so many.
What I want most and what excites me,
is to make an inflexible heart capitulate,
to convey suffering to an insensitive spirit,
to chain a captive stupefied by his irons,
vainly rebellious against a yoke he desires.
It was less difficult to disarm Hercules than Hippolytus.
He was conquered more often and defeated more quickly
and offered less glory to the one who tamed him.
But dear Ismene, see how imprudent I am!
All kinds of resistance will oppose me.
Humbly, in my anguish, you will perhaps hear me
lament over that same pride I admire today.
Might I have changed . . .

ISMENE.   You will hear this from Hippolytus himself.
He is coming here.

SCENE 2. *Hippolytus, Aricia, Ismene.*

HIPPOLYTUS.   Before leaving,
I wanted to tell you what you may expect.
My father is dead. My legitimate fears
foretold the reasons of his prolonged absence.
Death alone, limiting my father's dazzling work,
was able to hide him from the universe.
At last the gods gave over to the murderous Fates
the friend, the companion, the successor of Hercules.
I suppose that your hate, refusing him his greatness,
hears with displeasure these names that are due him.
One hope softens my painful grief.
I am able to free you from a severe bondage.
I revoke the laws whose harshness I deplored.
You are free in body and heart.
Here in Troezen which is now my kingdom,
where once my ancestor Pittheus ruled,
and where immediately I was recognized as king,
I set you free. You are freer than I am.

PHAEDRA

ARICIA. Your excessive kindness is embarrassing.
By honoring my misfortune with so generous an interest,
you place me, my lord, more than you realize,
under those austere laws from which you are freeing me.

HIPPOLYTUS. Athens, uncertain over the choice of a successor,
speaks of you, names me, and does not forget the
son of the Queen.

ARICIA. They speak of me?

HIPPOLYTUS.   I am not deceived,
and know that an insolent law rejects me.
Greece reproaches me for my foreign mother.
But if as a rival I had only my brother,
I have true rights over him
and could save him from ill-founded laws.
A more legitimate obstacle arrests my boldness.
I yield to you, or rather I give to you the place
and the scepter which long ago your ancestors received
from the famous mortal conceived by the Earth;
the adoption put it into the hands of Aegeus.
Athens, enriched and protected by my father,
joyously recognized so noble a king,
and relegated your wretched brothers to oblivion.
Athens now recalls you to within its walls.
Long enough has it suffered from such a quarrel.
The blood of your family sinking into its furrows
has nourished the field from which it arose.
Troezen will obey me. The countryside of Crete
has offered a rich asylum to the son of Phaedra.
Attica belongs to you. I leave now, and for you I will assemble
all the votes divided among us.

ARICIA. I am amazed and upset by all I hear.
I fear, yes, I fear a dream is deceiving me.
Am I awake? Can I trust such a plan?
What god conceived it in your heart, my lord?
How rightfully you are praised everywhere!
The truth about you is greater than your fame.
But for me, you sacrifice your own interests.
Isn't it enough that you don't hate me,
and that for so long a time you forbade your heart
a hatred . . . ?

HIPPOLYTUS. Hatred for you, my lady?
Despite the bad traits ascribed to my pride,
do people think some monster bore me in its womb?
What savage character, what hardened hate
would not be softened in your presence?
Could I resist the deceptive charm . . .

ARICIA. What are you saying, my lord?

HIPPOLYTUS. I have gone too far.
Reason, it is easy to see, has given me to Love.
Since I have begun the breaking of my silence,
my lady, let me continue. Let me tell you
of a secret my heart can no longer contain.
You see before you a pitiful prince,
the memorable example of presumptuous pride.
In proud revolt against love,
I long insulted the chains of its captives.
As I deplored the shipwrecks of weak mortals,
I thought I would always watch these storms from the shore.
But now, enslaved to the common law,
I am carried off far from myself by some fury!
One moment conquered my bold imprudence.
My soul which has been so proud is now dependent.
For six months, ashamed and desperate,
bearing everywhere the arrow which pierces my flesh,
I have tested myself in vain against you and against myself.
When you are here, I leave; when you are absent, I see you.
Your image follows me in the depths of the forest.
The light of day and the shadows of night
retrace before me your charms which I avoid.
The rebel Hippolytus has been caught by you.
As a result of my useless efforts,
I search for myself and cannot find myself.
I cannot remember the lessons of Neptune.
The woods resound only with my laments,
and my idle horses have forgotten my voice.
Perhaps the story of so wild a love
makes you, as you listen to it, blush at what you
    have caused.
These are mad words from a heart which bows before you,
and I am a strange captive for so beautiful a bond.
But the offering should be dearer to your eyes.
Remember that I am speaking in a foreign language

PHAEDRA

and do not reject these ill-expressed vows
which, without you, Hippolytus would never have said.

Scene 3. *Hippolytus, Aricia, Theramenes, Ismene.*

THERAMENES. My lord, the Queen is here. She follows me.
She wishes to see you.

HIPPOLYTUS. To see me?

THERAMENES. I do not know her purpose.
But she has asked to see you.
Phaedra wishes to speak to you before you leave.

HIPPOLYTUS. Phaedra? What can I say to her? What can she want?

ARICIA. My lord, you cannot refuse to see her.
Even if you are convinced she is your enemy,
you owe some degree of pity to her tears.

HIPPOLYTUS. In the meantime you are leaving, and I don't know
whether I have offended you,
whether the heart I have placed in your hands . . .

ARICIA. You may depart, Prince, and carry out your noble plans.
Make Athens tributary of my power.
I accept the gifts you offer me.
But, to me, the large glorious empire
is not the most precious of all your gifts.

Scene 4. *Hippolytus, Theramenes.*

HIPPOLYTUS. Is all in readiness? The Queen is coming.
Leave and see that everything is swiftly prepared
for the departure.
Give the signal and the orders, and then come back
to relieve me from this conversation I dread.

Scene 5. *Phaedra, Hippolytus, Oenone.*

PHAEDRA (*to* OENONE). There he is. All my blood mounts to my heart.
When I see him, I forget what I must say.

OENONE. Remember your son. You are his only hope.

PHAEDRA. I am told that you are about to leave us,
my lord. I am here to join my tears with yours.
I have come to you to speak of my alarm over my son.
He has no father now, and the day is not far off
which will make him the witness of my own death.
A thousand enemies are already attacking him
   in his childhood.
You alone can take up his defense against them.
But a secret remorse upsets my mind.
I fear I have closed your ears to his cries.
I tremble lest your just anger
will persecute him because of his hated mother.

HIPPOLYTUS. I would not stoop so low, my lady.

PHAEDRA. I would not complain if you hated me.
You have seen me bent upon bringing you harm.
But you were not able to read the deep meaning of
   my heart.
I took care to show you only my enmity.
Wherever I lived in this land, I could not bear your
   presence.
I had spoken against you publicly and secretly,
and wanted to be separated from you by oceans.
By specific law I even forbade
your name being said in my presence.
Yet if suffering is measured by the offense,
if hate alone can call up hate in you,
never was a woman more worthy of pity,
and less worthy, my lord, of your enmity.

HIPPOLYTUS. A mother, jealous of the rights of her own
   children,
rarely pardons the ways of a stepson.
I know this, my lady. Constant suspicions
are the commonest results of a second marriage.
Another woman would have been equally jealous of me
and I would have been perhaps more outraged by her.

PHAEDRA. I swear to you, my lord, that Heaven
exempted me from this common law
and that a very different matter rages within me.

HIPPOLYTUS. There is no reason to be upset any longer.
It is possible that your husband still lives.
Heaven may yet grant to our tears his return.

PHAEDRA

Neptune may protect him. My father's prayers
to his patron god may be efficacious.

   PHAEDRA. It is not possible to cross the river of
      twice.
If Theseus saw those dark banks,
no god can send him back to you.
The greedy Acheron will not release its prey.
But what am I saying? He is not dead since he breathes
   in you.
I believe I still see my husband standing before me.
I see him. I speak to him, and my heart . . . What madness,
my lord! In spite of myself, I am telling you of my passion.

   HIPPOLYTUS. I can see the marvelous power of your love.
Dead as he is, you can still see Theseus,
Your soul is still enflamed by his love.

   PHAEDRA. Yes, Prince, I suffer and burn for Theseus.
I love, not the man seen by hell,
the fickle worshiper of so many mistresses,
who will dishonor the god of the dead;
but the faithful man, proud, even a bit barbaric,
seductive, young, enflaming all the hearts he passes,
the man like our gods, or like you as I see you now.
He had your bearing, your eyes, your speech,
and the noble modesty which colors your countenance,
when he crossed the waters to Crete.
The daughters of Minos had reason to think of him.
What were you doing then? Why, without Hippolytus,
did he assemble the heroes of Greece?
You were still too young, but why weren't you
on the ships which brought him to our shore?
The monster of Crete would have perished at your hand
in spite of all the detours of his vast retreat.
To unravel the uncertain complexity,
my sister would have armed your hand with the fatal thread.
No! For I would have preceded her in this plan.
Love would have instantly inspired me with the right thought.
Prince, it is I, Phaedra, who would have served you
and taught you the detours of the labyrinth.
For your beauty I would have undertaken every risk.
A mere thread would not have asserted a woman's love
   for you.
I am the companion you needed in your peril.

.. would have walked ahead of you.
Phaedra going down into the labyrinth at your side,
would have been lost or saved with you.

HIPPOLYTUS. What are these words? Have you forgotten
that Theseus is my father and your husband?

PHAEDRA. What makes you think I have forgotten him?
Is it possible I have lost all sense of honor?

HIPPOLYTUS. Forgive me, my lady. I blush when I confess
that I wrongfully accused an innocent speech.
My shame will not allow me to stay here
and I am leaving . . .

PHAEDRA. You have heard too much, cruel Hippolytus!
I have told enough for you to understand all.
So, know Phaedra and know all her fury!
I am in love. But do not think that in this love
I approve of myself and find myself innocent,
or that any cowardly complacence has fortified the poison
of the mad love which bewilders my reason.
I am the wretched victim of heavenly vengeance
and hate myself more than you detest me.
The gods are my witnesses; those gods who in my heart
kindled the fire fatal to all of my family.
Those are the gods who took a cruel pride
in depraving the heart of a weak woman.
You yourself can remember the past.
It was not enough to avoid you, cruel Hippolytus, I
  exiled you.
I tried to appear odious and inhuman.
In order better to resist you, I sought to
  provoke your hate.
What profit came from all these useless efforts?
Your hate grew as my love grew.
Your sorrow gave you more charm than ever.
In tears and passion I languished and lost strength.
You needed only your eyes to be convinced of this,
if for one moment your eyes would look at me.
What am I saying? This shameful confession which I
  have just spoken,
can you believe it is voluntary?
Trembling for a son I did not dare betray,
I came to beg you not to hate him.
Feeble projects of a heart too full with what it loves!

PHAEDRA

Alas! I would speak to you only about yourself.
Avenge yourself, punish me for this odious love.
Worthy son of a hero who begot you,
free the universe of a monster who irritates you!
The widow of Theseus dares to love Hippolytus!
Believe me, this monster should not escape you.
Here is my heart. This is where your dagger should strike.
Eager to expiate its offense,
it moves forward to encounter your weapon.
Strike me. If you think my heart unworthy of your thrusts,
if your hate refuses me so sweet a punishment,
if your hand would be spotted with too vile a blood,
lend me your sword since I haven't your arm.
Give it over.

OENONE. What are you doing, my lady?
Someone is coming. We must avoid witnesses.
Come with me. Let us leave this shameful scene.

(They leave.)

SCENE 6. *Hippolytus, Theramenes.*

THERAMENES. Is it Phaedra who is leaving? or who is being taken away?
Why, my lord, all these signs of lamentation?
You are without a sword, speechless, colorless.

HIPPOLYTUS. Let us leave, Theramenes. My surprise is extreme.
I cannot look at myself without a feeling of horror.
Phaedra . . . No! Let this horrible secret
remain buried in deep oblivion.

THERAMENES. The ship is ready, if you wish to leave.
But Athens, my lord, has already spoken.
Its leaders have taken the votes of all the tribes.
Your brother has won. Phaedra has the upper hand.

HIPPOLYTUS. Phaedra?

THERAMENES. A herald, entrusted with the wishes of Athens,
is coming to place the control of the state in her hands.
Her son is king, my lord.

HIPPOLYTUS. Oh! you gods who know her,
is it her virtue you are rewarding?

THERAMENES. Yet meanwhile a new rumor says the King is alive.
It is believed that Theseus has been seen in Epirus.
But I who looked for him there, know better . . .

HIPPOLYTUS. No matter. We must listen carefully to every rumor.
Let us track down the source of this last report.
If it does not warrant putting off my departure,
we will leave. Whatever the cost may be,
we will put the scepter into the hands worthiest of bearing it.

ACT III

SCENE 1. *Phaedra, Oenone.*

PHAEDRA. Take away all the honors that are being sent to me.
Stop bothering me. I will see no one.
My poor mind will not be deceived, do you hear?
It is better to hide me. I have said too much.
My passionate outburst became too visible.
I said what never should have been heard.
And how he listened to me! With endless tricks
he eluded my speech like a man heartless.
All he wanted was to get away as fast as possible.
The blush on his face increased my shame.
Why did you obstruct my plan for death?
When his sword was about to pierce my heart,
did he turn pale because of me? did he snatch it away from me?
It was enough that my hand touched it but once—
it has become something loathsome for him.
The wretched sword would now profane his hands.

OENONE. In your affliction, these complaints
feed a passion you should extinguish.
Wouldn't it be better for you, a worthy descendant of Minos,
to seek repose in some other way,
to rule in opposition to an ingrate who plans to flee,
and fix your attention on the governing of the state?

PHAEDRA. You want me to rule? to submit a state to my law,
when my weak mind cannot rule itself?
when I have given up the control of my own senses?
when I can barely breathe under my shameful yoke?
when I am dying!

OENONE. You must leave.

PHAEDRA. I cannot leave him.

OENONE. You dared banish him. Haven't you the courage to avoid him?

PHAEDRA. There is no time left. He knows my insane passion.
I have moved beyond the fixed limits of modesty.
I have shown my shame to the eyes of my conqueror,

and hope, in spite of myself, has entered my heart.
You yourself, revived my weakened strength,
and my life which was expiring through my lips;
you gave me new hope by your deceptive advice
and made me see that I could love him.

OENONE. Innocent or guilty of your afflictions,
I was capable of any act in order to rescue you.
But if ever an offense distressed you,
could you forget the scorn of a proud man?
He looked at you with stubborn heartlessness
and left you almost prostrate at his feet.
His barbaric pride made him odious to me.
I wish you had seen him through my eyes at that moment.

PHAEDRA. Oenone, he may set aside this pride which is offensive to you.
Brought up in the forest, he has its savagery.
Hardened by those barbaric principles, Hippolytus
is hearing about love for the first time.
Perhaps astonishment explains his silence,
and perhaps we have complained too bitterly.

OENONE. Remember that a barbarian woman gave him birth.

PHAEDRA. She was a Scythian and barbarian, but she knew love.

OENONE. He was destined to hate all women.

PHAEDRA. Then I shall never have a rival.
Your advice is unseasonal, Oenone.
Serve my madness and not my reason.
To love he opposes an inaccessible heart;
to attack it let us find the most vulnerable spot.
The attractiveness of an empire seemed to affect him.
Athens appealed to him and this he did not conceal.
His ships were already pointed in that direction
and the sails abandoned to the wind.
Seek out this ambitious youth in my name,
Oenone, and tempt him with my sparkling crown.
Let him put on his own brow the sacred diadem.
All I wish is the honor of attaching it.
I will yield to him the power I cannot keep.
He will teach my son the art of command.
Perhaps he will serve as a father to him.
In his control I place both mother and son.

PHAEDRA

Try every means to bend his will.
Your words will be more heeded than mine.
Urge him and weep in his presence.
Do not fear begging him with your voice.
I approve of whatever you do. You are my one hope.
Go now. When you return, I will decide my fate.

Scene 2. *Phaedra.*

PHAEDRA. Relentless Venus, who knows the shame
of my ancestors, am I sufficiently humiliated?
You could not increase your cruelty.
Your triumph is complete; every arrow has reached its mark.
If you now seek a new glory,
turn to an enemy more rebellious than I.
Hippolytus avoids you, and defying your wrath
he has never knelt before your altars.
Your name seems to offend his proud ears.
Goddess, avenge yourself! My cause is yours!
Make him fall in love.
Have you returned already,
Oenone? He hates me and will not listen to you.

Scene 3. *Phaedra, Oenone.*

OENONE. You must stifle all thought of this impossible love,
my lady. Bring back your past virtue.
The King, who was believed dead, is about to appear before you.
Theseus has come. Theseus is in Troezen.
The crowds are rushing to see him.
By your order, I had gone out and was looking for Hippolytus,
when a great wave of shouting . . .

PHAEDRA. My husband is alive, Oenone! Say no more.
I have confessed a guilty love which will outrage him.
He is alive. I wish to know nothing else.

OENONE. What are you saying?

PHAEDRA. I predicted this, but you would not listen.
Your tears prevailed over my remorse.
This morning, had I died, I would have been wept for honorably.
I took your advice and now I will die dishonored.

OENONE. You will die?

PHAEDRA. This is my fatal day.
My husband is going to appear and his son with him.
I will see the witness to my adulterous love
watch the way I dare greet his father.
My heart will be heavy with the sighs he did not hear,
and my eyes wet with tears spurned by him.
He is sensitive to Theseus' honor; do you think
he will conceal the love with which I am burning?
Will he allow the betrayal of his father and his king?
Will he be able to suppress the horror he feels toward me?
But what if he does keep silent? I know my infidelity,
Oenone, and I am not one of those bold women
who enjoy tranquillity in crime
and who show a countenance that never blushes.
I know all my madness and can call it back to mind.
Even now I can feel that these walls and ceilings
are going to speak out, and, prepared to accuse me,
they are waiting for my husband in order to disillusion him.
Let me die. Let me be freed from such horror.
Is dying so great a disaster?
Death creates no fear for the unhappy.
All I fear is the name I will leave after me.
What a dire heritage for my wretched children!
The blood of Jupiter will have to swell their courage.
Yet despite the pride in such noble blood,
a mother's crime is a heavy burden.
I tremble lest one day words of too much truth
will reproach them for having had a guilty mother.
Oppressed by such a weight, I tremble
lest neither one nor the other ever dare to raise his eyes.

OENONE. Have no doubt, my lady, I pity both of them.
Never was fear more justified than yours.
But why expose them to such insults?
Why take up arms against yourself?
The die is cast. It will be said that Phaedra, guilty,
fled the presence of her deceived husband.
Hippolytus is fortunate in that
your death will lend support to his words.
And how will I answer your accuser?
In his presence I shall be easily silenced.
I will see him rejoice over his frightful triumph,

relating your share to any ear that will listen.
Rather than see this I would be devoured by a flame from heaven!
Do not deceive me now. Do you still love him?
What are your sentiments now for this bold prince?

PHAEDRA. He has become for me a terrible monster.

OENONE. Why grant him then a complete victory?
You fear him. Be the first to accuse him
of the crime he may impute to you today.
Who will contradict you? Everything is against him:
his sword is fortunately left with you,
your present sorrow, your past irritation,
your persistent warnings to his father,
and his exile already obtained by you.

PHAEDRA. Are you asking me to persecute and blacken an innocent man?

OENONE. My zeal needs only your silence.
I tremble as you do, and feel some of your remorse—
I would be swifter in facing a hundred deaths—
but I will lose you except for this unfortunate remedy;
there is nothing I would not do to save you.
I will speak. Theseus, angered by what I will tell him,
will limit his vengeance to exiling his son.
A father, when he punishes, remains a father.
His anger will be appeased with some slight rebuke.
But even if innocent blood has to be shed,
your threatened honor has the right to demand anything.
It is too rich a treasure to be compromised.
Whatever law it dictates, you must submit to it.
Your honor is in peril and to save it
you must sacrifice everything, even virtue.
People are coming. I see Theseus.

PHAEDRA. And I see Hippolytus.
In his insolent eyes I see my defeat.
Do what you wish. I yield to you.
In my anxiety I can do nothing myself.

Scene 4. *Theseus, Hippolytus, Phaedra, Oenone, Theramenes.*

THESEUS. Fortune is no longer against me,
my lady, and into your arms it puts . . .

PHAEDRA.   Stop, Theseus,
and do not profane such pure joy.
I do not deserve your tender attentions.
You have been offended. Jealous fortune
has not spared your wife in your absence.
Unworthy of pleasing or embracing you,
I can now think only of hiding.

Scene 5. *Theseus, Hippolytus, Theramenes.*

THESEUS. My son, what is this strange welcome
I have received?

HIPPOLYTUS. Phaedra alone can explain the mystery.
But if my ardent prayers are able to move you,
allow me, my lord, not to see her anymore.
Allow your disturbed son forever
to disappear from the city your wife inhabits.

THESEUS. You intend to leave me?

HIPPOLYTUS.   I did not seek her out.
It was you who brought her to these shores.
You were pleased, my lord, when you left, to entrust
Aricia and the Queen to my care.
I was charged with the duty of watching over them.
But now no duty keeps me here.
My idle youth has practiced its skill
for long enough in the forests on insignificant enemies.
This is an unworthy leisure. Allow me to leave
and dip my javelins in more glorious blood.
You had not yet reached my present age,
when more than one tyrant, more than one
   savage monster
had felt the strength of your arm.
You had already persecuted violence
and made safe the banks of the two seas.
The free traveler had no fear of attack.
Hercules, hearing the skill of your exploits

PHAEDRA

was resting from his labors because of you.
And I, the unknown son of so famous a father,
am still unequal to the fame of my mother.
Let my courage at last be put to the test.
If some monster has escaped you,
allow me to place at your feet its honorable remains,
or allow the enduring memory of a noble death,
immortalizing a life so worthily cut short,
to prove to the universe that I was your son.

THESEUS. What is this? What horror in this house
causes everyone to flee from my presence?
If I am so little wanted and so feared,
why was I taken from my prison?
I had only one friend. His imprudent desire
was to abduct the wife of the tyrant of Epirus.
Against my will I served his passionate plan.
But angry fate blinded both of us.
The tyrant caught me unarmed and without defense.
I saw Pirithous, whom I wept for,
delivered by that barbarian to the cruel beasts
he fed on the blood of wretched men.
He locked me up in dark caverns,
deep in the earth and close to the empire of the dead.
At last, after six months, the gods took pity on me.
I was able to trick my guards
and I purged the world of a perfidious enemy.
He himself became food for his beasts.
And now when joyfully I draw near
to those I hold dearest in the world,
what do I find? When my soul, recovering,
wants to behold again these dear ones,
they welcome me in trembling and fear.
Everyone leaves, all refuse to embrace me.
As I feel the terror I inspire,
I wish I were still in the prisons of Epirus.
You must speak. Phaedra complains that I have been outraged.
Who has betrayed me? Why have I not been avenged?
Has Greece, which I have served so often,
given refuge to the criminal?
You don't answer? Is my own son
an accomplice of my enemies?
I must know. This doubt is too heavy to bear.

What is the crime and who is guilty?
Phaedra will have to explain why she is troubled.

Scene 6. *Hippolytus, Theramenes.*

HIPPOLYTUS. What was the meaning of Phaedra's speech?
It chilled me. She is still a prey to her extreme fury.
Does she intend to accuse herself and destroy herself?
What will the King say? What deadly poison
has love spread throughout the house!
I am consumed by a love he will hate and blame.
Today I am the same as he once knew me,
though I am terrified by black forebodings.
But innocence has nothing to fear.
Let me find some way
by which I may move my father to pity
and tell him of my love, which he may oppose
but which he is powerless to destroy.

ACT IV

Scene 1. *Theseus, Oenone.*

THESEUS. Ah! What are you telling me? What kind of traitor
prepared this outrage to his father's honor?
How relentless this fate of mine!
I don't know where I am or where I am going.
Is this the reward for a father's care?
Could any plan or thought be more loathsome?
In order to succeed with this criminal love,
he resorted to force.
I know this sword which he used in his passion.
I armed him with it, but for a nobler use.
Couldn't he be restrained by the bonds of family?
Why did Phaedra put off his punishment?
Why did she protect him by her silence?

OENONE. My lord, she was protecting you, his father.
Ashamed of the attempt of her passionate lover,
ashamed of the criminal light in his eyes,
Phaedra was dying. With her own hands
she would have taken her life.
I saw her raise her arm and I ran to save her.
I saved her life for your love.
And because I pitied both her dismay and your alarm,
I have interpreted, in spite of myself, her tears to you.

THESEUS. The liar! He couldn't help turning pale,
through fear, when he saw me. I saw him tremble.
I was surprised by his lack of joy.
He embraced me coldly and my love was chilled.
But had he felt already in Athens
this guilty love which devours him?

OENONE. My lord, remember how the Queen complained.
This criminal love was the cause of her hate.

THESEUS. And so the passion began again in Troezen?

OENONE. I have told you everything that took place.
But I have left the Queen too long with her grief.
Allow me to leave you and go to her.

Scene 2. *Theseus, Hippolytus.*

THESEUS. There he is! By his noble bearing
anyone else would be deceived as I was.
How is it that on the countenance of an adulterer
there shines the expression of virtue and innocence?
Shouldn't we be able to recognize
by certain signs the heart of a traitor?

HIPPOLYTUS. May I ask you what chagrin,
my lord, has changed your noble face?
Won't you trust me with your secret?

THESEUS. Liar! How do you dare come into my presence?
Monster, whom Heaven has spared too long!
You are the last of the bandits. I have slain all the others.
After the passion of a horrible love
bore you to your father's bed,
you dare come before the man you wronged,
you come into this place reeking with your infamy.
You will not find, under a foreign sky,
any land where my name is unknown.
Leave now. Do not come here defying my hate
and tempting an anger which I can scarcely restrain.
I have my share of eternal opprobrium
for having begotten so criminal a son,
and must not allow your death, which would shame my
  memory,
to desecrate the glory of my work.
Go, I say. If you do not want a sudden punishment
to add you to the rogues I have punished,
see to it that the sun which lightens our world
never beholds you again walking on these shores.
Once more, go! Go forever
and purge my land of your presence.
Hear me, Neptune. If once my courage
rid your banks of infamous cutthroats,
remember that as a reward for my efforts,
you promised to grant the first of my prayers.
During the long cruel days in prison
I did not call upon your immortal power.
Greedy for the help I expect from you,
I held back my prayers for a greater need.
Today I beseech you. Avenge a wretched father.

PHAEDRA

I give over this traitor to the fullness of your anger.
Stifle with his own blood his licentious desires.
Theseus will measure your generosity by your wrath.

HIPPOLYTUS. So Phaedra accuses Hippolytus of a criminal
love!
Such horror makes me speechless.
So many attacks rain on me at once
that I have no words to say and no voice with which to
speak them . . .

THESEUS. Traitor, you imagined that in cowardly silence
Phaedra would bury your brutish insolence.
When you fled, you should not have left
in her hands the sword which condemns you.
Or rather you should have completed your attack,
and taken from her both speech and life.

HIPPOLYTUS. I should tell the truth
of so black a lie that has overwrought you.
But I will not reveal a secret concerning you.
Please approve of the respect which forbids me to speak.
Do not increase the torments you already have.
Examine my life and remember who I am.
Small crimes always precede major crimes.
A man who has first transgressed the laws,
can violate then the most sacred rights.
Crime has its degrees as virtue has.
Never have you seen timid innocence
suddenly pass to extreme licence.
One day is not enough to make of a virtuous man
a perfidious murderer and an incestuous coward.
Conceived in the womb of a chaste heroine,
I have not betrayed the origin of her blood.
Pittheus, looked upon by all men as a sage,
was my teacher when I left my mother's care.
I do not wish to boast or speak of myself,
but I think I have shown hatred
for the crimes that are ascribed to me.
Hippolytus is known for this in all of Greece.
I have made virtue blunt.
The unbending rigor of my temperament is known.
Daylight is not purer than the depths of my heart.
And yet you say Hippolytus, intoxicated with profane love,
has . . .

THESEUS. This is the very pride which condemns you.
I can see the odious principle of your coldness.
Phaedra alone bewitched your senses,
and for any other woman your heart
scorned an innocent love.

HIPPOLYTUS. No, father—I have concealed this too long—my heart
did not scorn an innocent love.
At your feet I will confess my real crime.
I am in love, but in defiance of your law.
Aricia has enslaved me to her law.
The daughter of Pallas has conquered your son.
I worship her. Rebellious to your command,
my heart breathes and yearns only for her.

THESEUS. You love Aricia? This is an obvious trick.
You acknowledge one crime in order to escape another.

HIPPOLYTUS. My lord, I have avoided her for six months, and I still love her.
I came here in great fear to tell you.
Will nothing clear away your error?
What awesome oath is needed to reassure you?
By heaven and earth and all of nature . . .

THESEUS. Perjury is always the recourse of scoundrels.
Spare me any more of your words,
if they are the only pledge of your false virtue.

HIPPOLYTUS. It seems false and deceptive to you.
Phaedra in her heart does me better justice.

THESEUS. Your impudence arouses my anger.

HIPPOLYTUS. How long will you banish me and to what place?

THESEUS. If you were beyond the column of Alcides,
I would still think you too close.

HIPPOLYTUS. Charged with the terrible crime you suspect me of,
who will pity me when you send me away?

THESEUS. Seek out those friends whose fatal character
honors adultery and applauds incest,
traitors and ingrates without honor, without principle,
worthy of protecting a man like you.

HIPPOLYTUS. You keep speaking to me of incest and adultery.
I will hold my tongue. But Phaedra comes from a mother,
Phaedra is from a lineage—and my lord, you know this—
more filled with horrors than mine.

THESEUS. Now your rage has lost all restraint.
For the last time, leave my presence.
Leave now. Do not wait for an angry father
to expel you shamelessly from this land.

Scene 3. *Theseus.*

THESEUS. Hippolytus, you are rushing to your death.
Neptune, god of the sea, who is feared by other gods,
gave me his word and will carry it out.
An avenging god is at your heels. You will not escape him.
I loved you once, and in spite of your crime
my heart feels for you now.
But you forced me to condemn you.
Never has a father been more outraged.
Gods in heaven, see my grief!
Why did I ever beget so criminal a child?

Scene 4. *Phaedra, Theseus.*

PHAEDRA. My lord, I have come to you in terror and fear.
Your loud voice reached my ears.
I am afraid your threat was carried out too swiftly.
If there is still time, spare your son.
Don't turn against your family, I beg you.
Save me from the horror of hearing your blood cry out.
Do not plunge me into everlasting grief
for spilling your own son's blood.

THESEUS. Phaedra, I have spilled no blood.
Yet the ingrate has not escaped.
An immortal has charge of his death.
Neptune has promised me this. You will be avenged.

PHAEDRA. Neptune has promised? What angry prayers . . . ?

THESEUS. Are you afraid they will not be heeded?
Join yours with my just prayers.
Tell me his crimes in all their blackness.
Stir up my anger which has been too slow.
You do not yet know all of his crimes.

His fury lashed out at you,
and said your mouth is full of lies and deceit.
He insists that Aricia is the mistress of his heart,
and that he loves her.

PHAEDRA.   What, my lord?

THESEUS.   He said it to me.
But I saw through this obvious trick.
Let us hope for swift justice from Neptune.
I myself am going to his altars
to urge him to carry out his immortal promises.

SCENE 5. *Phaedra, Oenone.*

PHAEDRA. What is this he said to me?
What fire flares up again in my heart?
What thunderbolt, O gods, what fatal news!
I came here to save my son.
I pulled myself away from terrified Oenone
and gave over to the remorse which has tormented me.
How far would this repentance have taken me?
I would have perhaps at last accused myself.
Perhaps, if my voice had not been cut off,
the terrible truth would have escaped from me.
Hippolytus feels nothing for me!
Aricia has his love and his faith!
When before my prayers the ruthless ingrate
armed himself with a haughty look and a proud countenance,
I believed that his heart, always closed to love,
was hostile equally to all women.
But one woman did affect his feelings.
One woman did find grace before his cruel eyes.
Perhaps he does have a heart easy to move.
I am the only one he could not bear.
Should I take on, then, the duty of defending him?

SCENE 6. *Phaedra, Oenone.*

PHAEDRA. Dear Oenone, do you know what I have just learned?

OENONE. No, but I can't conceal that I am terrified for you.
I tremble at the reason which made you come here.
I fear some madness that will be fatal.

PHAEDRA. Who would have believed it, Oenone? I had a rival.

OENONE. What, my lady?

PHAEDRA. Hippolytus is in love, and I cannot doubt it.
That wild enemy who could not be tamed,
who was offended by respect and irritated by complaints,
that tiger whom I never approached without fear,
submissive and docile has recognized a conqueror.
Aricia found the way to his heart.

OENONE. Aricia?

PHAEDRA. This suffering I had not yet felt!
I had saved myself for this new torment.
Whatever I suffered up until now: fears and passion,
the fury of love and the horror of remorse,
the unbearable pain of a cruel refusal—
all that was but a weak foretaste of the torment I endure now.
They are in love! By what spell were my eyes deceived?
How did they meet? How long have they loved? Where did they meet?
You knew this. Why did you let me be tricked?
Couldn't you have told me about their furtive passion?
Were they often seen speaking and looking for one another?
Did they hide in the depths of the forest?
Ah! It was permissible for them to see one another.
Heaven approved the innocence of their sighs.
Without remorse they could heed their instincts for love.
Every day rose clear and serene for them.
But I hid from the day and escaped from the light
as if I were rejected by all nature.
The only god I dared beseech was death.
I waited for the moment of death,
and fed on sorrow and tears.
Yet when I was too closely watched in my suffering
I did not dare give full vent to your tears.
As I trembled, I felt that fatal pleasure,
and with a serene face disguising my anguish,
I had often to deprive myself of my own tears.

OENONE. But what will come of their vain love?
They will not meet again.

PHAEDRA. Their love will continue always.
At this very moment—oh! let me not think of it!—
they are defying the fury of a jealous woman.
Even despite the exile which will separate them,
they swear a thousand times not to leave one another.
I cannot bear their happiness which insults me,
Oenone. Take pity on my jealous rage.
Aricia must be killed. We must arouse the anger
of my husband against a hated family.
He must not stop with easy penalties.
The sister's crime exceeds her brothers'.
I will implore him in my jealous rage.
What am I doing? Have I lost control of my mind?
I am jealous! and Theseus is the man I am to implore!
My husband is living, and I still burn with passion.
And for whom? to whose heart are my prayers addressed?
Every word I say adds to my panic.
My crimes have become monstrous.
They include incest and imposture.
My hands of an assassin, so eager for revenge,
are about to plunge into innocent blood.
And I continue to live. I am still seen
by the holy sun from which I am descended.
My ancestor is the father and the master of the gods.
The heavens, the entire universe is full of my ancestors.
Where can I hide? Let me turn to the darkness of Hades.
What am I saying? There my father holds the fatal urn.
The gods placed it in his severe hands.
In hell Minos judges the pale ghosts of men.
How his terrified spirit will tremble
when his daughter comes before him
and confesses these misdemeanors
and crimes which are unknown to hell!
Father, what will you say at such a horrible spectacle?
I can see the solemn urn drop from your hands.
I can see you looking for some new punishment
and becoming the executioner of your own family.
Forgive me. A cruel god laid waste to your family.
Behold his vengeance in the madness of your child.
Alas! my unhappy heart did not gather the fruit
of the terrible crime whose shame haunts me.
Pursued by woe until my last breath,
I relinquish in torment a painful life.

PHAEDRA

OENONE. My lady, you must repulse this ill-founded terror.
Consider differently an excusable error.
You are in love. Such a fate cannot be overcome.
You were impelled by some magical power of the gods.
Is this so unusual a prodigy for mankind?
Are you the only victim of love?
Weakness is innate in all of us.
You are mortal and you are involved in the fate of mortals.
You complain of a yoke imposed for all time.
Even the gods, inhabitants of Olympus,
who by scandal terrify criminals,
have sometimes suffered from illicit passion.

PHAEDRA. What are you saying? What advice do you dare offer me?
Are you bent on poisoning me to the very end,
wretched Oenone? This is how you ruined me.
You turned me back to the daylight I was fleeing.
Your entreaties made me forget my duty.
I was avoiding Hippolytus, and you forced me to look upon him.
What right did you have? Why did your imperious words,
as they accused him, blacken his life?
He may die because of this, and the sacrilegious vow
of a wrathful father is perhaps already carried out.
I will heed you no longer, for you are a monster.
Leave my presence.
I wish now to be alone with my tortured fate.
May the justice of heaven reward you,
and may your punishment forever terrify
all those who, like you, with loathsome means,
feed the weakness of unhappy rulers,
urge them to submit to the desires of their heart,
and dare open up the way to crime!
Detestable flatterers, they are the most pernicious gift
the anger of the gods can give to princes!

OENONE (*alone*). I gave up everything and did everything in order to serve her.
I deserve the reward she has now given me.

ACT V

Scene 1. *Hippolytus, Aricia.*

ARICIA. Can you be silent in such extreme danger?
Can you permit your loving father to remain in error?
Cruel Hippolytus, if you scorn the power of my tears,
if, without pain, you consent to seeing me no more,
you will leave and we shall separate,
but at least safeguard your life.
Defend your honor from a shameful reproach,
and force your father to withdraw his vows.
There is still time. Why, through what caprice,
are you leaving the way open to your accuser?
Inform Theseus.

HIPPOLYTUS. I have said everything I could.
Should I have revealed the wrong of his wife?
In telling him the full details,
should I have covered his face with unworthy shame?
You alone saw through the hateful mystery.
I have only you and the gods with whom I can speak.
This is the measure of my love: I could not hide from you
what I wanted to hide from myself.
But remember the seal of secrecy under which I told you all.
You must forget, if you can, that I spoke to you.
Your lips that are so pure,
must never tell this horrible adventure.
I will trust the justice of the gods.
It is for their own good to justify me.
Phaedra one day will be punished for her crime,
and will not escape a deserving ignominy.
This is the one mark of respect I demand from you.
Everything else I permit my free anger.
Leave the slavery to which you have been reduced.
Dare to follow me, dare to come with me in my flight.
You must pull yourself away from this fatal, profaned place
where virtue breathes a poisoned air.
To conceal your abrupt departure,
profit from the confusion created by my disgrace.
I can assure you of the means for this flight.
Your only guards here are my men.
Powerful defenders will take our side.

PHAEDRA

Argos has asked us to come, and Sparta.
We will speak of our cause to our common friends
and prevent Phaedra, as she gathers what fortune we abandon,
from expelling both of us from the paternal throne
and promising her son my death and yours.
This is the right moment for us to seize.
What fear holds you back? You seem uncertain.
Your rights and your interest guide me in this plan.
I am burning with anticipation, and you seem coldly indifferent.
Are you afraid of following in the steps of an exile?

ARICIA. How precious, my lord, such an exile would be!
If I could join with your fate, how joyously
I would live far from the rest of mankind!
But we are not united in marriage.
Can I honorably escape this place with you?
I know that I can free myself
from your father without harming even the strictest honor.
It would not be an escape from my own family.
Escape is permitted if it is escape from a tyrant.
But you love me, my lord, and my honor . . .

HIPPOLYTUS. No, no! I have not forgotten your reputation.
A nobler plan brings me here before you.
Flee from your enemies and follow your husband.
Since it is the will of Heaven, we are free in our woes.
The pledge of our word depends on no one.
Marriage is not always surrounded by torches.
At the gates of Troezen, in the midst of tombs,
ancient sepulchers of the princes of my race,
is a sacred temple which does not allow perjury.
In that place men do not dare take false oaths.
The dishonest man would receive a swift punishment.
He would fear inevitable death.
The consequence of a lie would be too fearful.
There, if you believe my words, we will take
the solemn oath of eternal love.
Our witness will be the god we revere in that temple.
We will pray that he be a father for us.
I will call upon the names of the most sacred of the gods.
Chaste Diana, proud Juno,
all of the gods, witnesses of my affection,
will vouch for the sincerity of my holy promises.

ARICIA. The King is coming. You must leave, Hippolytus, at this very moment.
I will stay briefly to conceal my departure.
Go. Leave me a faithful guide
who will direct my timid steps to you.

SCENE 2. *Theseus, Aricia, Ismene.*

THESEUS. O gods, bring me light and show me
the truth I am searching for in this palace.

ARICIA. Make preparations, dear Ismene, and be ready for our flight.

SCENE 3. *Theseus, Aricia.*

THESEUS. You change color, my lady, and seem embarrassed.
What was Hippolytus doing here?

ARICIA. My lord, he was saying a last farewell.

THESEUS. Your eyes subjugated his rebellious heart.
His first sighs were because of you.

ARICIA. My lord, I cannot hide the truth from you.
He did not inherit the unjust hate you feel.
He did not treat me as a criminal.

THESEUS. I know. He swore eternal love to you.
Do not put your trust in his inconstant heart.
He swore the same love to others that he swore to you.

ARICIA. Hippolytus, my lord?

THESEUS. You should have made him less fickle.
How could you stand sharing him with someone else?

ARICIA. And how can you allow such horrible words
to darken the days of so noble a life?
Have you so little knowledge of his heart?
Can't you discern the difference between crime and innocence?
Must you be the only one who cannot see
his virtue which shines forth for everyone else?
You have given him over to the malice of gossip.
You must repent of your homicidal prayers.
You should fear, my lord, that Heaven in its rigor
hates you enough to carry out your wishes.
In its wrath Heaven often receives our victims.
Its gifts are often the punishment for our crimes.

THESEUS. It will do you no good to cover up his sin.
Your love blinds you in favor of the ingrate.
I have put my faith in certain irreproachable witnesses.
I have seen the sincere tears of a woman.

ARICIA. Take care, my lord. Your invincible hands
have delivered mankind from countless monsters.
But all of them are not destroyed, and you allow
one of them to . . . Your son, my lord, has forbidden me to speak.
I know of the respect he will always have for you.
If I spoke now, I would grieve him.
Let me imitate his discreetness and leave your presence
so that I will not be forced to break my silence.

SCENE 4. *Theseus.*

THESEUS. What is she trying to say? What is concealed
in the words which she only half uttered?
Are they bent on confusing me by some vain pretense?
Are they both agreed to torture me?
In spite of the severity of my judgment,
I can hear a plaintive cry in the depths of my heart.
A secret pity has taken hold of me and is affecting me.
I will question Oenone a second time.
I must learn more about the entire crime.
Guards, have Oenone come here alone.

SCENE 5. *Theseus, Panope.*

PANOPE. My lord, I do not know what the Queen is planning,
but from her terrible state I fear the worst.
Her face shows a deathlike despair.
Already she has the pallor of death.
Oenone, whom she sent away in shame,
has already hurled herself into the sea.
We do not know how this madness came about,
but the waves have taken her from us forever.

THESEUS. What are you saying?

PANOPE.   Her death did not quiet the Queen.
The anguish of her heart seemed to get worse.
From time to time, to diminish her secret grief,

she lifts up her children and covers them with tears,
and then suddenly, forgetting her maternal love,
she pushes them aside with horror.
She wanders about aimlessly.
Bewildered, she does not recognize us.
Three times she began to write, and changing her mind,
three times she tore up the letter.
I beg you to see her, my lord, I beg you to help her.

THESEUS. So, Oenone is dead, and Phaedra wants to die.
Call back my son, let him come and defend himself!
I want him to speak. I am ready now to hear him.
Do not pour down your fatal blessings,
Neptune! I prefer now not to have my prayers heeded.
I have perhaps believed witnesses who were not trustworthy.
I raised my cruel hands to you too early.
Such vows I have taken would lead me to despair!

SCENE 6. *Theseus, Theramenes.*

THESEUS. Is it you, Theramenes? What have you done with my son?
I gave him to you at an early age.
But what is the reason for your sadness and your tears?
What has happened to my son?

THERAMENES. Your solicitude comes too late.
Your affection is useless. Hippolytus is dead.

THESEUS. Ah!

THERAMENES. I have seen the most loving of mortals perish,
and I can say also, my lord, the least guilty.

THESEUS. My son is dead? When I am opening my arms to receive him,
did the impatient gods hasten his end?
How has he been taken from me? What thunderbolt fell?

THERAMENES. We had just left the gates of Troezen.
He was on his chariot. His grieving guards,
drawn up around him, were silent as he was.
Sadly he was taking the road to Mycenae.
His hand had loosened the reins on his horses.
These proud beasts which could be seen once
ardent and noble obeying his voice,
now with sad eyes and lowered heads,
seemed to respond to his grieving thought.

PHAEDRA

A terrible cry, coming from below the waves,
at that moment cut through the quiet of the scene.
From the bowels of the earth a formidable voice
wailed in answer to the fearful cry.
Our blood froze in our hearts.
The attentive horses reared in terror
while over the flat surface of the sea
a gigantic wave of foam rose up.
It came close, broke and spewed out in full sight,
in its waves of foam, a raging monster.
Its broad head was armed with dangerous horns.
Yellowish scales covered its body.
Was it an untamed bull or a bold dragon?
Its back was twisted in coils.
Its long shrieks shook the seacoast.
Heaven was horrified at seeing such a wild monster.
The earth was shocked and the air grew infected.
The wave, which had brought it, recoiled in terror.
Everyone fled—a man's courage would have been useless—
and sought shelter in the neighboring temple.
Only Hippolytus, as the worthy son of a hero,
stopped his horses, seized his spear,
and rushing at the monster, hurled his weapon with good aim
and tore a wide gash in the animal's side.
It leaped, and roaring with rage and pain,
fell at the feet of the horses,
rolled over, and opened a flaming mouth.
Fire, blood, and fumes covered them.
Fright overcame them, and this time deaf,
they heeded neither the reins nor their master's voice.
Vainly Hippolytus tried to control them.
They reddened their bridles with bloody foam.
Some say that in this great melee a god was seen
flogging their dust-covered sides.
Through fear they plunged from the rocks.
The axle creaked and broke. Courageous Hippolytus
saw his broken chariot split into fragments.
He himself fell, twisted into the harness.
Forgive my grief. This cruel picture
will be for me an eternal source of sorrow.
My lord, I saw your poor son
dragged by the horses his hand had fed.
He tried to call them, but his voice frightened them.

They kept running until all of his body was an open wound.
The field resounded with our cries of grief.
They finally slowed their wild race,
and stopped, not far from those ancient tombs
where lie the cold remains of his royal ancestors.
Anguished I rushed up and his guard followed me.
The trail of his noble blood led us.
The rocks were covered with it and the thorns
bore blood-stained bits of his hair.
I reached him and called to him. Then stretching out his hand,
he opened his eyes and closed them again.
"Heaven," he said, "is snatching from me an innocent life.
After my death, take care of poor Aricia.
Dear friend, if one day my father learns the truth,
and pities the fate of a falsely accused son,
tell him, if he wishes to appease my blood and my unquiet shade,
to treat his captive with gentleness,
to give back to her . . ." At those words the hero died
and left in my arms a disfigured body,
in which the anger of the gods triumphed,
and which his own father would not recognize.

THESEUS. Oh son! You were the hope I have lost!
Oh! relentless gods, you served me too well.
Nothing remains now but mortal grief.

THERAMENES. Modest Aricia came then.
My lord, she was fleeing your wrath
and accepting him as husband in the sight of the gods.
On drawing near, she saw the grass streaked with blood,
and then she saw (what an object for the eyes of a lover!)
Hippolytus stretched out, mangled and without color.
For some time she would not believe her affliction,
and not recognizing the hero she loved,
she kept calling for Hippolytus.
Finally she realized he was there before her,
and turning her face toward heaven,
cold, grieving, and almost lifeless,
she fell in a faint at the feet of her lover.
Ismene was close by. Ismene weeping
brought her back to life, or rather to tears.
And I, cursing my life,
came here to tell you the last wish of a hero,

PHAEDRA

and acquit myself of the painful duty
he asked of me as he died.
But I see his mortal enemy coming.

SCENE 7. *Theseus, Phaedra, Theramenes, Panope, Guards.*

THESEUS. My son is dead, Phaedra, and you are triumphant.
I was right in my fears and suspicions
when I excused him in my heart.
But now he is dead. Take your victim.
Gloat over his loss, whether just or unjust.
I will not be undeceived, Phaedra.
I believe him guilty since you have accused him.
His death gives me enough reason for lament
without my looking for some terrible enlightenment,
which would not bring him back to life
but would only increase my sorrow.
Far from you and far from these shores,
let me flee the image of my bleeding son.
Obsessed with this memory of death,
I will banish myself from the entire universe.
Everything rises up against my injustice.
The glory of my name increases my suffering.
If I were less well known by men, I could hide more easily.
I detest now the help which the gods have given me.
I am going away in order to bewail their murderous favors,
and I shall stop beseeching them with useless prayers.
Whatever their power be, their fatal generosity
cannot replace what they have taken from me.

PHAEDRA. No, Theseus, I must break my silence.
I must give your son his innocence.
He was not guilty.

THESEUS.   Wretched father that I am!
It was on your word I condemned him.
Cruel Phaedra, how can you be forgiven?

PHAEDRA. I have but few moments left. You must hear me, Theseus.
I was the impure, the incestuous one
who hated to look at chaste respectful Hippolytus.
Heaven put this fatal love in my heart.
Wicked Oenone did all the rest.
She feared that Hippolytus, learning of my madness,

would tell of a passion which so horrified him.
Profiting from my extreme weakness,
she hastened to denounce him to you.
She has punished herself, and escaping from my wrath,
she sought in the sea an easy death.
The sword would have already severed my life,
if I had not allowed my suspected virtue to lament.
I wanted to tell you of my remorse
and descend by a slower path to the dead.
I have taken a poison which Medea brought to Athens.
It is coursing now through my veins.
It has already reached my heart
and has cast an unknown cold upon it.
There is a cloud over my eyes.
I can hardly see the sky and you whom my presence insults.
Death, stealing the light from my eyes
gives back to the day all of its purity.

PANOPE. She is dying, my lord!

THESEUS.   Would that the memory
of so black a deed might die with her!
Now that I know my error,
I want to mingle my tears with the blood of my son.
I want to embrace what is left of his body
and expiate the madness of a vow I loathe.
I will give him the honors he deserves,
and to appease his troubled spirit,
I will, despite the plottings of her guilty family,
ask Aricia to be my daughter from today on.

INDEX OF PROPER NAMES

Acheron, river in Hell.
Aegeus, father of Theseus.
Alcides, columns of Hercules.
Amazon, one of a race of female warriors.
Antiope, mother of Hippolytus.
Argos, town in Greece.
Ariadne, daughter of Minos and sister of Phaedra.
Cercyon, fighter of Arcadia.
Cocytus, river in Hell.
Crete, island in the Mediterranean.

PHAEDRA

Diana, goddess of the forest and the hunt.
Elis, country of ancient Greece.
Epidaurus, city of ancient Greece.
Epirus, country of ancient Greece.
Erechtheus, king, ancestor of Aricia.
Hercules, Greek hero, celebrated for his strength.
Icarus, son of Daedalus, the architect who invented the labyrinth in Crete. Together they fled Crete on wings of feather and wax. Icarus flew too close to the sun, his wings melted, and he fell into the sea and drowned.
Juno, goddess of marriage.
Jupiter, god of the heavens. Minos descended from him.
Medea, wife of Jason, magician famous for her poisons.
Minerva, goddess of Athens.
Minos, father of Phaedra.
Minotaur, half-bull, half-man, offspring of Pasiphaë and a white bull. Was confined to labyrinth built by Daedalus. Theseus went to Crete to kill the Minotaur.
Mycenae, city of Greece.
Neptune, god of the sea.
Olympus, mountain in Thessaly, abode of the Olympian gods.
Pallantides, the sons of Pallas, brothers of Aricia. Theseus had them killed because he believed them a threat to his rule of Athens.
Pallas, father of Aricia, king of Athens.
Pasiphaë, mother of Phaedra.
Periboea, maiden who was to be sacrificed to the Minotaur and whom Theseus saved.
Pirithous, friend of Theseus.
Pittheus, maternal ancestor of Theseus.
Procrustus, brigand of Attica.
Salamis, city of Cyprus.
Scythia, ancient name of parts of Europe.
Sinnis, brigand of Corinth.
Sirron, brigand of Megarus.
Sparta, chief city of the Peloponnesus.
Taenarus, today Cape Matapan.
Venus, goddess of love.

The Intellectual Ladies
(LES FEMMES SAVANTES)
1672

A COMEDY IN FIVE ACTS

BY

MOLIÈRE

translated by WALLACE FOWLIE

Molière
(1622-1673)

Molière exceeds and overflows the limits of academic categories. His exuberance and breadth seem to belie the formal aspects of his plays, which are in harmony with academic rules. He is of the academy and of something else which is solely Molière. He is a necessity of life, not a mere luxury, for the French. They recognize themselves in Molière and in a form acceptable to their taste for arrangement and swiftness. The morality of the plays is palatable to them because of the laughter and the contortions with which it is served. Molière is not a playwright of frivolity, and the French theater is not solely a source of amusement. It is a process of action and response to action, an institution which exists for the good of all and thanks to the support of all. The principal theater of France is rightfully called *la maison de Molière,* and its actors the "children of Molière." When the theatrical season is poor in Paris, producers have simply to revive a comedy of Molière and the vitality of the French theater is once again restored. Molière is one of the common memories of the French, of their childhood, of their classroom, of their first visit to Paris and the *matinées classiques* on Thursday at the Comédie-Française. He is their common memory and also their standard of a kind of balance by which they learn to live—a balance between vehemence and discretion, between passion and self-control.

Several of the major comedies of Molière are written in verse: *L'École des Femmes, Tartuffe, Le Misanthrope, Les Femmes savantes,* etc. As Racine did in the case of tragedy, Molière, in his treatment of comedy, fused language with situation, poetry with characterization. Molière's language is at all times vigorous and varied and colorful. He knew the language of the people, of the bourgeoisie and of the *précieux.* In the high comedies, such as *Les Femmes savantes,* one has the impression of listening to conversation, and at the same time of listening to something more substantial, in the skillful organization of the sentence, in the lilt of the rhythm and the resounding rhymes. Molière's style is purely theatrical. The dramatic suitability of the poetic expression is his guiding rule.

Les Femmes savantes (*The Intellectual Ladies*) was first performed at the Théâtre du Palais-Royal, March 11, 1672—just one year before Molière's death. At first there was some hostility toward the play, on the part of the *précieuses,* but the King liked it as did most of the first spectators. Between 1680 and 1952, there were 1,454 performances at the Comédie-Française.

At the beginning of Molière's career as playwright, in 1659, he had satirized the provincial form of preciosity in *Les Précieuses ridicules*. During the years the *précieuses* had tended to become *savantes*. Mme de Sévigné had demonstrated interest in theology, Mme Dacier was a student of Greek, and Mme de la Sablière (a possible model for Philaminte in Molière's play) studied mathematics and physics. Of the three *savantes* in the comedy, Bélise is closest to the type of *précieuse,* but she has recently become involved in literary pedantry. Armande is trying hard to follow the example of her mother, but has still many of the coquettish traits of the young girl. Philaminte is the only really sincere and noble-minded *savante* in her search for knowledge. She is willful by temperament, and irreproachable in her moral conduct.

The comic characters, Trissotin and Vadius, are both based on real poets of the day. Trissotin is Abbé Cotin, a *précieux* poet of the Hôtel de Rambouillet who had written madrigals and enigmas. (His name is obviously drawn from *triple sot*.) Vadius is Ménage, a scholar who had engaged in many pedantic quarrels and was known for his gallantry. Chrysale is the materialistic, thick-skinned bourgeois, concerned with his food, and carrying out his duties of father and husband without any sense of dignity or authority.

The ideal production of *Les Femmes savantes* should attempt to bring out the mechanical neatness which characterizes the manners and modes of thought of that rationalistic age—when the universe seemed to tick like a clock. The theatrical conventions of vaudeville have some of this deceptive patness; and Molière's theater was based on the vaudeville of his time—the *commedia dell'arte*.

The authenticity of Molière's speech—a trait which perhaps explains why he is the most universal French writer—is due largely, of course, to his genius. But it is also due to the literary form he elected. His diversity and his vision and his sense of humanity are perhaps less important to the world than

THE INTELLECTUAL LADIES

Racine's poetry and sense of tragic intensity. But Racine's very perfection prevents his being appreciated to any large extent outside of France. The universality of Molière is doubtless due to his imperfections. In any strict sense, he is the least classical of the classical writers of Louis XIV. He risked too much. He ranged too far—from buffoonery to high comedy that is almost tragedy. His extraordinary sense of the theater and of the public made it unnecessary for him to undergo the rigors of a Racine.

During the past one hundred years the number of monographs on Molière which have been written and published is overwhelming. Scholars have examined and re-examined all the available documents (which are not very plentiful) and advanced a variety of theories. As the study of Molière became more and more intellectualized, it moved progressively farther away from its source, which is the stage. The majority of his critics made Molière into a writer. But he was essentially an actor, a man of the theater. Whereas Corneille and Racine may be studied solely as dramatic poets, the poet in Molière may not be separated from the art of the comic actor. The art of the playwright is perhaps best explained by seeing it within the context of the career of an ambitious and gifted actor who for thirty years lived in the world of the theater. This thesis is supported by René Bray in his book *Molière, Homme de Théâtre* (1954), in which the critic argues that Molière's activity as actor conditioned, controlled, and explained his activity as playwright.

ie. you don't question th propriety ⟶
of stepmothers marrying sons —
it is a given.

The Intellectual Ladies

CHARACTERS

CHRYSALE, a rich bourgeois of Paris
PHILAMINTE, his intellectual wife
BÉLISE, his intellectual sister
ARMANDE, his intellectual daughter
HENRIETTE, his unintellectual daughter
CLITANDRE, in love with Henriette
ARISTE, Chrysale's brother and ally
TRISSOTIN, an author
L'EPINE, Trissotin's valet
VADIUS, another author
JULIEN, Vadius' valet
MARTINE, Chrysale's cook
NOTARY

Scene: Paris.

ACT I

SCENE 1. *Armande, Henriette.*

ARMANDE. Is it possible, my sister, that you want to give up the title of "maiden" and that you can even rejoice in the vulgar scheme of marriage? [1]*

HENRIETTE. Yes, sister Armande.

ARMANDE. Oh, that "yes." Can I bear it? The very thought turns my stomach.

HENRIETTE. But how can marriage in itself, my sister . . .

ARMANDE. Ah! Poh!

HENRIETTE. What?

ARMANDE. Ah! Poh! I say. Don't you see all the repulsive suggestions in the word? The queer picture it paints tortures me. How can you, Henriette, face the consequences of marriage?

* Notes follow the translation, pp. 167–168.

HENRIETTE. Consequences? But marriage simply means a husband, children, a home. There is nothing in that to terrify or torture me.

ARMANDE. Heavens! Are such bonds able to seduce you?

HENRIETTE. What better thing could a girl at my age do than accept a husband who loves her and whom she loves? And then in this innocent union, lead a life of love and affection. Am I wrong in wanting this?

ARMANDE. In what sunken condition is your mind! How small of you to hole yourself up at home and to see nothing beyond an adoring husband and little brats of children! It's a pastime for the vulgar. *You* must aim higher, Henriette. You must learn to love the noblest delights and, like the rest of us, give yourself completely to things of the mind. Our mother is an example for us. She is honored everywhere as an intellectual. We must be worthy of her and open our hearts to the love of study. Rather than be a slave to a man, my dear sister, marry Philosophy, who controls the animal side of our nature. When I see . . .

HENRIETTE (*interrupting*). Heaven, when we are born, doesn't decide that we should all become philosophers. Your mind may well be suited to the speculations of scholars, but mine is much inferior and loves the practical side of things. Let's not upset the rulings of Heaven. Let each one of us obey her own instincts. You, with your genius, can mount to the lofty spheres of philosophy; whereas I, down here, will be drawn into the worldly pleasure of matrimony. You see, in this way, we shall both imitate our mother. You will imitate her soul and her noble desires; I, her senses and her grosser pleasures.

ARMANDE. When you pretend to pattern yourself on someone, you should resemble her in her *best* traits. She is hardly your model if you merely cough and spit as she does.

HENRIETTE. If my mother had only a noble side to her nature, you would hardly be today, dear sister, what you pride yourself on being. It is lucky for you that she didn't give all her attention to philosophy. Please now, Armande, grant me a few of the "low consequences" of marriage to which you owe your very life, and don't suppress some little scholar who wants to be born.

ARMANDE. I see you can't be cured of this madness of getting a husband. At least, I trust you're not placing your hopes on Clitandre?

THE INTELLECTUAL LADIES

HENRIETTE. And why not? Would Clitandre be so bad a match?

ARMANDE. No. But it would be indelicate to walk off with another's prize. It is well known in our circle that Clitandre loves me.

HENRIETTE. Yes, but without much result, since you've given up marriage forever and since philosophy has all your affection. How can it matter to you if someone else loves Clitandre?

ARMANDE. Even if reason controls my senses and I refuse to marry a man, nothing prevents me from keeping him on as a suitor.

HENRIETTE. I didn't stop his playing suitor to your charms and I didn't listen to him until you had flatly refused to marry.

ARMANDE. But can you trust a lover who's been jilted? Do you think that he really loves you so deeply and that all his passion for me is dead?

HENRIETTE. He tells me so, Armande, and I believe him.

ARMANDE. If he tells you he loves you, he's deceiving himself too.

HENRIETTE. It won't be hard to find out. I see him coming, and on this point he can enlighten us completely.

SCENE 2. *Henriette, Armande, Clitandre.*

HENRIETTE. Clitandre, I am worried over what my sister has just said. You must tell us now which of us it is you really love.

ARMANDE. No, no, your love must not be tried in this way. I will not have you embarrassed by a public confession.

CLITANDRE. I have no fear of a public confession, Mademoiselle, and can say frankly that my love is all your sister's. Don't let this disturb you in the least. It is only what you wished. Your charms held me captive once and you had my tenderest sighs and my warmest ardors. But you did not think me worthy—and in your service I suffered nothing but your scorn. Now I have found a more humane conqueror and softer chains. Nothing could tear me away. Please don't try to recall me from the gentle passion in which I am resolved to die.

ARMANDE. And who wants to, Monsieur? I find you rather impertinent to insinuate so much.

HENRIETTE. Remember, dear sister, the animal side of your nature. We must transcend all anger.

ARMANDE. Gently, Sister! Do you wish to transcend your

duty? How can you accept this man without permission from our parents? You are permitted to love only at their pleasure and they have absolute authority over your heart.

HENRIETTE. Many thanks for the lesson on duty. I shall model my conduct on yours. Clitandre, you must get the approval of Mother and Father so that I may love you without committing a crime.

CLITANDRE. I shall set to work at once. Your permission was all I wanted.

ARMANDE. You are triumphant, Sister! You seem to think this hurts *me*.

HENRIETTE. Not at all. I see that your reason has completely subdued your senses. And instead of suspecting you of envy, I am sure you will do all you can to hasten the happy moment of marriage. Please do! I can suggest . . .

ARMANDE. You are trying to be witty. You are proud of the love I tossed you.

HENRIETTE. If I tossed it back again, you would not be too proud to try to catch it.

ARMANDE. I shall not stoop to answer you. I refuse to hear such nonsense.

HENRIETTE. Thank you for the inconceivable delicacy you have shown us!   (*Exit* ARMANDE.)

SCENE 3. *Henriette, Clitandre.*

HENRIETTE. Your frankness must have surprised her.

CLITANDRE. She deserved it. Her pride warranted a lesson. And now, let me go to your father, Henriette . . .

HENRIETTE. No! The best move would be to win over my mother. My father will consent to anything she says. She runs the house and dictates the law. You must try to please my mother and my aunt a little more than you do. If, in their presence, you would approve of some of their ideas . . .

CLITANDRE. It is hard for me to flatter your mother. Lady intellectuals are not to my taste. I agree that a woman should have some enlightenment, but she shouldn't gloat over becoming learned simply in order to be learned. I should rather have her know enough *not* to know a few things, and not to quote authors, nor say long words . . . Now I have great respect for your mother; but I don't approve of all her habits and particularly the way she praises her idol, her hero of wit, her Monsieur Trissotin. He bores me beyond words. And I

THE INTELLECTUAL LADIES

hate to see her respect a ninny whose pedantry is hissed and hooted everywhere else.

HENRIETTE. I agree his books are tiresome and his conversation is tiresome, but he has great power over Mother. You must try to bear him. When a lover woos a lady, he should try to win over everyone in the house—even the dog.

CLITANDRE. You are right, of course. But I should lose my self-respect if I tried to praise his writings. I read them before meeting him and saw all his interminable pedantry, his presumption, his lazy conceit.

HENRIETTE. How intelligent you were to see that!

CLITANDRE. I even knew what he looked like by the verses he wrote; and one day when I came across a man in the Palais de Justice, I bet he was Trissotin and I won my bet.

HENRIETTE. What a story!

CLITANDRE. No, no, it's true. Henriette, I see your aunt coming. Let me tell her how much I love you and win her over to our side.

(*Exit* HENRIETTE.)

SCENE 4. *Clitandre, Bélise.*

CLITANDRE. Pardon me, Madame. Will you let a lover take this opportunity to tell you about the great love which he . .

BÉLISE. Take care lest you say too much. You have taken your place among my lovers, but you must let only your eyes speak for you. Love me, pine for me, perish for me, but don't let me know it. If you spoil everything with speeches, I shall be forced to exile you forever from my sight.

CLITANDRE. Don't be alarmed, Madame. Henriette is the one I love and I beg you to help me in winning her suit.

BÉLISE. Ah! how ingenious of you! In all the novels I have read, I have not found such subtlety.[2]

CLITANDRE. It's not subtlety, Madame, but the simple truth. Heaven has bound me to the charms of Henriette. Henriette has full sway over my heart. Madame, will you approve of my wooing Henriette?

BÉLISE. I see through your request, and I know what you mean by "Henriette." Let me answer—to keep your figure of speech—that "Henriette" will not marry and that without hoping for very much, you must still pine for her.

CLITANDRE. Madame, what is the good of this? Why do you believe in something that does not exist?

BÉLISE. Please, no more complications! Stop denying what

your eyes have told me often. I respect your figure of speech and I shall accept your homage provided its ecstasy, enlightened by honor, offers on my altar only the purest of vows.

CLITANDRE. But . . .

BÉLISE. Farewell! This should content you. I have said more than I meant to say.

CLITANDRE. But you are wrong in . . .

BÉLISE. Enough! I am blushing, and my modesty is sorely tried!

CLITANDRE. I'll be hanged if I love you and if . . .

BÉLISE. No, no, I can bear no more today. (*Exit.*)

CLITANDRE. Devil take her hallucinations! Did you ever see anything like it? I must get help from a wise gentleman I know.[3] (*Exit.*)

ACT II

Scene 1. *Ariste, Clitandre.*

ARISTE. I'll give you their answer as soon as I know it. Yes, I'll urge them and praise you to the skies. *(Exit* CLITANDRE.) Whew! what a lover's impatience and what a flow of words! ...

(CHRYSALE *enters.*)

Scene 2. *Ariste, Chrysale.*[4]

ARISTE. Ah! Good afternoon, brother. Do you know why I'm here?

CHRYSALE. Not yet, but I hope you'll tell me.

ARISTE. Have you seen very much of this Clitandre?

CHRYSALE. Why, yes! He comes here often enough.

ARISTE. Frankly, what do you think of him?

CHRYSALE. He's an excellent fellow, mannerly, distinguished ...

ARISTE. I am glad you think well of him because it is he who sent me.

CHRYSALE. I knew his late father when I was in Rome.

ARISTE *(to himself)*. Good!

CHRYSALE. He was a fine gentleman.

ARISTE. So I have heard.

CHRYSALE. We were only twenty-eight then, and if I do say it, a couple of sports.

ARISTE *(to himself)*. I heard that, too.

CHRYSALE. They used to talk about our skill with the Roman ladies. Yes, brother, we made many a husband jealous.

ARISTE. Excellent! But let me speak of the matter which brought me here ...

(BÉLISE *enters and listens.*)

Scene 3. *Ariste, Chrysale, Bélise.*

ARISTE. Clitandre asked me to speak for him. He's in love with Henriette.

CHRYSALE. You don't say! With my little daughter?

ARISTE. Yes! I've rarely seen anyone hit so hard!

BÉLISE. No, no. I have overheard you and you don't understand the situation.

ARISTE. What do you mean, sister?

BÉLISE. Clitandre is making a fool of you. He is in love with someone else.

ARISTE. Are you saying it's not Henriette he loves?

BÉLISE. It is not Henriette.

ARISTE. He told me so himself.

BÉLISE. Of course!

ARISTE. And I am supposed to ask Chrysale for her hand.

BÉLISE. Of course!

ARISTE. He urged me to make all haste.

BÉLISE. Better and better! He could not play a more gallant trick. Henriette is only a pretext, a veil covering another love to whose secret I hold the key.

ARISTE. Since you know so much about this, tell us the name of this other woman.

BÉLISE. You really want to know?

ARISTE. Yes, who is she?

BÉLISE. It is myself.

ARISTE. You!

BÉLISE. Me! (*The men laugh.*) Why this laughter? Don't you know there are many men dying to marry me? Have you forgotten about Dorante, Damis, Cléonte, Lycidas?

ARISTE. Do those men love you?

BÉLISE. Yes, with all their might.

ARISTE. Have they told you so?

BÉLISE. Not one dared go that far, but their eyes have spoken and told me all that is in their hearts.

ARISTE. Damis hardly ever comes here.

BÉLISE. That is to show me his complete respect.

ARISTE. Dorante says rather biting things about you.

BÉLISE. He is jealous and mad.

ARISTE. Cléonte and Lycidas have both married.

BÉLISE. Through despair, dear brother.

ARISTE. Ah! sister, how bright is your intelligence!

CHRYSALE (*to* BÉLISE *as he points to his forehead*). You must get rid of all these ideas. (BÉLISE *laughs softly, then louder, until she is almost screeching.*)

BÉLISE. Ideas! You call them ideas! That's a fine thing to call them. I didn't know I had ideas. (*Exit* BÉLISE.)

SCENE 4. *Chrysale, Ariste.*

CHRYSALE. Our sister is mad, that's all.

ARISTE. It gets worse every day. But come back to our subject.

THE INTELLECTUAL LADIES

Clitandre wants to marry Henriette. What answer shall I give him?

CHRYSALE. Tell him he has my consent and that I'm proud to have him in the family.

ARISTE. You know that he is not very rich and . . .

CHRYSALE. That isn't of prime importance. He's rich in merit, and his father and I were the best of friends.

ARISTE. Shouldn't we speak to your wife and . . .

CHRYSALE. You have my word. I give my consent.

ARISTE. Yes, but it might be well to get Philaminte's consent too . . .

CHRYSALE. Are you joking? It is not necessary. I answer for my wife and take full responsibility.

ARISTE. But . . .

CHRYSALE. You have nothing to fear. I'll settle everything.

ARISTE. Very well. I must see Henriette now and I'll return shortly.
(*Exit* ARISTE.)

SCENE 5. *Chrysale, Martine.*

MARTINE (*enters crying*). Oh! what a stew I'm in! Why did I ever come into this house? It's true! If you want to drown a dog, just begin by calling him mad.

CHRYSALE. What's all this? What's the matter with you, Martine?

MARTINE. Matter?

CHRYSALE. Yes.

MARTINE. I just got my walking papers.

CHRYSALE. Your what?

MARTINE. Madame told me to get out.

CHRYSALE. I can't understand you. Speak more clearly.

MARTINE. She told me if I didn't get out, she'd have me thrown out.

CHRYSALE. No, no, my girl. I'm satisfied with you and you'll stay. My wife gets a little excited at times, but I don't . . .

(PHILAMINTE *and* BÉLISE *enter.*)

SCENE 6. *Chrysale, Martine, Philaminte, Bélise.*

PHILAMINTE. Are you still here, you beast? Get out, you little fool. Quick! Leave these premises at once and never come back.

CHRYSALE. Softly now.

PHILAMINTE. No, it is all settled.

CHRYSALE. What is settled?

PHILAMINTE. She must go.

CHRYSALE. But what has she done to be sent away?

PHILAMINTE. Are you taking sides with her?

CHRYSALE. No, not in the least.

PHILAMINTE. Are you taking sides against me?

CHRYSALE. Zounds, no! I'm just asking what her crime was.

PHILAMINTE. Would I dismiss her without good reason?

CHRYSALE. Of course not, my dear, but we must . . .

PHILAMINTE. She must leave this house, I repeat.

CHRYSALE. Quite so, quite so!

PHILAMINTE. I want no obstacle in my way when I'm running the house.

CHRYSALE. Neither do I.

PHILAMINTE. And if you were a real husband, you would be on my side and share in my anger.

CHRYSALE. And so I will. (*To* MARTINE.) You're a wretch and your crime can't be pardoned.

MARTINE. What have I done then?

CHRYSALE. I don't know. (*To* PHILAMINTE.) Did she break a mirror or a china dish? [5]

PHILAMINTE. Do you think I'd lose my temper over such a trifle?

CHRYSALE. You mean it was worse than that?

PHILAMINTE. It certainly was. Do you think I am unreasonable?

CHRYSALE. Did she lose a vase or a silver platter?

PHILAMINTE. I should not have minded that.

CHRYSALE (*to* MARTINE). Oh! you villain, you! (*To* PHILAMINTE.) Did you catch her being dishonest?

PHILAMINTE. It is worse than that.

CHRYSALE. Worse than that?

PHILAMINTE. Worse.

CHRYSALE (*to* MARTINE). Why, you devil! What did you . . . (*Whispers to* PHILAMINTE.) Did she . . .

PHILAMINTE. After my giving her thirty lessons, she deliberately used a low vulgar word which Vaugelas decisively condemns.[6]

CHRYSALE. Is that all the . . .

PHILAMINTE. In spite of all our efforts, she ignored grammar, the fountain of all science, which makes even kings obey its laws.

CHRYSALE (*to himself*). I thought her guilty of a great crime.

THE INTELLECTUAL LADIES

PHILAMINTE. Don't you consider this unpardonable?

CHRYSALE. Yes, indeed.

PHILAMINTE. *You* could, I suppose, excuse her.

CHRYSALE. I don't want to.

BÉLISE. She wrecks every known construction and we've given her language drill over and over.

MARTINE. I know all you preach is beautiful, but I'll never learn to speak your jargon.

PHILAMINTE. She calls our language, founded on reason and good usage, jargon!

MARTINE. It's enough when you're understood and all your fine sayings ain't no good.

PHILAMINTE. There's a sample of her style: "ain't no good."

BÉLISE. O indocile brain! Haven't we told you over and over that "ain't" isn't said and that if it were, it is already negative and does not need "no" after it?

MARTINE. I ain't studied like you and I speaks like they speak at home.

PHILAMINTE. Ah! can we bear it?

BÉLISE. What a horrible solecism! [7]

PHILAMINTE. Death to a sensitive ear!

BÉLISE. Your mind is utterly material. "Speaks" is for the third person pronoun. "I" is first person. Will you outrage grammar all your life?

MARTINE. Who said anything about gran'ma or gran'pa?

BÉLISE. I've told you where "grammar" comes from.

MARTINE. Lord o' mercy! I don't much care if she comes from Paris or Pontoise.

BÉLISE. What a rustic creature! Grammar teaches us the laws of the verb and the subject, of the adjective and the substantive.

MARTINE. I never met them people.

PHILAMINTE. This kills me.

BÉLISE. They are names of words and we must see to it they agree with one another.

MARTINE. I don't much care if they agree or if they fight.

PHILAMINTE. It's no use! Don't go on. (*To* CHRYSALE.) Now, don't you want her to leave?

CHRYSALE (*to himself*). I'll have to give in this time. (*To* MARTINE.) You'd better go, Martine. Don't upset her any more.

PHILAMINTE. How obligingly you speak! Are you afraid of offending her?

CHRYSALE (*firmly*). Not I! Come now, off with you! (*In a low voice.*) Good-by, my child.   (*Exit* MARTINE.)

SCENE 7. *Chrysale, Philaminte, Bélise.*

CHRYSALE. You are satisfied. She's gone. But she was good at her task and you have sent her away for a trifle.

PHILAMINTE. What! She drove me out of my wits with her barbarisms and her fishwives' proverbs.

BÉLISE. Every day she committed neologisms and cacophony.

CHRYSALE. But she was a fine cook and I prefer that she repeat a hundred times over any vulgar word you choose than to burn my meat or put too much salt in my stew. I live on good soup and not on fine speech. Vaugelas doesn't teach how to cook a meal and Malherbe [8] and Balzac [9] would have been idiots in the kitchen.

PHILAMINTE. How coarsely you are speaking! How can you so completely forget the spirit and lower yourself to material cares? Can you attach any importance to this body of ours, this piece of rubbish?

CHRYSALE. Why, my body is me! This piece of rubbish is the apple of my eye!

BÉLISE. The body plays its part with the spirit, my brother, but the spirit must lead the body, and our greatest care should be to nourish it on science.

CHRYSALE. Yes, and every one says that you're feeding your spirit on rather fatuous food and that you have no care, no solicitude for . . .

PHILAMINTE. Oh! that word "solicitude" is outmoded.

BÉLISE. Yes, the word is certainly stilted.

CHRYSALE. Do you want me to speak clearly? Everywhere you are called fools and . . . (PHILAMINTE *glares,* CHRYSALE *turns to* BÉLISE.) I'm speaking to you, sister. Any misused word sets you off. Why do we need all these books around? All I want is one good Plutarch to press my neckbands in. You ought to burn all the stuff in this house and give science back to the scientists, and I mean burn that long spyglass in the attic and give up watching the moon and see what's going on in your own home. It isn't right for a woman to study and know so much. She should bring up her children, run her house, keep an eye on the servants, and economize. That should be her philosophy. My father always said that a woman knows enough when she can tell the difference between a doublet and a pair of breeches. Women in his time sewed on the trousseau of their daughters and didn't want to write and become authors. Now you want to play about with modern science and you know everything except what you ought to know. You know all about the moon, the North Star, Venus, Saturn, and Mars, but you don't know how my pot roast is cooking. The servants are taking up science to please you. To reason has become the law of the house and all the reasoning that goes on here has banished common sense. One poor servant girl was left who was not contaminated and she's gone, and with what a scene!—just because she doesn't use Vaugelas' grammar. I can't stand all these Latin friends of yours and particularly that Monsieur Trissotin. I think he's the main cause of this fad. You try to understand what he has said after he has said it. If you ask me, his head is cracked.

PHILAMINTE. What an ugly soul and what ugly language my husband has!

BÉLISE. His spirit is composed of bourgeois atoms! I can hardly believe I am of the same race, and I shall retire in confusion. (*Exit* BÉLISE.)

SCENE 8. *Chrysale, Philaminte.*

PHILAMINTE. Have you any more criticisms to make?

CHRYSALE. I? No, I don't want to fight any more. But I want to talk to you about something else. Armande doesn't seem to care much about marriage. You have made her into a philosopher, and that's that. But I think that Henriette is about ready to . . .

PHILAMINTE. I have thought about this too, and Monsieur Trissotin, who hasn't the honor of being liked by you, is the man I have chosen for her husband. I am in a better position than you to judge his worth. Don't oppose me on this because I have made up my mind. And above all, don't speak to Henriette first. I want to tell her myself.

(*Exit* PHILAMINTE; ARISTE *enters*.)

SCENE 9. *Chrysale, Ariste.*

ARISTE. I see you have just been talking with your wife.
CHRYSALE. Yes.
ARISTE. Is the marriage arranged for?

CHRYSALE. No, not yet.
ARISTE. Did she refuse?
CHRYSALE. No.
ARISTE. Is she hesitating?
CHRYSALE. No.
ARISTE. What then?
CHRYSALE. She has another son-in-law in mind.
ARISTE. Another? What's his name?
CHRYSALE. Monsieur Trissotin.
ARISTE. What! That Trissotin who . . .
CHRYSALE. Yes, who speaks in verse and Latin.
ARISTE. Did you give in?
CHRYSALE. God forbid!
ARISTE. What did you say?
CHRYSALE. Nothing. And I'm glad I didn't speak, so as not to commit myself.
ARISTE. Good! You're making progress. Did you mention Clitandre?
CHRYSALE. No, I thought I had better not since she mentioned someone else.
ARISTE. That's prudent indeed. You're a man after all. Aren't you ashamed of giving absolute power to your wife?
CHRYSALE. But I hate an uproar so. You don't know how I love peace and harmony. And my wife is terrible. Although she makes a great fuss over being a philosopher, she can throw a fit of anger. If I go against anything she wants, I'm in for a week of storming. She makes me tremble, but all the same, I've got to call her "my love" and "my sweet."
ARISTE. Nonsense. Just between ourselves she rules you because you're a coward. Can't you make a woman give in to your will and buck up enough to say: "You do this"? Your daughter is now going to be sacrificed to a nincompoop who, because he has said six words in Latin, is called a philosopher. You're a coward, brother, and you deserve to be laughed at.
CHRYSALE. You're right. I must be more forceful.
ARISTE. Well said!
CHRYSALE. It's a terrible thing to be under the sway of a woman.
ARISTE. Bravo!
CHRYSALE. She has taken advantage of my kindness.
ARISTE. Good words.
CHRYSALE. And of my willingness.
ARISTE. Exactly.

CHRYSALE. And I'll let her know today that my daughter is my daughter and I'll choose her husband for her.

ARISTE. That's the way I like to see you.

CHRYSALE. Get Clitandre for me. Have him come right away.

ARISTE. Good! I'm off!

CHRYSALE. I've been underdog long enough. Now I am going to be master. (*Exeunt.*)

ACT III

SCENE 1. *Philaminte, Armande, Bélise, Trissotin, L'Epine.*

PHILAMINTE. Come let us sit here and listen in peace to each word and each comma in the verse of Monsieur Trissotin.

ARMANDE. I burn with desire to see some.

BÉLISE. We shall die before he speaks.

PHILAMINTE (*to* TRISSOTIN). Whatever you say bewitches me.

ARMANDE. Your verse is unique and sweet.

BÉLISE. For my ears it is food.

PHILAMINTE. Don't you hear our desires panting?

ARMANDE. Do not delay any longer.

PHILAMINTE. Yes, give us your epigram.[10] Give our impatience your words.

TRISSOTIN. My epigram, alas! It is a newborn babe, Madame. His fate indeed should move you, for I gave him birth, just now, in your courtyard.

PHILAMINTE. The father's fame assures me I shall love him.

TRISSOTIN. Your approval, Madame, will be his mother.

BÉLISE. Mother Approval! Oh! what a wit!

SCENE 2. *Henriette (enters and tries to withdraw).*

PHILAMINTE (*to* HENRIETTE). Stop! Where are you running to?

HENRIETTE. I fear I'll disturb your meeting.

PHILAMINTE. Come here and share our pleasure in hearing these marvels.

HENRIETTE. But mother, I don't understand the beauties of verse.

PHILAMINTE. No matter! Stay now, for after the reading, there's a great secret you must learn.

TRISSOTIN (*to* HENRIETTE). The sciences do not inspire you. Or rather, you have your own science which is that of enchanting the world.

HENRIETTE. I assure you, Monsieur, I have no desire to . . .

BÉLISE. The newborn babe! I beseech you! Do we forget?

PHILAMINTE. Quickly, little boy, a chair for Monsieur. (L'EPINE *falls.*) How ungraceful! Must you fall after learning the equilibrium of matter?

BÉLISE. Stupid boy, do you see the cause of your fall? It has

THE INTELLECTUAL LADIES

removed you from the fixed point we name the center of gravity.

L'ÉPINE. Yes, I saw it. Madame—on the floor.

PHILAMINTE. How heavy! How clumsy!

TRISSOTIN. How fortunate the boy isn't of glass!

ARMANDE. His wit never dries up.

PHILAMINTE. Serve us, I beg you, at once, your charming repast.

TRISSOTIN. For this hunger exposed to my eyes, one lone dish of eight lines is too small. I might add, if you will, to my epigram the relish of a sonnet which in a princess's boudoir was thought to be rather delicate. Throughout, it is spiced with the Attic salt. You will find it, I think, in good taste.

ARMANDE. I have no doubt, Monsieur Trissotin.

PHILAMINTE. We extend you our ears.

BÉLISE (*interrupts* TRISSOTIN). Even now my heart swoons with delight . . . With passion I love poesy when the lines are gallant.

PHILAMINTE. If we continue to speak, he won't read.

TRISSOTIN. So——

BÉLISE (*to* HENRIETTE). Be quiet, my niece!

TRISSOTIN. SONNET TO PRINCESS URANIA ON HER FEVER.[11]

> Has prudence gone to sleep within your breast?
> You entertain with pomp magnificent
> And house with pride as in some lavish tent
> Your very enemy and cruel pest.

BÉLISE. What a pretty beginning!

ARMANDE. With such a gallant turn. "Prudence gone to sleep" is a find.

BÉLISE. "To house in some tent" is my preference.

PHILAMINTE. I like "magnificent" and "lavish." They give adjectival strength to the stanza.

BÉLISE. Will you give us the rest?

TRISSOTIN.

> Make her depart, whate'er for you the test,
> Depart from out your rich apartment
> In which the wretch with wrath so insolent
> Attacks your charming life and wrecks your nest.

BÉLISE. No more, no more, let me catch my breath.
ARMANDE. Give us, we beg you, some leisure to marvel.
PHILAMINTE. From these lines to the depths of my soul there flows some strange liquid which makes me faint.
ARMANDE.

> Make her depart, whate'er for you the test,
> Depart from out your rich apartment.

"Rich apartment" is so well said! The whole metaphor is constructed with wit.
PHILAMINTE.

> Make her depart, whate'er for you the test.

"Whate'er for you the test" is in admirable taste. If I am any critic, it is priceless.
ARMANDE. I also am in love with "whate'er for you the test."
BÉLISE. You are right. "Whate'er for you the test" is skillfully put.
ARMANDE. I wish I had written it.
BÉLISE. It is worth a whole sonnet.
PHILAMINTE. But do you all understand its subtleties?
ARMANDE and BÉLISE. Oh! Oh!
PHILAMINTE.

> Make her depart, whate'er for you the test.

Here the poet speaks of the fever. Give heed to no gossip, he says.

> Make her depart, whate'er for you the test.

Whate'er for you the test, whate'er for you the test. This "whate'er for you the test" is a greater test than it seems. I wonder if you all feel, as I do, the many tests it suggests.
BÉLISE. In truth, it says much for its size.
PHILAMINTE. When you wrote "whate'er for you the test," did you feel all its force? Did you know how much wit there was in it?
TRISSOTIN. Hey! Hey!
ARMANDE. I can't forget "the wretch with wrath." That "wretch" of a fever, so unjust, so dishonest, who destroys her own hostess.

THE INTELLECTUAL LADIES

PHILAMINTE. The quatrains have bewitched us. Is it time for the tercets? [12]

ARMANDE. Once more, once more, "Whate'er for you the test."

TRISSOTIN.

Make her depart, whate'er for you the test.

PHILAMINTE, ARMANDE, and BÉLISE. "Whate'er for you the test."

TRISSOTIN.

Depart from out your rich apartment.

PHILAMINTE, ARMANDE, and BÉLISE. "Your rich apartment."

TRISSOTIN.

In which the wretch with wrath so insolent

PHILAMINTE, ARMANDE, and BÉLISE. That "wretch" of a fever!

TRISSOTIN.

Attacks your charming life and wrecks your nest.

PHILAMINTE. "Your charming life."
ARMANDE and BÉLISE. Ah!
TRISSOTIN.

Without respect, without esteem she wars,
In fury bent, upon your very blood.
By day, by night, by sun, by moon, she gnaws.

When to the baths you lead her all aflame,
With thoughts of victory, with thoughts of flood,
Do drown her by your hands, do drown the flame.

PHILAMINTE. I'm speechless.
BÉLISE. I've almost fainted.
ARMANDE. Yes, it's a joy that slays. "When to the baths you lead her all aflame."
BÉLISE. "With thoughts of victory, with thoughts of flood."
PHILAMINTE. "Do drown her by your hands, do drown the flame." Drown her, drown her in the baths themselves.

ARMANDE. At each step in your verse there is a charming scene.

BÉLISE. We walk there with delight.

PHILAMINTE. They are little avenues of roses.

TRISSOTIN. Tell me what you think of my sonnet.

PHILAMINTE. Admirable, original, beautiful.

BÉLISE (*to* HENRIETTE). Can't you say anything, my niece? Aren't you moved by the sonnet?

HENRIETTE. We all have our own tastes and I cannot make myself into a great intellectual.

TRISSOTIN. Perhaps my verses bore Mademoiselle.

HENRIETTE. Oh, no. I just don't listen.

PHILAMINTE (*trying to relieve the strain*). Now let's have the epigram.

TRISSOTIN. ON A RED CARRIAGE GIVEN TO A LADY BY HER FRIEND.[13]

PHILAMINTE. His titles have always a surprise.

TRISSOTIN.

> So dearly Love has sold to me its chains,
> Their price to half my wealth and goods attains,
> And when one day you see this carriage red
> Embossed and rich with gold on wood and lead,
> When it astounds the countryside with grace
> And shows to all, my lady's charming face,
> Don't say: what brilliant red! what chariot speed!
> But say: the man is poor, the man's in need.

ARMANDE. Oh! oh! oh! What an unexpected ending!

PHILAMINTE. Only you can write with such taste.

TRISSOTIN (*to* PHILAMINTE). Wouldn't you read something of yours, so we could admire that too?

PHILAMINTE. I have done nothing in verse, but I hope soon to show you eight chapters on the Academy we are forming. Plato didn't go beyond a rough draft when he wrote his *Republic*, but I want to put the idea into practice. It will be a revenge for us women over the men who shut us out from their academies and want us to spend our time on trifles.

ARMANDE. It is an insult to think our intelligence is satisfied by judging a skirt or a coat or the beauties of a piece of lace.

BÉLISE. We must rise above this inequality and emancipate our intelligence.

TRISSOTIN. You all know how much I respect the fair sex. I

write of their shining eyes, but I also honor the light of their wit.

PHILAMINTE. And we are grateful to you, Monsieur Trissotin. We must prove to other men that we can have our own learned societies conducted with the best regulations, where fine language and science mingle and where nature is discovered in a thousand experiments.

TRISSOTIN. I personally like peripatetic teaching.

PHILAMINTE. For idealism I prefer Plato.

ARMANDE. Epicurus delights me.

BÉLISE. I rather like atoms and molecules, and I cannot accept the vacuum.

TRISSOTIN. Descartes agrees with me about the magnet.

ARMANDE. I love his vortices.

PHILAMINTE. I, his comets and shooting stars.

TRISSOTIN. We expect much from your studies and experiments.

PHILAMINTE. I must not brag, but I have seen men in the moon.

BÉLISE. I haven't seen men yet, but I've seen church spires as clearly as I see you.

ARMANDE. As well as physics, we will study grammar, history, poetry, morals, and politics.

TRISSOTIN. What admirable plans!

ARMANDE. With our laws we'll become the judges of all new works and we'll censure everything in prose and verse. No one will be intellectual except us and our friends.

SCENE 3. *L'Epine (enters), Trissotin, Philaminte, Bélise, Armande, Henriette, Vadius.*

L'EPINE (*to* TRISSOTIN). Monsieur, there is a gentleman outside who wishes to speak to you. He is dressed in black and speaks very softly.

TRISSOTIN. It is my learned friend Vadius, who begs to meet you.

PHILAMINTE. You were quite right in having him come. (L'EPINE *and* TRISSOTIN *go out; ladies rise.*) Let us rise to our reputation, ladies. (*To* HENRIETTE, *who tries to escape.*) Henriette, I have told you distinctly that I need you here.

HENRIETTE. But why, Mother?

PHILAMINTE. You will see very shortly.

TRISSOTIN (*presenting* VADIUS). Here is the man who longs

to meet you. He will take his place, I assure you, Madame, among the best intellectuals of today.

PHILAMINTE. Since you introduce him, Monsieur, we know already his worth.

TRISSOTIN. He studies our ancient authors and, Madame, he knows Greek as well as any man in France.

PHILAMINTE. Greek! Great heavens! Sister, he knows Greek!

BÉLISE. Did you hear, my niece? He knows Greek!

ARMANDE. Greek? How wonderful!

PHILAMINTE. Monsieur, you know Greek? Allow us, in the name of Greece, to embrace you. (*He kisses all except* HENRIETTE, *who says:*)

HENRIETTE. Excuse me, Monsieur. I don't understand Greek.

PHILAMINTE. I have great respect for books in Greek.

VADIUS. I trust, Madame, that I chose the right day to pay you my homage. Did I interrupt some learned discussion?

PHILAMINTE. Oh, with Greek, Monsieur, you can interrupt anything.

TRISSOTIN. He writes as well in verse as in prose and if urged, might show you something.

VADIUS. Authors are too often tyrants in conversation and tireless readers of their own works. Nothing is more irritating than a poet who goes about everywhere begging for incense and forcing everyone to listen. I have never had this crazy habit and follow a Greek on this point who expressly forbids authors to read from their own books. (*He draws out a paper.*) Here are some verses about love I should like you to criticize for me.

TRISSOTIN. Your verse has an original kind of beauty.

VADIUS. Venus and all the muses are in your verse.

TRISSOTIN. You have given us eglogues which have more charm than those of Theocritus and Virgil.

VADIUS. In your odes, my friend, so noble and delicate, you have outdistanced Horace himself.

TRISSOTIN. Nothing is more refreshing than your rondeaux.[14]

VADIUS. Your madrigals [15] are the wittiest of our time.

TRISSOTIN. If our age paid any heed to its artists . . .

VADIUS. You would ride about in a gilded coach.

TRISSOTIN. If France recognized your worth . . .

VADIUS. You would have statues in every village. (*Unfolds a paper.*) This is a ballade,[16] and I want you to . . .

TRISSOTIN. Have you seen the sonnet on the fever of Princess Urania?

THE INTELLECTUAL LADIES

VADIUS. Yes, it was read to me yesterday.

TRISSOTIN. Do you know who wrote it?

VADIUS. No, but his sonnet, whoever he is, is piffle.

TRISSOTIN (*suffocating*). Yet, many think it quite good.

VADIUS. If you had seen it, my friend, you would agree with me.

TRISSOTIN. But I don't agree! There are few poets capable of writing such a sonnet.

VADIUS. God keep me from writing any like it!

TRISSOTIN. I maintain that you couldn't do better. I happen to know, because I wrote it. (*Silence.*)

VADIUS (*timidly*). You did?

TRISSOTIN. I *did*.

VADIUS. I don't understand.

TRISSOTIN. Too bad I was not able to please you.

VADIUS. I must have been distracted, or perhaps it was badly read. But let me read my ballade.

TRISSOTIN. I have always thought the ballade a rather insipid form. It is out of fashion today.

VADIUS. It is not any the worse for that.

TRISSOTIN. It attracts all the pedants.

VADIUS. Yet it doesn't seem to please you.

TRISSOTIN. Off with you, scribbler, scratcher!

VADIUS. Off with *you*, penny-a-liner, disgrace to the profession!

TRISSOTIN. Hack writer, plagiarist!

VADIUS. Schoolteacher!

PHILAMINTE. Gentlemen! What are you saying?

TRISSOTIN. You'd better restore all your thievings from the Greeks and Romans.

VADIUS. Horace flounders about in your poetry.

TRISSOTIN. Don't forget about your book and what little attention it got.

VADIUS. Why, your publisher has become a beggar. My pen will teach you what kind of a man I am.

TRISSOTIN. And mine will show you your master.

VADIUS. I defy you in verse, prose, Greek, and Latin.

TRISSOTIN. We'll meet alone at the print shop.

(*Exit* VADIUS.)

SCENE 4. *Trissotin, Philaminte, Henriette, Bélise, Armande.*

TRISSOTIN. Don't reproach my anger, Madame. I was defending your judgment of the sonnet he dared attack.

PHILAMINTE. I shall endeavor to patch up this quarrel. But let us change the subject. Come here, Henriette. I have been worried for some time because you seem to have no mind. But I have found a way to change all this.

HENRIETTE. There is no need to go to any fuss. I don't care about learned arguments. I prefer to live without all that agony. I have no ambition to think up brilliant remarks. I like being stupid much more.

PHILAMINTE. It is shameful for a daughter of mine to say such things. The beauty of the face is a frail ornament, a passing flower which does not penetrate under the epidermis. But the beauty of the intellect is strong and durable. For a long time I have sought a means to give you the beauty which years cannot harvest, to inculcate the desire for learning in you; and so I have decided to give you as husband a man of the intellect. This man is none other than Monsieur Trissotin.

HENRIETTE. For me, Mother?

PHILAMINTE. Yes, for you. Now don't be silly.

BÉLISE (*to* TRISSOTIN). I understand. Your eyes have been pleading for my consent. You may—even if your heart is mine —I allow you to marry.

TRISSOTIN. How can I tell you my joy, Mademoiselle? This marriage will . . .

HENRIETTE. Not so fast, Monsieur, we are not married yet.

PHILAMINTE. What an answer, Henriette! (*To* TRISSOTIN.) Never fear, Monsieur, she will behave. Come, let us leave her.

(*Exeunt* PHILAMINTE, BÉLISE, *and* TRISSOTIN.)

SCENE 5. *Henriette, Armande.*

ARMANDE. Mother couldn't have chosen a more illustrious husband for you.

HENRIETTE. If he is such a prize, why don't you take him?

ARMANDE. He is for you and not for me.

HENRIETTE. But you are older than me and I'll give him up.

ARMANDE. If marriage attracted me as it does you, I'd accept your offer.

HENRIETTE. If I were as mad about pedants as you, I'd find him a good match.

ARMANDE. We must obey our parents, Sister, and if you think you can resist . . .

SCENE 6. (*Enter* CHRYSALE, ARISTE, CLITANDRE.)

CHRYSALE (*presenting* CLITANDRE *to* HENRIETTE). Come here, my daughter, you must approve of my choice. Take this man's hand. You are to consider him henceforth as the man whom I want you to marry.

ARMANDE. This seems to excite you a bit more, Sister.

HENRIETTE. We must obey our parents, dear Sister.

ARMANDE. Then we must obey our mother, too.

CHRYSALE. What's all this?

ARMANDE. I am afraid you and Mother do not agree on this point. She has chosen someone else for . . .

CHRYSALE. Close your mouth, you chatterbox. Go and philosophize your fill with her and don't meddle with what I do. Tell her what I've decided and tell her I don't want any scene. (*Exit* ARMANDE.)

ARISTE. Bravo! You are working miracles.

CLITANDRE. Oh, my love! How happy I am! This is a day of such joy.

CHRYSALE (*to* CLITANDRE). Come, take her hand. You two go before us. Take her in. (CLITANDRE *and* HENRIETTE *go out; to* ARISTE.) Ah! the tender scene! My old heart is waking up again! I can remember when I was first in love.

(*Exeunt* CHRYSALE *and* ARISTE.)

ACT IV

Scène 1. *Armande, Philaminte.*

ARMANDE. She took such pride in her obedience, and in my very presence she gave over her heart in the twinkling of an eye. But she seemed less bent on obeying her father than on defying the orders of her mother.

PHILAMINTE. I shall teach her who should govern by rights of reason, her mother or her father, the spirit or the body, the soul or matter.

ARMANDE. I think that Monsieur Clitandre owes you some courtesy. Does he expect to become your son-in-law in spite of you?

PHILAMINTE. He is not in the family yet, my dear. When he was paying court to you, I found him quite handsome, but his conduct always displeased me. He certainly knows that I write, God be praised, and he has never asked me to read him anything.

Scène 2. *Clitandre (enters and listens).*

ARMANDE. If I were you, I would never allow him to marry Henriette. It would be wrong to think that I have any interest in him left, or that the cowardly trick he played on me has made me angry. Philosophy has fortified my soul against such attacks. But it's the way he treats you, Mother. I never felt he had any admiration for you.

PHILAMINTE. The fool!

ARMANDE. He always seemed icy in praising you, whenever he had to.

PHILAMINTE. The brute!

ARMANDE. And twenty times over I read him some of your poetry, which he did not like.

PHILAMINTE. How impertinent!

ARMANDE. We often quarreled about it and you'll never believe . . .

CLITANDRE. May I ask for a little charity, Mademoiselle, or at least for some consideration. What have I done to you? How have I offended you that you want to make me disliked by your family? Please tell me in all frankness and let Madame be the judge.

ARMANDE. Have I no reason to be offended when you know

THE INTELLECTUAL LADIES

as well as I do, that your first love has sacred rights on your soul and that it were better to lose all and even die, than love a second time? An unfaithful heart is a monster in morals.

CLITANDRE. Do you call it infidelity when I simply obey your pride? It is true that I loved you constantly for two years and I paid you the tribute of duty, respect, and service. But it had no effect upon you and you opposed my dearest desires. So, what you refused, I offered to another. Was it my fault or yours? Would I have changed, if you had not urged me to? Was it I who left you, or you who drove me away?

ARMANDE. Do you think I was opposing your dearest desires, when I was trying to relieve them of all their vulgarity and reduce them to the purity of perfect love? Your thoughts never conquered the power of the senses and you never yearned for the union of hearts where the body has no role. You always wanted those bonds of matter—a marriage—and all the implications of marriage. Great souls never burn with such terrestrial flames. They love for love and for nothing else. All their ecstasy comes from their spirit alone and they never realize they have a body.

CLITANDRE. Well, I must confess, Mademoiselle, with your permission, that I have a body as well as a soul—and it is too important to neglect completely. Heaven has not revealed to me your philosophy, and my body and soul walk along together. I agree that there is nothing more beautiful than your purified desires which concern only the spirit. But I am a little coarse, as you say, and the love I feel comes from the whole person. I think this is very common in the world. It is not usually punished very severely, and most people would see no offense in my asking to become your husband.

ARMANDE. Well, Monsieur, well . . . since your animal sentiments must be satisfied and since you need bonds of the flesh and corporeal chains, I am ready to consent in this matter, if my mother agrees.

CLITANDRE. It is too late, Mademoiselle. Another has taken your place. I could never betray the kindness which was my refuge from your pride.

PHILAMINTE. Monsieur, are you counting on my consent to this dream of yours? Do you know, pray, that I *have* a husband for Henriette.

CLITANDRE. Oh, Madame, don't humiliate me. Don't make me the rival of Trissotin. You couldn't have given me a less noble opponent, a man whom the bad taste of the age has put on a pedestal. Outside of this house, his writings may be judged for what they're worth. Here I am always dumfounded to hear you praise to the skies his drivel which, had you written it yourself, you would disown.

Scene 3. *Trissotin (enters).*

Trissotin. I come with great news, Madame. We were almost killed in our beds last night. A comet passed right through our vortex and if it had collided with our earth on its way, it would have shattered us into bits.

Philaminte. We shall speak of this at another time. Monsieur (*Pointing to* Clitandre.) is hardly interested. He professes to embrace ignorance and to hate the spirit and science.

Clitandre. That speech needs some correction, Madame. I only hate science when it spoils people. It is good in itself, but I'd rather be ignorant than learned like *some*.

Trissotin. I don't see how science can spoil anything.

Clitandre. It is my conviction that science can make fools.

Trissotin. That's a dark paradox.

Clitandre. The proof would be simple. Rather celebrated examples are not lacking.

Trissotin. Personally I don't see any examples.

Clitandre (*looking away from* Trissotin). They blind me.

Trissotin. I always thought that it was ignorance that made fools and not science.

Clitandre. You are wrong. I assure you that a wise fool is more of a fool than an ignorant fool.

Trissotin. Public opinion is against you since ignorant and fool are synonyms.

Clitandre. If we consider the use of the word, there is a strong connection between pedant and fool.

Trissotin. Idiocy is quite apparent in one.

Clitandre. And study swells the nature of the other.

Trissotin. Study in itself is of eminent importance.

Clitandre. A fool is out of place studying.

Trissotin. Ignorance must have great fascination for you, since you fight so valiantly for it.

Clitandre. Yes, it has had an attraction for me since the day I met certain scholars.

Philaminte (*to* Clitandre). It seems to me, Monsieur . . .

Clitandre. I beg you, Madame, Trissotin is strong enough without your helping him.

THE INTELLECTUAL LADIES

ARMANDE. But the bitterness of each word you say . . .

CLITANDRE. Another opponent! I give up the fight.

TRISSOTIN. Of course, I don't wonder at the side Monsieur has taken in this quarrel. He's in well at court. Enough said! As you know, the court is not for the intellect.

PHILAMINTE. This anger, Monsieur, reveals your true nature and I'm sure it is the name of rival which excites . . .

SCENE 4. *Julien (enters).*

JULIEN. The scholar who just paid you a visit and whose valet I have the honor of being, prays you to read this letter, Madame.

PHILAMINTE. No matter how important this letter may be, my man, you should never interrupt a conversation in this way but should go first to the servants and be let in by them.

JULIEN. I will note that down in my book, Madame.

PHILAMINTE (*reads*). "Trissotin has boasted he will marry your daughter. I warn you that his philosophy aims only at your wealth and that you should not conclude the marriage until you have seen the poem I am composing against him. I content myself for the moment with sending you Horace, Virgil, Terence, and Catullus where I have indicated in the margins all the passages he has pillaged." Another attack on the marriage I planned. (*To* JULIEN.) Take this letter back at once to your master and tell him, so that he will know what weight I give to his warning, that I am giving my daughter in marriage to Monsieur Trissotin tonight. (*Exit* JULIEN; *to* CLITANDRE.) You, Monsieur, may come to the signing of the marriage contract if you wish. Armande, be sure to send for the notary, and tell your sister of my plans.

ARMANDE. There's no need to tell my sister, for Monsieur Clitandre will tell her the news as fast as he can and prepare her to rebel.

PHILAMINTE. We shall see who will teach my daughter her duty. (*Exeunt* PHILAMINTE *and* TRISSOTIN.)

ARMANDE. I regret, Monsieur, that everything does not seem to fit in with your plans.

CLITANDRE. I intend, Mademoiselle, to do all in my power to relieve you of that regret.

ARMANDE. I fear that your efforts may not reach success.

CLITANDRE. Perhaps your fear will be allayed.

ARMANDE. I hope so.

CLITANDRE. I am sure of it—and am sure of your help.
ARMANDE. Yes, I am going to help all I can.
CLITANDRE. And I shall be grateful to you. (*Exit* ARMANDE.)

SCENE 5. (*Enter Chrysale, Ariste, Henriette.*)

CLITANDRE (*to* CHRYSALE). Without your help, Monsieur, I am lost. Your wife has rejected my suit and she has chosen Trissotin for her son-in-law.

CHRYSALE. The ideas she gets in her head! Why the devil does she want Trissotin?

ARISTE. He's won over Clitandre because he rhymes in Latin.

CLITANDRE. She wants the marriage to take place this very night.

CHRYSALE. Tonight?

CLITANDRE. Tonight.

CHRYSALE. Then, just to trick her, I'll marry you and Henriette tonight.

CLITANDRE. She sent to the notary's for the contract.

CHRYSALE. I'll have him draw up the right contract.

CLITANDRE. And Henriette's to be told by her sister about this marriage they are making.

CHRYSALE. And I command her to give her hand to you. I'll show them who is master in this house. (*To* HENRIETTE.) We'll be back, so wait for us. Come, follow me, Brother, and you too, Son.

HENRIETTE (*to* ARISTE). I pray my father will not weaken.

ARISTE (*going out*). I'll do my best to back him up.

(*Exeunt* ARISTE *and* CHRYSALE.)

CLITANDRE. In spite of all this help, still my greatest hope is you, Henriette.

HENRIETTE. I'll never change in my feelings for you and if I don't become your wife, I'll go into a retreat and marry no one else.

CLITANDRE. God grant I never need that proof of your love!

ACT V

Scene 1. *Henriette, Trissotin.*

HENRIETTE. It is about this marriage, Monsieur, that I wished to speak to you; and I believe that even with all this commotion I can still speak frankly with *you*. I know you think that I shall bring to the man I marry a large dowry, but of course that would have no enticement for a true philosopher.

TRISSOTIN. It is indeed not your dowry which attracts me. Your shining eyes, your graciousness, your beauty—these are the treasures with which I am in love.

HENRIETTE. Monsieur, I am very grateful for this generous love, and I esteem you so highly that I wish I might return it. But there is an obstacle: one girl's heart cannot belong to two men, and Clitandre has mine. I know he has less merit than you. I hate myself for being so silly. My reason tells me I am blind . . .

TRISSOTIN. When you give me your hand, you will give me your heart. And I dare think that I know a thousand subtle ways of making myself loved.

HENRIETTE. No, Monsieur! My heart is caught. This confession should not shock *you*. I can be so frank with *you*. Love, you know, has nothing to do with merit. Why, if I loved intelligently, I should be all yours. Please leave me in my blindness, and I beg of you, do not use force. A man of honor should owe nothing to the power parents have over a girl. Don't love me, but give someone else the homage of a heart so valuable as yours.

TRISSOTIN. How can I obey? I can't *not* love you, while my eyes feast upon these heavenly charms, these . . .

HENRIETTE. Ah, Monsieur, let's have no foolishness! In your poetry there are so many Irises and Philises [17] who are so charming, and to whom you swear such eternal devotion . . .

TRISSOTIN. That is only my mind speaking, not my heart. It is only the poet who's in love with *them*. But I love the adorable Henriette.

HENRIETTE. Please!

TRISSOTIN. If this offends you, I must still offend. This flame, which has so far been hidden, burns eternally. I can't refuse your mother's help in consummating such tender devotion—and in short, I must get you and I don't care how.

HENRIETTE. But do you realize that violence is dangerous for *you* too? To put it plainly, don't you know that when you marry a girl in spite of her wishes, she will have her revenge? This should terrify the husband.

TRISSOTIN. Such threats do not affect me. The philosopher is prepared for everything. He rises above all that is beyond his control.

HENRIETTE. Really, Monsieur, I am charmed with you. I never knew that philosophy was so noble and taught *such* fortitude in *such* misfortune! This great, this unique strength of soul is worthy of a better mate who could lovingly add to the luster of its glory. To this I could never dare to aspire and I renounce all hope of having you for my husband.

TRISSOTIN. We shall see very soon. They have already called for the notary. (*Exit* TRISSOTIN.)

SCENE 2. *Chrysale, Clitandre, Martine, Henriette.*

CHRYSALE. I'm happy you're here, Daughter. It is time to do your duty and submit to a father's will. I'm going to teach your mother to behave, and for the first lesson I have brought back Martine to cast in her teeth.

HENRIETTE. May you not change in that resolution, Father! Don't give in to the kindness of your heart! Stand your ground before Mother!

CHRYSALE. What are you saying? Do you think I'm a simpleton?

HENRIETTE. Heaven forbid!

CHRYSALE. Am I weak-minded?

HENRIETTE. I didn't say that.

CHRYSALE. Do you think I have no conviction of my own?

HENRIETTE. No, Father.

CHRYSALE. Do you think my wife leads me about by the nose?

HENRIETTE. Oh, no, Father!

CHRYSALE. Uh! What can you be thinking of?

HENRIETTE. I never expected to shock you.

CHRYSALE. My will is absolute.

HENRIETTE. Very well, Father.

CHRYSALE. No one except me has the right to give orders in this house.

HENRIETTE. You are right.

CHRYSALE. I am the head of the house.

HENRIETTE. I agree.

CHRYSALE. Heaven gives me full power over your fate.

HENRIETTE. Oh, yes!

CHRYSALE. In taking a husband, I'll show you that you must obey your father and not your mother.

HENRIETTE. Oh! I hope that you'll be obeyed!

CHRYSALE. We'll see if my wife dare rebel against . . .

(*Enter* PHILAMINTE, BÉLISE, ARMANDE, TRISSOTIN, NOTARY.)

CLITANDRE. She is coming now with the notary.

CHRYSALE. All of you must back me up!

MARTINE. Count me in for that.

SCENE 3. *All the above.*

PHILAMINTE (*to* NOTARY). Couldn't you modify that uncouth style of yours and draw up a contract in fine language?

NOTARY. The style is, Madame, correct, and I'd be a fool to change a word.

BÉLISE. Such barbarism in France! But at least for the sake of science, please, Monsieur, instead of in pounds and francs, write out the dowry in mines and talents [18] and give the dates in ides and calends.[19]

NOTARY. If I did, I'd be hooted at by the whole profession.

PHILAMINTE. We sigh in vain under this barbarity. Come, Monsieur, you can write at this table. (*Sees* MARTINE.) Ah! ah! is that impudent girl here again? Why did you bring *her* back?

CHRYSALE. I will tell you in a little while. We have something else to settle first.

NOTARY. Let's get on with the contract. Where is the bride?

PHILAMINTE. It is my younger daughter I am giving in marriage.

NOTARY. Very good.

CHRYSALE. Yes, and here she is, Monsieur. Her name is Henriette.

NOTARY. Very good. And the man?

PHILAMINTE (*showing* TRISSOTIN). The husband I am giving her is this gentleman.

CHRYSALE (*urged by* MARTINE, *shows* CLITANDRE). And the husband I am giving her is this gentleman.

NOTARY. Two husbands! It is not usual.

PHILAMINTE. Why do you pause? Put down Trissotin for my son-in-law.

CHRYSALE. Put down Clitandre for mine.

NOTARY. Put down your dispute and decide on a husband.

PHILAMINTE. Follow *me*.

CHRYSALE. Do what *I* say.

NOTARY. Which am I to listen to?

PHILAMINTE. What? you dispute my *orders*?

CHRYSALE. I don't want any man to marry my daughter for the money that happens to be in the family.

PHILAMINTE. Money! A very worthy question for a philosopher.

CHRYSALE. Well, I have chosen Clitandre.

PHILAMINTE. I have chosen *him*. (*Pointing to* TRISSOTIN.) It is all decided.

CHRYSALE. Uh! That tone is pretty harsh.

MARTINE. The wife don't decide. I'm for giving in to the man.

CHRYSALE. Well said.

MARTINE. Even if you run me out again, the hen don't crow before the cock.

CHRYSALE. That's right.

MARTINE. And when the wife wears the pants, they cackle.

CHRYSALE. True.

MARTINE. If I had a man, I'd want him to be the boss. I couldn't love a ninny. If I argued or talked too loud, I'd expect a few cuffs to take me down.

CHRYSALE. Good girl.

MARTINE. Monsieur is right to want a good husband for his daughter.

CHRYSALE. Yes.

MARTINE. Why not give her Monsieur Clitandre, young and handsome as he is? And why that wordy professor? She wants a husband, not a lecturer. She don't want to learn Latin and so what does she want with M. Trissotin?

CHRYSALE. Absolutely right.

PHILAMINTE. Of course she must be allowed to expound at her ease.

MARTINE. Professors can't do nothing but talk. I've said a thousand times I'd never *marry* brains. You don't want brains around the house, and you don't want books. My husband would have to have *me* for his book, and not be a doctor of nothing but his wife.

PHILAMINTE (*to* CHRYSALE). Is that all? Have I listened long enough to your excellent interpreter?

CHRYSALE. She has said wise words.

PHILAMINTE. Well, to conclude the discussion, my wish must be carried out. Henriette and Monsieur will be married immediately. I have spoken. You know what I want. Don't speak back. And since you have promised Clitandre, he can marry Armande.

CHRYSALE. That may be a way out. (*To* HENRIETTE *and* CLITANDRE.) What do you say to that?

HENRIETTE. Father!

CLITANDRE. Monsieur!

BÉLISE. You might make him a proposal he would like better, but our kind of love shall be as pure as the day star. Thought may be included in this love, but never the vulgar matter which has extension.

SCENE 4. (*Enter Ariste.*)

ARISTE. I regret disturbing this happy ceremony by bringing you two letters of bad news. I have already felt the grief they will bring you. (*To* PHILAMINTE.) This one for you was sent me by your lawyer. (*To* CHRYSALE.) And the other for you comes from Lyons.

PHILAMINTE. What misfortune worthy of disturbing us can this be? (*Reads.*) "Madame, I have asked your brother to give you this letter which will inform you of what I dared not tell you in person. The great negligence you show in business matters has caused you to lose the lawsuit you ought to have won."

CLITANDRE. You have lost the suit!

PHILAMINTE. Don't be so upset. I am not at all shaken by the news. You must stand up, as I do, under all adversities. (*Reads.*) "This negligence will cost you forty thousand francs and you are condemned by court decree to pay this sum." Condemned! What a shocking word! It is only for criminals.

ARISTE. Of course he is wrong. He should have said: the court humbly begs you to pay forty thousand francs and expenses at once.

PHILAMINTE. What does your letter say?

CHRYSALE (*reads*). "Monsieur, the friendship I have for your brother gives me an interest in all that affects you. I know that you entrusted your fortune to Argante and Damon and I warn you that they have both today gone into bankruptcy." My God! we have lost everything.

PHILAMINTE. Fie! What a shameful exclamation! For the true sage there can be no tragic reversal. He may lose all his possessions; he will still possess himself. Come back to the marriage and forget your dismay. Monsieur Trissotin's fortune is large enough for all of us.

TRISSOTIN. No, Madame, do not insist. I see now that everyone is against this marriage, and I don't wish to force anyone.

PHILAMINTE. This thought, Monsieur, is sudden. It follows fast upon our misfortune.

TRISSOTIN. I am weary at last of so much resistance. I prefer to give up the whole idea. I do not want a heart which is unwilling.

PHILAMINTE. I see something in you which up until now I have refused to believe, and it is not to your credit.

TRISSOTIN. You are free to see in me what you will. I am not a man to suffer the infamy of an insulting refusal. I am worth more consideration. My homage to all those who do not realize my worth. (*Exit* TRISSOTIN.)

PHILAMINTE. How clearly he has shown his mercenary soul! How unphilosophic his action!

CLITANDRE. I don't pretend to be a philosopher, Madame, but may I offer you the help which my small fortune might provide?

PHILAMINTE. I am moved by your generosity, Monsieur. Yes, and I will requite your love with Henriette's hand.

HENRIETTE. No, Mother. I have now changed my mind. I must disobey you.

CLITANDRE. Is it now you who oppose me, when everyone else has given in to . . .

HENRIETTE. I know what limited means you have, Clitandre. I have always wanted to marry you, but in the light of these new adversities, I refuse to be a burden.

CLITANDRE. I want my life with you—without you I cannot live.

ARISTE. Is this your only motive for refusing Clitandre?

HENRIETTE. Yes. My whole heart is his. I am leaving him only to cherish him the more.

ARISTE. Well, you can be married then, for the news I brought is false. It was only a stratagem to serve your love and reveal the wiles of our philosopher-poet.

CHRYSALE. God be praised! (*He kisses all.*)

THE INTELLECTUAL LADIES

PHILAMINTE. I am happy when I think of Trissotin's chagrin. His avarice will be well punished when he sees this brilliant marriage.

CHRYSALE (*to* CLITANDRE). I knew that you would marry her.

ARMANDE. So you sacrifice me to their happiness.

PHILAMINTE. Not at all! It is not you who are sacrificed. You have the support of philosophy, and now you may smile upon the consummation of their love.

BÉLISE. I hope he takes care that I am not in his heart. Men often marry through despair and are sorry for it all their lives.

CHRYSALE (*to* NOTARY). Monsieur, give me the marriage contract which you have drawn up.

NOTES

1. The repulsiveness of marriage was a common theme for the *précieuses* about the middle of the seventeenth century.
2. The favorite novelists of the *précieux* society were Honoré d'Urfé, Mlle de Scudéry, and Mme de la Calprenède.
3. The *wise gentleman* is Ariste whose name means *wisdom*.
4. Chrysale's role was first played by Molière.
5. Mirrors and porcelain (*China dish*) were very expensive in the seventeenth century since they were not yet manufactured in France.
6. Vaugelas, a famous grammarian (1585–1640). The *précieux* looked upon him as the arbiter of good taste in language.
7. *Solecism*, a mistake in syntax. The word "solecism" had been recently introduced into French by the grammarians.
8. François de Malherbe (1555–1628) inaugurated the classical age by his reforms in poetry.
9. J.-L. Guez de Balzac (1594–1654) performed a similar function for prose and founded the eloquent *précieux* style.
10. *Epigram*, a poem of eight lines.
11. This sonnet is in the *Œuvres Galantes* of Cotin, where it is called *Sonnet à Mlle de Longueville, à présent duchesse de Nemours, sur sa fièvre quarte*.
12. *Tercets*. A sonnet has fourteen lines and is divided into two stanzas of four lines each (quatrains) and two stanzas of three lines each (tercets).
13. This epigram is taken from the *Œuvres Galantes* of Cotin, where it is entitled *Sur un carrosse de couleur amarante, acheté pour une dame*.

168   MOLIÈRE

14. *Rondeau,* a short French poem, usually of thirteen lines.
15. *Madrigal,* a short poem on a galant theme.
16. *Ballade.* The French *ballade,* unlike the English ballad, has three stanzas and a refrain.
17. *Irises and Philises,* heroines of pastoral poems and plays.
18. *Mines and talents,* Greek money.
19. *Ides and calends,* the fifteenth and the first of each month, in the Roman calendar.

This translation of *The Intellectual Ladies* was first used at Bennington College, June 1939.

CAST

CHRYSALE	Wallace Fowlie
PHILAMINTE	Lucy Glazebrook
BÉLISE	Virginia Todahl
ARMANDE	Florence Lovell
HENRIETTE	Honora Kammerer
CLITANDRE	Chilton Ryan
ARISTE	John Blackburn
TRISSOTIN	Edward Thommen
L'EPINE	Herbert Shaw
VADIUS	Chandler Cowles
JULIEN	Chandler Cowles
MARTINE	Vida Ginsberg
NOTARY	Herbert Shaw

CHARACTERS IN THE BALLET INTERLUDES

PANTALONE	Mary-Averett Seeyle
HIS FOUR DAUGHTERS	Jane Perry
	Carolyn Gerber
	Adele Bookman
	Jane Hartington
DOTTORE	Carol Channing
AMOROSO	Dorothea Hanwell
ZANI	Raymond Malon

Play directed by Francis Fergusson
Settings designed by Arch Lauterer
Ballet interludes composed and directed by Martha Hill
Music under the direction of Otto Luening

The Game of Love and Chance
(LE JEU DE L'AMOUR ET DU HASARD)
1730

❦

A COMEDY IN THREE ACTS
BY
PIERRE DE MARIVAUX

❦

translated by WALLACE FOWLIE

Pierre de Marivaux
(1688–1763)

An Italian troupe of actors (La Comédie-Italienne) occupied the Hôtel de Bourgogne in Paris for seventeen years at the end of the seventeenth century. They returned to Paris in 1716. It was a freer and easier theater to work with than the Comédie-Française, and Pierre de Marivaux gave his best comedies to *les Italiens*. He was concerned with satirizing the prejudices and social institutions of his day. He was a modernist, fairly close to the beliefs of Fontenelle, although he had none of the violence of Fontenelle.

In one of his early comedies, *Arlequin poli par l'amour* (1720), one can find most of the important traits of his art: a deft but penetrating analysis of love, a study of the human soul in its impulses, a refined but very real sensuality. Marivaux's comedies developed a style and tone which have come to be called *marivaudage*. This term suggests the beginnings of the emotion of love, the first tender sentiments as expressed in refined language which is without any trace of affectation. (The language of *marivaudage* is not to be confused with the language of *préciosité*.) As an analyst of nascent love, Marivaux is without a peer in the history of French comedy.

He does not treat love as being either comic or tragic. It is a principle by which happiness and suffering are experienced. It is a principle characterized by its truth and tenderness and even by its profundity. Marivaux is skillful in his ability to indicate very slight changes and shifts in sentiments. The almost imperceptible impulses of the heart are indicated. His comedies contain, in addition to this analysis of love, many other themes and characterizations: egoism, distrust, class prejudice, shyness. Such traits as these are usually conceived of as being obstacles in the development of love. Repeatedly in the comedies of Marivaux (as in *Le Jeu de l'Amour et du Hasard*) a man and a woman, before they actually fall in love, try to know one another. They are placed in one another's company where they study and observe one another. As the action of the comedy continues, each sets a trap for the other in an effort to test the nascent sentiment.

The Game of Love and Chance is the comedy of two characters, each of whom is bent upon preserving his own integrity and egoism. It is an inner action we follow, as Silvia reveals more frankness and perhaps more susceptibility in the beginnings of her love, and as Dorante, more positive and more sincere, reveals a greater willingness to accept his feelings and acknowledge them. The comedy does not present studies of character as much as it presents moments, which are universal moments, in the lives of the characters. The father is indulgent and the servants are almost knaves in their cleverness. Sentiment is everywhere, and it is never platitudinous or insipid.

Le Jeu de l'Amour et du Hasard was first performed on January 23, 1730, at the Comédie-Italienne. Recently the Comédie-Française celebrated its thousandth performance of the play. During his career, Marivaux knew more failures than successes. In fact, he never had an overwhelming success in the theater. But during the past half century in France he has been rediscovered and acclaimed as a leading French dramatist.

His art has been defined as a special form of comedy. There are perhaps five masterpieces in the thirty-four plays which Marivaux wrote, and they contain traits of subtlety in wit and emotion, an elegance and clarity of speech, a sense of proportion in structure and suitability in tone which have often been ascribed to French art. The paintings of Watteau combine in somewhat the same way tones of refinement and discreetness in the amorous scenes. After the first meeting of the two who are destined to love, there is grace and ease and wit in their encounters, but the art of the playwright concentrates on all that has to be said and understood before the avowal of love and its success.

The ancestors of the characters of both Molière and Marivaux were the stock characters of the *commedia dell'arte*: Arlequino, Pantalone, il Dottore, Scaramouche, Scapin. But the French playwrights did not adhere to the principle of improvisation. They wrote a text which is still used without alteration in today's performances. Marivaux himself did not have a high esteem for Molière. Doubtless, in trying to avoid the overpowering influence of Molière, he gave to the theme of love a greater importance, and in this he recalled Racine.

Marivaux, however, does not use history and the tragic legends of lovers as does Racine. His characters bear a closer resemblance to the *commedia dell'arte* figures, as seen in the paintings of his contemporaries, with their masks, their graceful and somewhat coy posturings, their malice, and the familiar prop of the guitar.

A double action unfolds throughout the Marivaux play. In the first place, there is an outer action which is concerned with disguises, encounters, and quarrels. At the same time, an inner action is going on, which is the birth and the very gradual development of the sentiment of love. The sentiment is tested, rejected, revived, discouraged, encouraged, until at the end it burns with a clear flame. It is not important, in such an art, for the characters to be presented in full delineation. In truth, there is no character of the stature of Alceste or Tartuffe in Marivaux's comedies. The art is in the flexibility and gracefulness of the scenes, in the precision of gesture and speech, in the sense of abiding morality which pervades the action, in the climate which love creates and sustains. Love is an obsession in this theater, but it is a generous youthful spirit, a *marivaudage* which will return to some degree in the comedies of Alfred de Musset in the nineteenth century and in the plays of Jean Giraudoux in the twentieth.

The Game of Love and Chance

CHARACTERS

MONSIEUR ORGON
MARIO, his son
SILVIA, his daughter
DORANTE, suitor to Silvia
LISETTE, Silvia's maid
HARLEQUIN, Dorante's valet
A FOOTMAN

Scene: Paris.

ACT I

SCENE 1. *Silvia, Lisette.*

SILVIA. Tell me once more why you are interfering this way. How can you speak for my sentiments?

LISETTE. It is because I thought that on this occasion your sentiments would be like everyone else's. Your father asked me if you were happy he is giving you in marriage, if you were overjoyed about it. I told him yes, it was obvious. You are perhaps the only girl in the world for whom that *yes* was not true. A *no* is not natural.

SILVIA. A *no* is not natural! What idiotic silliness! So marriage would have great attractions for you?

LISETTE. Most decidedly, *yes*.

SILVIA. Be silent! Go give your impertinent answers somewhere else. You must learn not to judge my heart by yours.

LISETTE. My heart is like everyone else's. Why should yours decide not to be like any other heart?

SILVIA. I am sure that if you dared, you would call me an eccentric.

LISETTE. If I were your equal, we would see.

SILVIA. Lisette, you are working hard to make me angry.

LISETTE. That is not my intention. But after all, tell me, what harm did I do to tell Monsieur Orgon that you were very happy to be given in marriage?

SILVIA. In the first place, it isn't true. I am not bored with being unmarried.

LISETTE. You haven't yet had time to be bored.

SILVIA. I don't want my father to think he is pleasing me by giving me in marriage. That makes him act with a confidence which will perhaps be frustrated.

LISETTE. What! You won't marry the man he has chosen for you?

SILVIA. How can I tell? Perhaps I won't like him, and that worries me.

LISETTE. They say that your future husband is one of the finest gentlemen in the world, handsome, kind, healthy, more witty than most men, and with a better disposition than most. What more can you ask? Can you imagine a sweeter marriage, a more delicious union?

SILVIA. Delicious! How silly you are to use such an expression!

LISETTE. Upon my word, Miss Silvia, it is lucky that a man like that is willing to go through the ceremony of marriage. Every girl I can think of, if he courted her, would be in danger of marrying him without ceremony. Kind and handsome—that is what you need for love; sociable and witty—that is what you need for social manners. My goodness, everything about that man is good. Whatever is useful and agreeable is found in him.

SILVIA. Yes, in the picture *you* are giving of him. And people say that he is like that. But it's what *people say*, and I might not have the same impression. He's a handsome man, they say, and that's almost a pity.

LISETTE. A pity! A pity! Well, that's a crazy idea!

SILVIA. It's a very sensible idea. A handsome man is usually fatuous. I have noticed this.

LISETTE. Oh! he's wrong to be fatuous. But he's right to be handsome.

SILVIA. They also say he's well built. That's all right!

LISETTE. Well, yes. That is pardonable.

SILVIA. I make no demands that he be handsome or of fine appearance. Those are superfluous decorations.

LISETTE. Glory be, if I ever marry, I will demand those superfluous decorations.

SILVIA. You don't know what you're saying. In marriage, a man's reasonableness is more important than his kindness. In a word, I only ask that he have a good disposition. And that is more difficult to find than you think. People praise his disposition, but who has ever lived with him? When men are witty, don't they counterfeit themselves? I have seen them with their friends behaving as if they were the best people in the world. Such sweetness and good sense and liveliness. Why, even their face is proof of the good qualities ascribed to them. Every day it was said of Ergaste: "What a fine gentleman and so intelligent." "He certainly is," people would answer. (I would say it myself.) "His face does not belie his character." Yes, you should trust such a sweet engaging face, which disappears in a quarter of an hour to become a face that is dark, brutal, wild, the terror of an entire household. Ergaste married. To his wife, his children, and his servant he showed only that kind of face, while everywhere else he showed the kind of face which we see and which is only a mask he puts on when he leaves his house.

LISETTE. What a freakish man with his two faces!

SILVIA. Everyone is so pleased with Léandre when he appears. But in his own house, he says nothing. He doesn't laugh, he doesn't scold. He has a frigid, lonely, inaccessible soul. His wife doesn't know him. He has nothing to do with her. She married a face that emerges from a study, sits down at the table, and kills with languor, cold, and boredom everything that surrounds him. Isn't he an amusing husband?

LISETTE. That story gives me the chills. But what about Tersandre?

SILVIA. Tersandre! The other day he had just flown into a rage with his wife when I called. I was announced. I beheld a man coming to me with open arms, serene and free. He seemed to be coming from a light chatty conversation, his mouth and his eyes still laughing. The cheat! That's what men are! Who believes that his wife is to be pitied? I found her depressed, her face ashen. She had just been crying. She looked as I will one day perhaps. My future portrait. At least I will run the risk of being a copy. I pitied her, Lisette. What if I caused you to pity me! Wouldn't that be terrible? You must not forget what a husband can be like.

LISETTE. A husband? What a husband can be like? You shouldn't have ended with that word. It reconciles me to everything else.

Scene 2. *Monsieur Orgon, Silvia, Lisette.*

ORGON. Good morning, Daughter! I wonder if you will be pleased with the news I have come to tell you. Your suitor arrives today. His father has told me in his letter. You do not answer. And you seem sad. Lisette won't look me in the eye. What does this mean? Tell me! What has happened?

LISETTE. Sir, a face which makes you tremble. Another face which chills you with its coldness. A soul, frozen and alone. A portrait of a woman with downcast face, dull complexion, eyes puffed from weeping. That is what we have been thoughtfully considering.

ORGON. What is the meaning of this gibberish? A soul? A portrait? Will you explain! I make nothing out of what you say.

SILVIA. I was telling Lisette the sad story of a wife mistreated by her husband, of Tersandre's wife whom I found the other day upset because her husband had just fought with her. I was giving Lisette my thoughts on the problem.

LISETTE. Yes, we were talking about the kind of face that changes, of a husband who wears a mask in society, and an ugly face with his wife.

ORGON. Daughter, I can understand that the idea of marriage may disturb you, especially since you do not know Dorante.

LISETTE. In the first place, he is handsome. And that is almost a pity.

ORGON. A pity! Are you dreaming, with your pity?

LISETTE. Oh! I repeat what I am taught. It is your daughter's theory. She is my teacher.

ORGON. Come, come, this is not the point. Dear child, you know how much I love you. Dorante is coming here to marry you. On my last trip to the country, I arranged this marriage with his father who is an old, intimate friend of mine. But it was on the condition that you would like one another, and that you would have full freedom to reach an agreement. I forbid that you merely give in to my whim. If Dorante does not please you, he will leave anyway.

LISETTE. A tender love duet will decide, just as at the opera. You want me, I want you. Quick, a notary! Or, do you love me? No! I don't either! Quick, my horse!

ORGON. I have never seen Dorante. He was not there when I was at his father's. But because of all the fine things I have

THE GAME OF LOVE AND CHANCE

heard about him, I am not afraid that you will just dismiss one another.

SILVIA. Father, I am deeply grateful for your kindness. You forbid that I be merely courteous to you. I will obey you.

ORGON. These are my orders.

SILVIA. But if I dared, I would ask, because of an idea I have, that you grant me one favor which would put my mind completely at rest.

ORGON. Tell me what it is. If it is possible, I will grant it.

SILVIA. It is possible, but I fear it would be taking advantage of your kindness.

ORGON. Well, take advantage. In this world you have to be a little overkind if you want to be kind enough.

LISETTE. Only the best of all men could say that.

ORGON. Daughter, explain your idea.

SILVIA. Dorante arrives today. Could I see him and examine him a bit without his knowing me? Lisette is very intelligent. She could take my place for a little while, and I would take hers.

ORGON (*aside*). An amusing idea! (*Aloud.*) Let me reflect a bit on what you suggest. (*Aside.*) If I allow this, something extraordinary will happen. She doesn't realize it herself. (*Aloud.*) So be it, my daughter, I permit the disguise. Do you think you can play your role, Lisette?

LISETTE. Sir, you should know who I am. There is no point in trying to deceive me. Show me disrespect, if you dare. This is my new bearing and an example of the fine manners I will show when you enter my presence. Tell me what you think of me. Do you recognize Lisette?

ORGON. Why! I myself would be taken in. But there is no time to lose. Go put on the right clothes for your part. Dorante might arrive unexpectedly. Hurry up. And tell all the servants.

SILVIA. All I need is an apron.

LISETTE. And I have to dress. Help me with my hair, Lisette. It will get you used to your duties. Be careful of the way you wait on me.

SILVIA. You will be satisfied, Madame. Let us go.

SCENE 3. *Mario, Monsieur Orgon, Silvia.*

MARIO. Sister, I congratulate you on the news. I am told we are going to see your suitor.

SILVIA. Yes, Brother. But I am in a hurry. There is serious business to attend to. My father will tell you. I leave you now.

Scene 4. *Monsieur Orgon, Mario.*

ORGON. Don't delay her, Mario. Come, I'll tell you what it is all about.

MARIO. Has anything new happened, sir?

ORGON. I will begin by asking you to be very discreet about what I am going to tell you.

MARIO. I will follow your orders.

ORGON. Today we are going to see Dorante. But he will be wearing a disguise.

MARIO. A disguise! Is he coming for a masked party? Are you giving a ball for him?

ORGON. Listen to this part of his father's letter . . . "But I don't know what you will think of an idea my son has had. He agrees that it is an unusual idea. The reason is pardonable and even scrupulous. He has urged me to allow him to come to your house dressed as his valet, who in his turn will play the part of his master."

MARIO. Ha, ha! That will be comical.

ORGON. Listen to the rest . . . "My son knows the seriousness of the engagement he is undertaking, and hopes, in this disguise which he will wear just a short time, to observe some of the character traits of his future bride, and know her better, and be guided thereafter by what he should do in terms of the freedom we agreed to give them. I have confidence in all you told me about your charming daughter, and gave my consent, and am now taking the precaution of warning you, although he asked me to swear you to secrecy. You will do with the young lady what you judge appropriate . . ." That is what the father wrote me. But that is not all. There is something else. Your sister, who herself is worried about Dorante, whose secret she does not know, has asked me to let her play the same comedy here, in order to observe Dorante, as Dorante wishes to observe her. What do you say to that? Is there anything more extraordinary? At this moment, mistress and maid are disguising themselves. What do you advise me, Mario? Shall I tell your sister, or not?

MARIO. Upon my word, Father, since matters are taking this turn, I shouldn't disturb these two young people, and I should respect the idea which inspired both of them. Under this disguise they will have to speak often to one another. Let us see if each will find out what the other is worth. Perhaps Dorante will take a liking to my sister, even if she is a maid, and that would be enchanting for her.

ORGON. We will see shortly how she will carry out this intrigue.

MARIO. It's an adventure which will not fail to amuse us. I want to be there at the beginning and irritate both of them.

SCENE 5. *Silvia, Monsieur Orgon, Mario.*

SILVIA. Here I am, Father. Do you approve of me as a maid? Apparently, Brother, you know what is up. What do you think of me?

MARIO. Upon my word, Sister, the valet is lucky and you will probably steal Dorante from your mistress.

SILVIA. Frankly, I should rather like to please him in this character I am playing. I would not be sorry if I could affect his common sense and bewilder him a bit over the distance between us. If my charms have that effect, I will be pleased and flattered. Moreover, it will help me to understand Dorante. As far as his valet goes, I am not afraid of his sighs. He will keep his distance. Something in my face will inspire in that fellow more respect than love.

MARIO. You will have to be cautious, Sister. That fellow will be your equal.

ORGON. He will certainly fall in love with you.

SILVIA. Well, the honor of attracting him will not be useless. Valets are by nature indiscreet. Love is talkative. I will make him the historian of his master.

(*A* VALET *enters.*)

VALET. Sir, a servant has just come who asks to speak to you. He is followed by a porter carrying a valise.

ORGON. Have him come in. It is probably Dorante's valet. His master may have stayed at the office on business. Where is Lisette?

SILVIA. Lisette is dressing, and in her mirror she finds us imprudent in giving Dorante over to her. She will be ready soon.

ORGON. Quiet! Someone is coming.

Scene 6. *Dorante (as a valet), Monsieur Orgon, Silvia, Mario.*

Dorante. I am looking for Monsieur Orgon. Have I the honor of bowing to him?

Orgon. Yes, my friend. I am Monsieur Orgon.

Dorante. Sir, you have doubtless received word about us. I belong to Monsieur Dorante who will be here soon, and who sent me on ahead to pay you his respects until he can pay them in person.

Orgon. You have graciously carried out your commission. Lisette, what do you think of this fellow?

Silvia. Sir, I would say he is welcome and that he shows promise.

Dorante. You are very kind. I do the best I can.

Mario. At least he is quite presentable. I hope your heart will stay in its place, Lisette.

Silvia. My heart! Just leave that to me!

Dorante. Do not be angry, Mademoiselle. What Monsieur said will not make me conceited.

Silvia. I like such modesty. See that you maintain it.

Mario. Very good! Now it seems to me that his calling you Mademoiselle is rather serious. Between servants a complimentary style should not be quite so heavy. You would always be on the alert. Speak to one another with greater ease. Your name is Lisette. What is your name, my good man?

Dorante. Bourguignon, sir, and your servant.

Silvia. All right, Bourguignon, so be it!

Dorante. I will call you Lisette, then, but nevertheless I am your servant.

Orgon. Ha, ha, ha, ha!

Silvia. You are making fun of me. Sir! The ice is broken, Bourguignon, and these gentlemen are amused.

Dorante. Thank you, Lisette. I am grateful for the honor you do me.

Orgon. Courage, my children. If you begin to fall in love, there won't be any ceremonies left.

Mario. Just a minute! Falling in love is something else. Perhaps you don't know that I desire the heart of Lisette. It is true that she is cruel to me, but I don't want Bourguignon to follow in my footsteps.

Silvia. Why do you take that attitude? I want Bourguignon to like me.

DORANTE. You are wrong to say I *want*, beautiful Lisette. You don't need to give such a command, in order to be served.

MARIO. Monsieur Bourguignon, you pillaged that gallant trait from somewhere.

DORANTE. You are right, sir. I found it in her eyes.

MARIO. Be silent. That is still worse. I forbid you to be so witty.

SILVIA. He isn't witty at your expense. If he finds it in my eyes, he has only to take it.

ORGON. Son, you are losing the debate. Let us leave. Dorante is coming soon and I must tell my daughter. You, Lisette, show this man his master's apartment. Good-by, Bourguignon.

DORANTE. Sir, you do me great honor.

SCENE 7. *Silvia, Dorante.*

SILVIA (*aside*). They are making a joke out of all this. But it's of no consequence, and I can profit from it. This fellow is not stupid, and I don't pity the maid who will get him. He is going to tell me stories, but that will be all right if I can learn something.

DORANTE (*aside*). This girl astounds me! The beauty of her countenance would honor any woman. (*Aloud.*) Since we are speaking on such friendly terms, and since we have renounced all formality, tell me, Lisette, is your mistress as fine a person as you are? She is courageous to have you as a maid.

SILVIA. Bourguignon, that question tells me that, in accordance with custom, you are now going to say some sweet things to me. Is that so?

DORANTE. I confess to you that I didn't come here with that intention. Even if I am a valet, I have never had any great affairs with the maids. I don't enjoy the domestic mind. But with you, it is different! You subdue me. I am almost shy. My familiarity would not dare relax in your presence. I have the inclination to treat you with such respect that you would laugh. What kind of a servant are you with your air of a princess?

SILVIA. Why, everything you say you felt on seeing me is exactly the story of all the valets who have seen me.

DORANTE. On my word, I shouldn't be surprised if it were also the story of all the masters.

SILVIA. That's a charming reply. But I repeat once more, I

am not susceptible to the coaxing of those whose wardrobe resembles yours.

DORANTE. So, my uniform does not please you?

SILVIA. No, Bourguignon. Let us leave love alone and be good friends.

DORANTE. Only that? Your short treatise is made up of two impossible clauses.

SILVIA (*aside*). How is this man a valet? (*Aloud.*) Yet it must be carried out. It was predicted that I will marry a man of rank, and I swore at that time not to listen to any others.

DORANTE. Why, that is almost comical! What you have sworn concerning a husband, I have sworn for a wife. I have taken an oath to love seriously only a young lady of rank.

SILVIA. Well, you mustn't forget your project.

DORANTE. Perhaps I am not forgetting it as much as we think. You seem very distinguished to me. Sometimes a girl is of high rank without knowing it.

SILVIA. Ha, ha, ha! I would thank you for your compliment, if my mother did not have to pay for it.

DORANTE. Well, take your revenge on mine, if my looks warrant it.

SILVIA (*aside*). They would warrant it. (*Aloud.*) But that isn't the question. Let's stop this banter. It was prophesied I will have a man of rank for a husband, and I won't change my mind.

DORANTE. On my word, if I were such a man, the prophecy would be a threat. I would be afraid to verify it. I have no faith in astrology, but I have a great deal of faith in your beauty.

SILVIA (*aside*). He is inexhaustible. (*Aloud.*) When will you stop this? The prophecy is of no importance to you, because it excludes you.

DORANTE. It did not predict that I would not love you.

SILVIA. No, but it said you would gain nothing from it, and I wish to confirm that.

DORANTE. Very good, Lisette. Such pride becomes you, and although it is hostile to me, I am glad to see you have it. As soon as I saw you, I hoped you would have it. You needed that one remaining grace, and I am reconciled at losing out, because you have won.

SILVIA (*aside*). But really, this fellow surprises me, although I have . . . (*Aloud.*) Tell me, who are you, to be speaking in this way?

DORANTE. The son of good people who were not rich.

SILVIA. With all my heart, I hope you find a better situation than the one you have. And I wish I could be of help. Fortune has been mistaken about you.

DORANTE. But love has made a bigger mistake than fortune. I would prefer to have the right to ask you for your heart than to have all the wealth in the world.

SILVIA (*aside*). Now, thank goodness, we are back in the predictable conversation. (*Aloud.*) Bourguignon, I cannot get angry over your speech, but I beg you, let us change the subject. Let us talk about your master. You can stop talking to me of love, can't you?

DORANTE. Can you stop making me feel love?

SILVIA. Oh! I'm going to get angry. You are going too far. Once more now, let us put love aside.

DORANTE. Then you had better turn your head aside.

SILVIA (*aside*). He is amusing, I must say. (*Aloud.*) So, you won't stop, Bourguignon? I will have to leave you, will I? (*Aside.*) I should have done that already.

DORANTE. Wait, Lisette. I wanted to speak to you about something else, but I can't remember what it was.

SILVIA. I too had something to say to you, but you have put every idea out of my head.

DORANTE. I remember asking you whether your mistress is as beautiful as you.

SILVIA. You are coming back to the main road by a detour.

DORANTE. No, Lisette, I assure you. I am thinking only of my master.

SILVIA. All right, then. I too wanted to speak to you about him, and I hope you will tell me in confidence what he is. Your devotion to him is in his favor. He must be somewhat worthy, since you are serving him.

DORANTE. Perhaps you will at least allow me to thank you for what you have just said.

SILVIA. Please forget my lack of discretion in saying it.

DORANTE. Another of those answers which devastate me. Do as you wish, I can't resist. I am wretched at being put off by the most lovable person in the world.

SILVIA. I wish I knew why I have the kindness to listen to you. This is most unusual.

DORANTE. You are right. Our adventure is unique.

SILVIA (*aside*). In spite of all of his speeches, I haven't left.

I am not leaving, I am still here, and I'm answering him. Truly, the joke has gone far enough. (*Aloud.*) Good-by.

DORANTE. Let us finish what we wanted to say.

SILVIA. Good-by, I say. When your master comes, on behalf of my mistress, I will try to know him myself, if he is worth the trouble. In the meantime, here is the apartment. It is yours.

DORANTE. Why, here is my master.

SCENE 8. *Dorante, Silvia, Harlequin.*

HARLEQUIN. Ah! here you are, Bourguignon! Have you and my valise been made welcome here?

DORANTE. Sir, we were graciously welcomed.

HARLEQUIN. One of the servants told me to come here and that he would tell my father-in-law, who is with my wife.

SILVIA. Sir, you doubtless mean Monsieur and his daughter.

HARLEQUIN. Why, yes! But you might as well say my father-in-law and my wife. I have come here to get married and they are expecting me for the marriage. It is all settled. All that remains is the ceremony, which is a bagatelle.

SILVIA. It is a bagatelle worthy of being remembered.

HARLEQUIN. Yes, remember it once, and that's all that is needed.

SILVIA (*in a low voice to* DORANTE). Bourguignon, being a man of quality in your house seems to be quite unique.

HARLEQUIN. What are you saying to my valet, pretty one?

SILVIA. Nothing. I merely said I was going to get Monsieur Orgon.

HARLEQUIN. Why don't you say my father-in-law, as I do?

SILVIA. Because he isn't that yet.

DORANTE. She is right, sir. There has been no marriage yet.

HARLEQUIN. Well, I'm all ready for it.

DORANTE. Wait until it is over.

HARLEQUIN. What difference is there between a father-in-law the day before and one the day after?

SILVIA. In truth, is there much difference between being married and not being married? Yes, sir, we are wrong. I will tell your father-in-law instantly of your arrival.

HARLEQUIN. And tell my wife too, please. But before going, tell me one thing. You, who are so pretty, are you the maid of the house?

SILVIA. Yes, sir.

HARLEQUIN. Very good, I am delighted. Do you think they will like me here? What do you think of me?

SILVIA. I find you agreeable.

HARLEQUIN. Good, fine! Don't change your mind. This may be an advantage for you.

SILVIA. You are very kind to say so. I am leaving now. They must have forgotten to tell your father-in-law, because he certainly would have come.

HARLEQUIN. Say that I am waiting for him with affection.

SILVIA. (*aside*). How strange fate is! Neither of these men is in his right place.

SCENE 9. *Dorante, Harlequin.*

HARLEQUIN. Well, sir! How was my beginning? The maid already likes me.

DORANTE. Dolt that you are!

HARLEQUIN. How is that? I made such a fine entrance.

DORANTE. You promised me over and over to give up your silly, trivial speech. I gave you careful instructions and advised you to be serious. I see now that I was stupid to have trusted you.

HARLEQUIN. I'll do better from now on. And since it isn't enough to be serious, I'll show a melancholy side. I'll weep if necessary.

DORANTE. I don't know what to do next. This adventure is driving me mad. What should I do?

HARLEQUIN. Isn't the girl nice?

DORANTE. Be still. Monsieur Orgon is coming.

SCENE 10. *Monsieur Orgon, Dorante, Harlequin.*

ORGON. My dear sir, a thousand pardons for having made you wait. But it is just this moment that I learned you were here.

HARLEQUIN. Sir, a thousand pardons are too many. Only one is needed when only one mistake has been made. Moreover, all my pardons are at your service.

ORGON. I will try not to need them.

HARLEQUIN. You are the master, and I am your servant.

ORGON. I assure you, I am delighted to see you. I was waiting for you impatiently.

HARLEQUIN. I would have come here immediately with Bourguignon, but after a trip, you know how worn out one is. I wanted to appear in a slicker state.

ORGON. You succeeded very well. My daughter is dressing. She has been a bit indisposed. While waiting for her to come down, may I offer you something to drink?

HARLEQUIN. I have never refused taking a nip with anyone.

ORGON. Bourguignon, you take care of yourself, my boy.

HARLEQUIN. That fellow is a tippler. He'll drink the best there is.

ORGON. Let him have all he wants.

ACT II

Scene 1. *Lisette, Monsieur Orgon.*

ORGON. Well, what can I do for you, Lisette?

LISETTE. I must talk to you for a moment.

ORGON. What about?

LISETTE. About the state of things here. It is important that you know about it, so you will have no reason to complain about me.

ORGON. Is it serious, then?

LISETTE. Yes, very serious. You gave permission for Mademoiselle Silvia's disguise, and I myself saw nothing wrong with it at first. But I was mistaken.

ORGON. And what is wrong with it?

LISETTE. Sir, it is not easy to praise oneself, but in spite of all the rules of modesty, I have to tell you that if you do not put some order into what is happening, your future son-in-law will have no heart left to offer to your daughter. He is on the point of making a declaration. One more day, and it may be too late.

ORGON. Why do you think he won't want my daughter when he knows her? Do you distrust her charms?

LISETTE. No. But you don't distrust mine enough. I warn you that they are following their own instincts, and I don't advise your letting them do so.

ORGON. My congratulations, Lisette. Ha! ha! ha!

LISETTE. There you go. You are joking, sir. You are making fun of me. I am sorry because you will be caught.

ORGON. Don't worry about this, Lisette. Just continue as before.

LISETTE. Let me repeat once more. Dorante's heart is making big strides. Right now he likes me very much. Tonight he will love me. Tomorrow he will adore me. I don't deserve this. It's in bad taste, you can say what you wish, but that won't stop it. Do you understand? Tomorrow he'll adore me.

ORGON. Well, why are you troubled? If he loves you that much, let him marry you.

LISETTE. What! You wouldn't stop him from doing that?

ORGON. No, on my honor, if he goes that far with you.

LISETTE. Sir, you must beware. Up until now I haven't enhanced any of my charms. I just let them be themselves. So he hasn't lost his head. But if I set about enhancing them, he will lose his head, and there won't be any remedy.

ORGON. Uproot, ravage, burn, in a word, marry him. I permit it, if you can.

LISETTE. With that permission, my fortune is made.

ORGON. Now, tell me. Has my daughter spoken to you? What does she think of her suitor?

LISETTE. We have hardly had a moment to talk together because the suitor is plaguing me. But from what I've seen, she isn't happy. She is sad and dreamy. I expect her to tell me to send him off.

ORGON. And I forbid that. I have good reason to want this disguise to continue. I want her to examine her future husband more carefully. But how is the valet behaving? Isn't he falling in love with my daughter?

LISETTE. He's a strange one. I notice that he plays the important man with her, because he is good-looking. He looks at her and sighs.

ORGON. Does that make her angry?

LISETTE. Well . . . she blushes.

ORGON. That's because she is indignant.

LISETTE. Have it your own way.

ORGON. Well, when you speak to her, tell her you suspect this valet of predisposing her against his master. If she gets angry, don't worry. That's my business. Here is Dorante apparently looking for you.

SCENE 2. *Lisette, Harlequin, Monsieur Orgon.*

HARLEQUIN. Ah! there you are, my charming lady! I was asking everyone where you were. Your servant, dear father-in-law, or almost.

ORGAN. Your servant. Good-by, my children. I will leave you alone. It is appropriate that you grow fond of one another before getting married.

HARLEQUIN. I could easily perform those two duties at the same time.

ORGON. Don't be impatient. Good-by.

SCENE 3. *Lisette, Harlequin.*

HARLEQUIN. He tells me not to be impatient. It's easy enough for the old fellow to say that!

LISETTE. I can hardly believe it is that difficult for you to wait, sir. You pretend to be impatient through gallantry. You have just arrived. Your love couldn't be that strong. At the most, it's just a budding love.

HARLEQUIN. You are wrong, my beauty. Love for you can't remain long in the cradle. Your first glance aroused my love. Your second gave it strength. And the third made it a big boy. Let's try to set him up in business as quickly as possible. Take care of him. You are his mother.

LISETTE. Do you think he is mistreated? Is he forsaken?

HARLEQUIN. Until he is provided for, just give him your beautiful white hand, and amuse him a bit.

LISETTE. You tease! Take it then, there will be no peace with you unless you're amused.

HARLEQUIN (*kissing her hand*). What a dear sweet toy! It makes me as happy as a delicious wine would. What a pity there is only a quarter-of-a-pint!

LISETTE. Here now! Stop! You're overanxious.

HARLEQUIN. I only want to be supported until I've come of age.

LISETTE. But you must have good sense!

HARLEQUIN. Good sense? Alas! I lost it. Your beautiful eyes were the thieves who stole it from me.

LISETTE. Is it possible you could love me so much? I can't be convinced.

HARLEQUIN. I don't give a hang for what is possible. I am madly in love with you, and you can see the reason in your mirror.

LISETTE. My mirror would only make me more unbelieving.

HARLEQUIN. Adorable sweetheart! Your humility is a hypocrite.

LISETTE. Someone is coming. It's your valet.

SCENE 4. *Dorante, Harlequin, Lisette.*

DORANTE. Sir, may I speak to you for a moment?

HARLEQUIN. No! Blasted be the flunkeys who won't leave us in peace!

LISETTE. You had better see what he wants.

DORANTE. Just let me say one word.

HARLEQUIN. If he says two, his dismissal will be the third. What is it?

DORANTE (*in a low voice to* HARLEQUIN). You're impertinent. Come here.

HARLEQUIN (*in low voice to* DORANTE). Those are names and not words. (*To* LISETTE.) Excuse me, my darling.

LISETTE. Please see to it.

DORANTE. You must stop this. Don't yield so fast. Be serious and pensive. And even unhappy. Do you understand?

HARLEQUIN. Yes, my friend. Don't worry. (*Aloud.*) You may leave.

SCENE 5. *Harlequin, Lisette.*

HARLEQUIN. If he hadn't come in, I would have said some wonderful things. But now I will speak only commonplaces, except of my love which is extraordinary. Now, speaking of my love, when will yours keep it company?

LISETTE. I hope that will come about.

HARLEQUIN. Do you think it will come about?

LISETTE. That's a pointed question. Do you know that you are embarrassing me?

HARLEQUIN. What can I say? I am burning and I cry "Fire!"

LISETTE. If I were permitted to explain this quickly . . .

HARLEQUIN. I have the feeling you can in good conscience.

LISETTE. The modesty of my sex won't allow it.

HARLEQUIN. In this case, it's not modesty which gives the permission.

LISETTE. What are you asking of me?

HARLEQUIN. Tell me just a bit that you love me. I love you. Now give me the echo. Repeat it, Princess.

LISETTE. How greedy you are! Well: I love you.

HARLEQUIN. Now, Madame, I can die. My happiness is too great. You love me! How wonderful!

LISETTE. Now it is my turn to be surprised at the promptness of your homage. Perhaps you will love me less when we know one another better.

HARLEQUIN. Ah! When we reach that point, I will be the loser. There will be a great deal to deduct.

LISETTE. You give me more virtues than I have.

HARLEQUIN. You do not know mine, and I should be speaking to you on my knees.

LISETTE. Remember that we are not masters of our fate.

HARLEQUIN. Father and mother have their own way.

LISETTE. As for me, my heart would have chosen you no matter what your condition had been.

HARLEQUIN. It is still free to choose me.

LISETTE. Am I right in thinking you feel the same about me?

HARLEQUIN. Even if you were Perrette or Margot. Even if I saw you carrying a candlestick and going down to the cellar, you would still be my princess.

LISETTE. I hope such fine sentiments will last!

HARLEQUIN. To fortify them, let us swear to love one another always, in spite of all the mistakes in spelling you will make because of me.

LISETTE. Such an oath means more to me than to you, and I take it with all my heart.

HARLEQUIN (*on his knees*). I am dazzled by your goodness, and I kneel before you.

LISETTE. Stop that. I won't allow you to stay in that position. I would be silly to allow that. Get up. Someone else is coming.

SCENE 6. *Lisette, Harlequin, Silvia.*

LISETTE. What do you want, Lisette?

SILVIA. I must speak to you, Madame.

HARLEQUIN. Is that so, girl? Come back in a quarter of an hour. Where I come from, chambermaids don't enter a room unless they're called.

SILVIA. Sir, I have to speak to Madame.

HARLEQUIN. And she is stubborn too. Sweetheart, send her away! Go back to where you came from, girl. We have to make love before we are married. Don't interrupt our obligations.

LISETTE. Can't you come back in a moment, Lisette?

SILVIA. But, Madame . . .

HARLEQUIN. That *but* is all I need to set me off!

SILVIA (*aside*). What a terrible man! (*Aloud.*) I assure you, Madame, it is very urgent.

LISETTE. Let me take care of the matter.

HARLEQUIN. The devil take her! Give me patience. I'll take a walk until it's over. How stupid some servants are!

SCENE 7. *Silvia, Lisette.*

SILVIA. Why did you force his vulgar manners on me? You should have sent him out immediately.

LISETTE. But, Madame, I can't play two roles at the same time. I have to be the mistress or the servant, the one who obeys or the one who gives orders.

SILVIA. Yes, I know. But since he is not here, listen to me as your mistress. You see clearly that that man does not please me.

LISETTE. You haven't had enough time to examine him.

SILVIA. There is no need for an examination. Do you have to see a man twice to judge how little civility he has? In a word, I have no interest in him. Apparently my father does not approve of the dislike he senses in me, because he avoids me and doesn't speak to me. At this point, it is up to you to get me out of this situation by skillfully telling the young man that you have no inclination to marry him.

LISETTE. I can't, Madame.

SILVIA. You can't? What is stopping you?

LISETTE. Monsieur Orgon forbade it.

SILVIA. He forbade it! That doesn't seem like my father.

LISETTE. He positively forbade it.

SILVIA. Well, I want you to tell him of my distaste, and convince him it is invincible. I am sure that after that he will not try to continue with the matter.

LISETTE. But, Madame, what is so disagreeable and repulsive about this man?

SILVIA. I tell you, I don't like him, and I don't like your attitude either.

LISETTE. Take the time to see what he is like, that is all I ask.

SILVIA. I dislike him enough now, without taking the time to dislike him more.

LISETTE. Isn't it true that his valet, who pretends to be so important, has turned you against him?

SILVIA. You are silly. His valet has nothing to do with this.

LISETTE. I don't trust him, because he is so intellectual.

SILVIA. Stop analyzing the man. There is no need of that. I have seen to it that this valet has said very little to me, but in all that he said, he always spoke wisely.

LISETTE. He is the kind of man who tells you crazy stories in order to make a show of his mind and wit.

SILVIA. But my disguise forces me to listen to very nice things. Why have you turned against him? Why are you so bent on giving this fellow a repulsiveness he doesn't have? You are forcing me to stand up for him. It is not a question of causing

THE GAME OF LOVE AND CHANCE

a rift between him and his master or of making a rascal out of him and a fool of me for listening to his stories.

LISETTE. When you defend him in that tone of voice, Madame, and you even seem angry, I must say nothing further.

SILVIA. What is this tone of voice you have when you say this? What do you mean by these words? What is going on in your mind?

LISETTE. Madame, I have never seen you this way before. I don't understand your bitterness. So, if this valet said nothing, that is fine! There is no need to be angry in order to justify him. I believe you, and the matter is closed. I wouldn't disagree with the good opinion you have of him.

SILVIA. What a devious mind you have! How you turn things around! I am so indignant . . . I could cry . . .

LISETTE. Now, Madame, what strange meaning are you giving to my words?

SILVIA. Strange meaning? You think I am quarreling because of him? So I have a high opinion of him! Your disrespect goes that far! High opinion! Good heavens! What answer can I give to that? What does it mean? Whom are you speaking to? Will you please explain?

LISETTE. There is nothing to explain, but I won't recover for some time from the surprise you've given me.

SILVIA. You say things that put me into a rage. Will you leave! I can't stand this any longer. I will take other precautions.

SCENE 8. *Silvia.*

SILVIA. I am still trembling from what I heard her say. The impudence servants treat us with in their minds! They degrade us. I'll never recover from this. I don't dare recall the terms she used. They terrify me! The way she said "valet." I must try to put all her insolent words out of my mind. Here is Bourguignon, the very man over whom I lost my temper. It isn't his fault, the poor fellow. I mustn't blame him.

SCENE 9. *Dorante, Silvia.*

DORANTE. Lisette, even if you feel far away from me, I must speak to you. Let us talk to one another as best we can. There is only a little time left. Let us not waste it by embarrassment.

SILVIA. So, your master is going to leave? It won't be a great loss.

DORANTE. Neither will my going be a great loss, will it? Isn't that part of your thought?

SILVIA. It might be, but I am not thinking of you.

DORANTE. And I can't get you out of my thoughts.

SILVIA. Once and for all, Bourguignon, stay, go, come back. Whatever you do can have no importance for me. I don't wish you good luck or bad luck. I don't dislike you. I don't like you. I shall never love you unless I lose my mind. That is how matters are. Reason doesn't permit me any other choice, and I should not even have told you this much.

DORANTE. You have made me wretchedly unhappy and have taken away from me all peace of mind.

SILVIA. What foolishness you have created for yourself! I am sorry. You must recover. You are speaking to me and I am answering. That is a great deal. It is perhaps too much. If you were educated, you would be pleased with me. You would find in me a kindness which I would criticize in any other girl. But I am not blaming myself for it. My heart reassures me that what I am doing is the right thing. I am speaking to you through charity. But it mustn't go on. Such charity is good only in a temporary way. I will not be able always to be sure of the purity of my intentions. What would become of such sentiments? So, let us put an end to it, Bourguignon, I beg you. Let's not look for meanings and let's stop talking about it.

DORANTE. How you make me suffer, dear Lisette!

SILVIA. You wanted to say something to me. When you came in just now you were complaining about me. What was it?

DORANTE. It was nothing at all. I simply wanted to see you and I needed a pretext.

SILVIA (*aside*). What can I say to that? If I became angry, there'd be no point to it.

DORANTE. As your mistress was leaving, she seemed to be accusing me of speaking improperly of my master.

SILVIA. She imagined that. If she speaks to you again about this, you may deny it flatly. I take the responsibility.

DORANTE. Oh! That isn't what bothers me.

SILVIA. If that is all you have to say, there is no reason for us to be together.

DORANTE. Let me at least have the pleasure of seeing you.

SILVIA. What a motive you are offering me! So I am here to amuse the passion of Bourguignon. Some day I will laugh at the memory of all this.

DORANTE. You are right to make fun of me. I don't know what I'm saying or what I am asking. Good-by.

SILVIA. Good-by. You have made a good decision. But with respect to your farewell, I must know one more thing. You say you are leaving. Is it serious?

DORANTE. I have to leave or I'll lose my mind.

SILVIA. I didn't stop you in order to hear that answer.

DORANTE. I made only one mistake—not to have left as soon as I saw you.

SILVIA (*aside*). Every moment I need to forget that I am listening to him.

DORANTE. Lisette, if you knew the state I'm in . . .

SILVIA. It isn't as interesting as the state I'm in, I assure you.

DORANTE. What can you reproach me for? I don't propose to play on your sentiments.

SILVIA (*aside*). They can't be counted on.

DORANTE. What could I hope for by trying to make you love me? Alas! even if I had your heart . . .

SILVIA. Heaven forbid! If you had it, you wouldn't know. And I would behave in such a way that I wouldn't know myself. What an idea!

DORANTE. Is it really true that you don't hate me, that you don't love me, and that you will never love me?

SILVIA. Yes.

DORANTE. Yes? What is so frightful about me?

SILVIA. Nothing! But that isn't the point.

DORANTE. Dear Lisette, tell me a hundred times that you will not love me.

SILVIA. Oh! I've said it enough times. Try to believe me.

DORANTE. I must believe it. This dangerous passion is despairing. Save me from the effects I fear. You don't hate me! You don't love me! You will never love me! Pound these certainties into my heart. I am acting on good faith. Please help me against myself. This is necessary. I beg you on my knees.

(*He falls to his knees. At that moment* MONSIEUR ORGON *and* MARIO *come in and say nothing.*)

SCENE 10. *Monsieur Orgon, Mario, Silvia, Dorante.*

SILVIA. So it has come to this! This is all that was needed in my adventure. I am truly unhappy. It was my considerate manner that put you there. Please stand up, Bourguignon, I beg you. Someone may come. I will say whatever you want me to. What do you want? I don't dislike you. Get up. I would love you if I could. I like you. That should be enough.

DORANTE. Why, Lisette, if I were not what I am, if I were rich, of a higher class, and if I loved you then as much as I love you now, would your heart feel disgust for me?

SILVIA. Of course not!

DORANTE. You wouldn't hate me? You would allow me to be here?

SILVIA. Willingly. But get up.

DORANTE. You seem to be saying it seriously, and if that is so, I am bewildered.

SILVIA. I said what you wanted to hear, and you don't get up.

ORGON (*coming forward*). It is a great pity to interrupt you. How well it is working out, my children! Courage!

SILVIA. I don't know how to keep this man off his knees, sir. I'm not able to make him behave.

ORGON. You suit one another perfectly. But I want a word with you, Lisette, and you will continue your conversation when we have left. Will you allow me, Bourguignon.

DORANTE. I am leaving, sir.

ORGON. Go and try to talk a bit more graciously with your master than you have.

DORANTE. Me, sir?

MARIO. Yes, you, Bourguignon. You are not renowned for the respect you show your master.

DORANTE. I don't understand.

ORGON. Go on, go on. You will explain another time.

SCENE 11. *Silvia, Mario, Monsieur Orgon.*

ORGON. Well, Silvia, can't you look at me? You seemed embarrassed.

SILVIA. Father, what reason is there for me to be embarrassed? Thank goodness, I am my usual self. I am sorry to say you are imagining things.

MARIO. There is something, Sister. Yes, there is something.

SILVIA. Something in your head, Brother. The only thing in *my* head is surprise over what you are saying.

ORGON. Is this fellow who just left the one who aroused in you the extreme dislike you have for his master?

SILVIA. Who? Dorante's servant?

ORGON. Yes, gallant Bourguignon.

THE GAME OF LOVE AND CHANCE

SILVIA. Gallant Bourguignon—I haven't heard that adjective—has not spoken to me about him.

ORGON. Yet I am told it is he who is ruining Dorante for you. That is the topic I want to talk to you about.

SILVIA. Don't go to that trouble, Father. No one but the master himself inspired in me the natural dislike I have for him.

MARIO. Don't try to argue, Sister. Your dislike for him is too strong to be natural. Someone must have instigated it.

SILVIA (*excitedly*). You say that, dear Brother, with such a mysterious tone. Now, who could have instigated it? Tell me!

MARIO. You are in a bad disposition, Sister. You are really angry.

SILVIA. I'm tired of this role I am playing. I would have taken off this disguise before now if I hadn't feared irritating my father.

ORGON. Be sure that you don't, Daughter. I am here to urge you not to. Since I was willing to allow you to wear this disguise, you must be willing to suspend your judgment on Dorante and see if the dislike someone gave you for him is legitimate.

SILVIA. Won't you listen to me, Father? I tell you that no one taught me to dislike him.

MARIO. You mean to say that the talkative fellow who just left did not incite you against him?

SILVIA (*angrily*). What you say is so unjust! Didn't incite me against him? You are using strong language, words that I am not used to. I am embarrassed. Something is wrong. Gallant Bourguignon turned me against Dorante? Go on talking, but I don't understand you.

MARIO. It's you something has happened to! Whom are you blaming? Why have you been so touchy? Why are you so suspicious?

SILVIA. Courage, Brother! It is fate that every word you say to me today shocks me. What kind of suspicion could I have? Do you have hallucinations?

ORGON. It is true. You are so upset that I don't recognize you. This attitude of yours is obviously the reason for Lisette's speaking to us as she did. She accused this valet of having prejudiced you against his master. She said, "Madame defended Bourguignon with such anger that I am still surprised." We quarreled with her because of this word "surprise." But such people don't know the consequence a word can have.

SILVIA. Nothing is more distasteful than the impertinence of that girl! I confess I was angered by a feeling of justice for the fellow.

MARIO. There is nothing wrong in that.

SILVIA. It's perfectly simple. Because I am fair and want no one to be harmed, because I want to save a servant from being slandered to his master, you say I have fits of anger and fury that surprise you! A moment later, an evil-minded girl begins to argue. You get angry, silence her, and take my side against her because of the consequence of what she says. My side! So I need to be defended and justified! Whatever I do is misunderstood. But what have I done? What are you accusing me of? Tell me, I beg you. Is it serious? Are you making fun of me? I am worried.

ORGON. You must quiet down.

SILVIA. No, Father, I will not quiet down. You talk about surprises and consequences. Explain yourself! What do you mean? You accuse this valet and you are wrong. All of you are wrong. Lisette is a fool and he is innocent. That's all there is to it. Don't talk to me any more about it. I am beside myself!

ORGON. You are holding back, Daughter. You would like to quarrel with me too. Let's do better than that. The valet is the only one under suspicion here. Dorante should dismiss him.

SILVIA. This wretched disguise! Don't let me see Lisette. I hate her more than Dorante.

ORGON. You will see her only when you want to. You must be pleased that the valet will leave. He is in love with you, and that must be very hard to stand.

SILVIA. I am not complaining about him. He thinks I am a servant, and he speaks to me in that way. But I take care he doesn't tell me what he really wants.

MARIO. You are not quite as powerful as you think you are.

ORGON. Didn't we see him get down on his knees, in spite of you? In order to make him stand up, didn't you have to tell him you liked him?

SILVIA (*aside*). How mean they are!

MARIO. Moreover, when he asked you whether you would love him, you had to say very tenderly that you were willing. Otherwise he'd still be here.

SILVIA. That was just a mild remark. I didn't like his action, and didn't want it repeated. Now, to be serious. When will you stop this game you are playing at my expense?

ORGON. The one thing I ask of you, Daughter, is not to

THE GAME OF LOVE AND CHANCE

refuse him until you have full knowledge of the facts. Wait a bit longer. I guarantee you will thank me for the delay I am asking.

MARIO. You will marry Dorante, and even with love, I predict it . . . But Father, you must pardon the valet.

SILVIA. Why *pardon?* I want him to leave.

ORGON. His master will decide that. Let us go.

MARIO. Good-by, Sister. No ill feelings.

SCENE 12. *Silvia, alone; Dorante, later.*

SILVIA. Oh! My heart! My poor heart! What an embarrassing situation I am in! This whole adventure oppresses me. I distrust everyone, and especially myself.

DORANTE. Ah! I was looking for you, Lisette.

SILVIA. I am sorry you found me. I was trying to keep away from you.

DORANTE (*detaining her*). Please stop, Lisette. I must speak to you for the last time. It is about an important matter which concerns your masters.

SILVIA. Go tell it to them. Every time I see you, you add to my troubles. Please leave me.

DORANTE. You have the same effect on me. But listen, I beg you. Things will change because of what I am going to say.

SILVIA. All right, speak! I am listening. It is fated that my submissiveness to you will be eternal.

DORANTE. Do I have your confidence?

SILVIA. I have never betrayed anyone.

DORANTE. I am telling you this secret only because of the confidence I have in you.

SILVIA. I believe you. But try to esteem me without telling me. It sounds like a pretext.

DORANTE. You are wrong, Lisette. You have given me your word and I will continue. You have seen how upset I am. I wasn't able to keep from loving you.

SILVIA. Here we are back again. I don't want to hear anymore. Good-by.

DORANTE. Stay. It isn't Bourguignon who is speaking.

SILVIA. Who are you then?

DORANTE. Ah! Lisette! Now you will judge the anguish that my heart has felt.

SILVIA. I am not speaking to your heart, but to you.

DORANTE. Is anyone coming?

SILVIA. No.

DORANTE. The predicament we are in forces me to say this. My sense of honesty urges me to put an end to it.

SILVIA. Do so then.

DORANTE. The man who is with your mistress is not the man you think he is.

SILVIA (*quickly*). Who is he then?

DORANTE. A valet.

SILVIA. And so?

DORANTE. I am Dorante.

SILVIA (*aside*). Ah! Now I understand my heart.

DORANTE. In this costume I wanted to get to know something about your mistress before marrying her. My father gave me permission to do this and the whole incident seems like a dream. I dislike the mistress whose husband I was to become, and I am in love with the maid who was to see in me only a new master. What must I do now? I blush for her in telling this, but your mistress has so little taste that she is in love with my valet, and ready to marry him if allowed. What is the solution?

SILVIA (*aside*). I must not tell him who I am. (*Aloud.*) Your position is most certainly unique. But, sir, first may I ask you to pardon me for all the unusual topics we have discussed together.

DORANTE (*quickly*). Don't say that, Lisette. Your excuses pain me. They remind me of the distance which separates us and which seems to me all the more regrettable.

SILVIA. Is your attraction to me serious? Do you like me that much?

DORANTE. Yes, I would give up all other associations since I am not permitted to join my lot with yours. The one happiness I could enjoy would be to know you did not dislike me.

SILVIA. A heart which chose me in my lowly condition is certainly worthy of being accepted. I would willingly offer my heart in return if I did not fear placing yours in a bond that would be harmful.

DORANTE. Haven't you enough charms as it is, Lisette? Your words now add noble-mindedness to them.

SILVIA. I hear someone. Be patient on the subject of your valet. Matters will not go out of control. We will meet again and look for ways to help you.

DORANTE. I will follow your advice. (*Exit* DORANTE.)

SILVIA. I wanted so much for him to be Dorante.

SCENE 13. *Silvia, Mario.*

MARIO. I have been anxious about you, Sister. We left you in a terrible state of worry. I want to help you. Listen to me.

SILVIA (*quickly*). Dear Brother, something new has happened.

MARIO. What is it?

SILVIA. Bourguignon is really Dorante.

MARIO. Which one do you mean?

SILVIA. I just learned it. He has told me himself.

MARIO. Who told you?

SILVIA. Don't you understand me?

MARIO. I don't understand a word you're saying.

SILVIA. Come, let's go. We must find my father. He must know this. I will need you too, Brother. I have a new idea. You must pretend to be in love with me. You have already hinted at this in a joke. But you must really keep it a secret, I beg you . . .

MARIO. I'll keep it a secret all right. I don't know what it is.

SILVIA. Come with me, Brother. There is very little time. Nothing like this has ever happened.

MARIO. I pray heaven she hasn't lost her mind.

ACT III

Scene 1. *Dorante, Harlequin.*

HARLEQUIN. Alas, kind sir and honored master, I beg you . . .

DORANTE. What is the matter?

HARLEQUIN. Have pity on my fine adventure. Don't wish bad luck to my happiness which is jogging along so nicely. Don't close the road.

DORANTE. Come now, you're making a joke of it. You deserve a hundred thrashes with the stick.

HARLEQUIN. I won't refuse them if I deserve them. When I've had them, allow me to deserve more. Do you want me to get the stick?

DORANTE. Knave!

HARLEQUIN. Knave if you will. But there is nothing against winning a fortune.

DORANTE. What a rascal! What an imagination he has!

HARLEQUIN. Rascal is another good term which suits me. A knave isn't dishonored by being called a rascal, but a rascal can make a good marriage.

DORANTE. You are insolent! You expect I will allow a gentleman to be tricked and allow you to use my name in marrying his daughter? If you ever again mention such a plot, as soon as I have told Monsieur Orgon who you are, I will dismiss you, do you hear?

HARLEQUIN. Let's come to an agreement. This young lady worships and idolizes me. If I tell her I'm a valet and if her tender heart, despite that, still wants to play around with me, won't you let the violins tune up?

DORANTE. As soon as they know who you are, I'll have nothing more to do with the matter.

HARLEQUIN. Good! I am going right away to tell her about my costume. I hope we won't have a fight over a piece of colored lace, and that her love will let me move up to the table, in spite of fate which placed me at the buffet.

Scene 2. *Dorante, alone, and then Mario.*

DORANTE. Everything that is taking place here, everything that has happened to me here, is unbelievable. I wish I could see Lisette and know the outcome of what she promised to do to extricate me from the problem with her mistress. Perhaps if I look, I can find her.

MARIO. Stay, Bourguignon, I have something to say to you.

DORANTE. I am at your service, sir.

MARIO. Are you making love to Lisette?

DORANTE. She is so charming that it is hard not to speak to her about love.

MARIO. How does she welcome what you say?

DORANTE. Sir, she makes a joke of it.

MARIO. You have a sense of humor. Aren't you playing the hypocrite?

DORANTE. No! But how would that affect you? Suppose that Lisette found me to her liking?

MARIO. To her liking? Where have you learned such words? For a valet, your language is very elegant.

DORANTE. Sir, I can't speak otherwise.

MARIO. It is apparently with this kind of speech that you are trying to win Lisette. You are playing the gentleman.

DORANTE. I assure you, sir, that I am playing no part. But you were not seeking me out to ridicule me. Don't you have something else to say? We were speaking of Lisette, of my love for her, and of the interest you have in all this.

MARIO. Why, there is a tone of jealousy in what you say. You must quiet down. You were saying that if Lisette found you to her liking . . . what then?

DORANTE. Why is there any need for your knowing this?

MARIO. All right. I will come to the point. In spite of the jesting tone I took just now, I would be angry if she loved you. Without going into this further, I forbid your speaking to her any more. It is not that I really fear she will fall in love with you. Her heart is too noble for that. But I would dislike having Bourguignon as a rival.

DORANTE. I don't blame you. And Bourguignon himself, I might say, is not very happy that you are his rival.

MARIO. He will be patient.

DORANTE. He will have to. But, sir, do you love her very much?

MARIO. Enough to attach myself seriously to her, as soon as I have taken certain measurements. Do you understand what that means?

DORANTE. Yes, I think I understand. And on that score, you are doubtless loved.

MARIO. What would you think? Am I not worthy of being loved?

DORANTE. I hope you don't expect to be praised by your own rivals.

MARIO. An excellent answer. I excuse you for it. But I am mortified not to be able to tell you she loves me. I am not telling you this just to inform you. But I must tell the truth.

DORANTE. You amaze me, sir. Doesn't Lisette know your plans?

MARIO. Lisette knows how much I think of her and doesn't seem to be very much interested. But I hope that common sense will win her heart for me. Good-by. Leave without making any disturbance. Her coldness to me, in spite of all I am offering her, will console you for the sacrifice you are making . . . Your livery is not enough to tip the balance in your favor. You are not the man to oppose me.

SCENE 3. *Silvia, Dorante, Mario.*

MARIO. Is that you, Lisette?

SILVIA. What is wrong, sir? You seem upset.

MARIO. Nothing is wrong. I was speaking to Bourguignon.

SILVIA. He is sad. Were you quarreling with him?

DORANTE. Monsieur Mario tells me he loves you, Lisette.

SILVIA. It isn't my fault.

DORANTE. And he forbids me to love you.

SILVIA. Does he also forbid me to appear lovable to you?

MARIO. I can't keep him from loving you, Lisette. But I don't want him to tell you.

SILVIA. He doesn't *tell* me any more. He just repeats it.

MARIO. At least he won't repeat it in my presence. You may leave, Bourguignon.

DORANTE. I am waiting for her to give the order.

MARIO. Again, you . . .

SILVIA. He says he is waiting. Be patient.

DORANTE. Do you feel any love for this gentleman?

SILVIA. Love? It won't be necessary to forbid that.

DORANTE. Aren't you deceiving me?

MARIO. What kind of a man am I? He must leave. Whom am I speaking to?

DORANTE. To Bourguignon, that's all.

MARIO. Well, have him leave!

DORANTE (*aside*). This is agony.

SILVIA. Do as he says. He is getting angry.
DORANTE (*in low voice, to* SILVIA). Perhaps that is what you want?
MARIO. Come now, that's enough!
DORANTE. You hadn't told me of this love, Lisette.

SCENE 4. *Monsieur Orgon, Mario, Silvia.*

SILVIA. Confess it, if I didn't love this man, I would be ungrateful.
MARIO (*laughs*). Ha, ha, ha, ha!
ORGON. What are you laughing at, Mario?
MARIO. At Dorante's anger. I forced him to leave Lisette.
SILVIA. What did he say to you in the little conversation you just had with him?
MARIO. I never saw a man more intrigued or in a worse humor.
ORGON. I am not sorry he is the dupe of his own stratagem. All in all, there is nothing more flattering or kinder for him than what you have done, Daughter. But you have gone far enough.
MARIO. Sister, how do matters stand now?
SILVIA. Brother, I confess to you that I have reason to be pleased.
MARIO. "Brother," she says to me! Do you feel the sweet peacefulness in her very words?
ORGON. Why, Daughter, do you hope he will go as far as proposing to you in your present costume?
SILVIA. Yes, dear father, I hope so.
MARIO. What a hussy you are, with your "dear father"! You're not scolding us now. You are speaking very sweetly.
SILVIA. I am following your example.
MARIO. Ha, ha! I'll have my revenge. Just now you were making fun of my speech. Now it is my turn to mock you for yours. Your happiness is as diverting as your worry was.
ORGON. You will have no reason to complain about me, Daughter. I give in to whatever you decide.
SILVIA. Oh! Father, if you knew how grateful I am to you! Dorante and I are made for one another. He must marry me. If you knew how I will remember all he did for me today. My heart will never forget the great tenderness he showed me. This will make our marriage all the more perfect. He will love me every time he recalls our story. I will love him every time I

think of it. You created our happiness for life by allowing me to play this trick. It will be a unique marriage, an adventure whose tale will make people cry, a more extraordinary and happy play of chance, the most . . .

MARIO. Ha, ha, ha! How chatty your heart has become, Sister! What eloquence it has!

ORGON. I must agree that the entertainment you are giving yourself is delightful, especially if you complete it.

SILVIA. When it is done, it will be worth something. Dorante is conquered. I am waiting for my captive.

MARIO. His irons will be more gilded than he thinks. But his soul is distressed and I am sorry for what he is suffering.

SILVIA. What it is costing him to make up his mind makes him all the more noble. He thinks he will dismay his father by marrying me. He believes he will betray his fortune and his birth. He has to reflect about such things. I shall be so happy to triumph. But I will have to snatch my victory. He will not offer it to me. I want a combat between love and reason.

MARIO. And you want reason to perish.

ORGON. That means you want him to feel the full extent of the impertinence he thinks he is committing. What insatiable vanity!

MARIO. It is the vanity of a woman, and the usual thing.

SCENE 5. *Monsieur Orgon, Silvia, Mario, Lisette.*

ORGON. Quiet! Here comes Lisette. We'll see what she wants.

LISETTE. Sir, a while ago you said you would give me Dorante, that you would give him over to my discretion. I took you at your word, and I have worked for my own good. You will see how well I have worked. He is in excellent condition. What shall I do with him now? Will your daughter give him to me?

ORGON. Once more, Daughter, have you any plans for him?

SILVIA. No. I give him to you, Lisette. I release all my rights to you. To use your words, I will never share a heart which I myself have not conditioned.

LISETTE. What! Will you allow me to marry him? And your father also will allow me?

ORGON. Yes, I give my consent.

MARIO. And I consent also.

LISETTE. And I too, and I thank all of you.

ORGON. Wait. Just one little stipulation. In order to exculpate us from whatever may happen, you must tell him a bit about who you are.

LISETTE. But if I tell him a bit, he will know the whole story.

ORGON. Well, his head is solid enough to stand that shock. I don't think his temperament is one to be frightened away.

LISETTE. Here he comes looking for me. Please be good enough to leave me alone with him. My masterpiece is at stake.

ORGON. That is only fair. Let us go.

SILVIA. With all my heart.

MARIO. We're off!

SCENE 6. *Lisette, Harlequin.*

HARLEQUIN. At last, queen of mine, I find you and I won't leave you again. I've missed you too much and I even thought you were avoiding me.

LISETTE. I have to confess there is some truth in what you say.

HARLEQUIN. Dear soul, dear heart, were you trying to bring about the end of my life?

LISETTE. No, dear man. Your life is too precious to me for that.

HARLEQUIN. Ah! those words bolster me up.

LISETTE. You must not doubt my affection.

HARLEQUIN. I want to kiss those little words and pick them from your mouth with mine.

LISETTE. You were urging me about our marriage. My father hadn't yet permitted me to answer you. I have just spoken to him, and I have his word that you may ask him for my hand when you wish.

HARLEQUIN. Before I ask him for your hand, let me ask you for it. I want to thank it for the kind charity it will show in wishing to take its place in mine, which is truly unworthy of it.

LISETTE. I don't mind lending it to you for a moment, on the condition that you will take it forever.

HARLEQUIN. Dear little round, chubby hand, I take you without further bargaining. I am not worried over the honor you are doing me. But I am worried over the honor I am doing you.

LISETTE. You will be doing me more honor than is needed.

HARLEQUIN. No, not at all! You don't know that arithmetic as well as I do.

LISETTE. But I look upon your love as a gift from heaven.

HARLEQUIN. That gift won't ruin heaven. It's rather measly.

LISETTE. For me it is magnificent.

HARLEQUIN. That's because you don't see it in full daylight.

LISETTE. I can't tell you how much your modesty is embarrassing me.

HARLEQUIN. Don't let yourself go to too much embarrassment. If I weren't modest, I'd be pretty brazen.

LISETTE. Do I have to tell you it is I who am honored by your affection?

HARLEQUIN. Aie! aie! I don't know where to turn.

LISETTE. Let me say once more: I know what I am.

HARLEQUIN. I too know what I am, and it's not a very fine acquaintanceship, and it won't be for you, when you've made it. That's the devilish part of knowing me. You don't know what's in the bottom of the bag.

LISETTE (*aside*). It isn't natural for a man to underrate himself this way. (*Aloud.*) Why are you saying this to me?

HARLEQUIN. There's the rub.

LISETTE. You worry me. After all, aren't you . . . ?

HARLEQUIN. Aie, aie! You're stripping me down!

LISETTE. I want to know what's up.

HARLEQUIN (*aside*). I have to prepare her for this. (*Aloud.*) Does your love have a robust constitution? Will it stand the shock I'm going to give it? Will a poor lodging terrify it? I'm going to house it shabbily.

LISETTE. Stop beating around the bush. Who are you?

HARLEQUIN. I am . . . Have you even seen counterfeit money? Do you know what a counterfeit gold louis is like? Well, I bear some resemblance to it.

LISETTE. Tell me all. What is your name?

HARLEQUIN. My name? (*Aside.*) Can I tell her it's Harlequin? No, that almost rhymes with worth-a-pin!

LISETTE. Tell me.

HARLEQUIN. I have to go gently. Do you despise the position of a soldier?

LISETTE. What do you mean by a soldier?

HARLEQUIN. For example, a soldier of the antechamber.

LISETTE. A soldier of the antechamber? So you're not Dorante?

HARLEQUIN. He's my captain.

LISETTE. You big ape, you!

HARLEQUIN. An ape that has taken a tumble!

LISETTE. For a whole hour I've been begging his pardon and humiliating myself before this beast.

HARLEQUIN. If you preferred love to glory, I would be as profitable to you as a gentleman.

LISETTE. Ha, ha, ha! I can't keep from laughing at him with his glory! There's only one way out of this. Come now, my glory pardons you. It's pretty tough.

HARLEQUIN. Do you really pardon me? How grateful my love is going to be!

LISETTE. Let's shake hands, Harlequin. I was duped. Monsieur's antechamber soldier is no better than Madame's hairdresser.

HARLEQUIN. Madame's hairdresser!

LISETTE. She's my captain.

HARLEQUIN. You're in disguise!

LISETTE. Take your revenge.

HARLEQUIN. So, you're the she-ape I've been mortifying myself before this past hour.

LISETTE. Let's come to the point. Do you love me?

HARLEQUIN. I certainly do. When you changed your name, you didn't change your face. You remember we promised to be faithful in spite of all mistakes in spelling.

LISETTE. There's no great harm. Let's make up. But we won't let on to anyone and let them laugh at us. Your master still doesn't know about my mistress. Don't tell him. Let's leave everything as it is. I think he is coming. Monsieur, I am your servant.

HARLEQUIN. Madame, I am your valet. Ha, ha, ha!

SCENE 7. *Dorante, Harlequin.*

DORANTE. Well, that was Orgon's daughter. Did you tell her who you are?

HARLEQUIN. Why, yes. The poor child! Her heart is gentler than a lamb's. It didn't even pant. When I told her my name was Harlequin and that I wore an orderly's uniform, she said to me, "Each one of us has his own name in life and his uniform. Yours cost you nothing and it is very pleasing."

DORANTE. What sort of a story are you telling me?

HARLEQUIN. Such a sort that I am asking her to marry me.

DORANTE. What! Does she agree to marry you?

HARLEQUIN. Yes! She must be badly off!

DORANTE. You're deceiving me. She doesn't know who you are.

HARLEQUIN. Damn it! Do you want to bet that I will marry her with my livery on my back, with a stable-coat on, if you make me mad? I want you to know that my kind of love isn't easy to disrupt, and that I don't need your clothes to make a move. Why don't you give me back my livery?

DORANTE. You're a cheat. This isn't possible, and I see I will have to warn Monsieur Orgon.

HARLEQUIN. Who? He's our father. Ah! the good man! He's at our disposal. He's the finest kind of man . . . We're highly pleased with him.

DORANTE. You're raving! Have you seen Lisette?

HARLEQUIN. Lisette? No! She perhaps passed in front of me, but a gentleman pays no attention to a chambermaid. You can do that part of the job for me.

DORANTE. You may leave. You have lost your head.

HARLEQUIN. Your methods are rather convenient. Habit explains them. Good-by. When I'm married, we'll live without any odds. Here is your maid. Hello, Lisette. I give you Bourguignon. A worthy young fellow.

SCENE 8. *Dorante, Silvia.*

DORANTE (*aside*). She inspires such love in me! Why did Mario have to caution me?

SILVIA. Where were you? Since leaving Mario, I haven't been able to find you to tell you what I said to Monsieur Orgon.

DORANTE. I haven't left the house. What do you wish to say?

SILVIA (*aside*). How cold he is! (*Aloud.*) I discredited your valet and pointed out how little deserving he was, but it was to no avail. I even pointed out that we could postpone the marriage, but he didn't even listen. I warn you that they are thinking of sending for the notary. It is high time for you to speak.

DORANTE. I intend to. I am going away *incognito,* and I will leave a note telling Monsieur Orgon everything.

SILVIA (*aside*). But I don't want him to go away.

DORANTE. Don't you approve of my plan?

SILVIA. No . . . not really.

DORANTE. I see nothing better to do in my present situation,

THE GAME OF LOVE AND CHANCE

unless I myself speak, and I can't bring myself to do that. Besides, there are other reasons which force me to leave. There is nothing else for me to do here.

SILVIA. As I don't know your reasons, I can neither approve nor oppose them. And I can't ask you what they are.

DORANTE. It is easy for you to imagine what they are, Lisette.

SILVIA. Well, I imagine you have some liking for Monsieur Orgeon's daughter.

DORANTE. Is that all you see?

SILVIA. There are other things also I could imagine. But I'm not angry and I'm not vain enough to believe them.

DORANTE. Nor courageous enough to speak of them. Because you would have nothing pleasant to tell me. Good-by, Lisette.

SILVIA. Take care. I don't believe you understand me. I am obliged to tell you this.

DORANTE. That's fine! And the explanation would not be favorable for me. Keep the secret until I have gone.

SILVIA. Seriously, are you going?

DORANTE. You are afraid I will change my mind.

SILVIA. How fortunate you are so well informed!

DORANTE. That is naïve. Good-by. *(Exit* DORANTE.*)*

SILVIA *(aside)*. If he goes, I will stop loving him, I will never marry him. *(She watches him go.)* Now he is stopping. He's thinking. He's looking to see if I have turned around. I mustn't call him back . . . It would be strange if he left after all I have done! . . . Well, it's over. He is going. I didn't have as much power over him as I thought. My brother is so clumsy. He went about it in the wrong way. Outsiders spoil everything. I've made no progress. What an ending! . . . There's Dorante again! I think he's coming back. I will change my mind. I still love him . . . I will pretend to leave so he will stop me. Our reconciliation must cost him something.

DORANTE *(stopping her)*. Stay, I beg you. I have something else to tell you.

SILVIA. To tell me?

DORANTE. I can't leave unless I convince you I am not wrong in leaving.

SILVIA. There is no reason why you have to justify yourself. No reason at all. I am only a servant, and you have made me realize it.

DORANTE. Have I, Lisette? Should you complain? You've seen me make up my mind, and you have said nothing to me.

SILVIA. Hum! If I wanted to, I could answer that.

DORANTE. Please answer. All I want is to be wrong. But what am I saying? Mario loves you.

SILVIA. That is true.

DORANTE. You are receptive to his love. I saw that just now in your great desire to have me leave. So you couldn't love me.

SILVIA. I am receptive to his love? Who told you that? And I couldn't love you? How do you know that? You make up your mind very fast.

DORANTE. Lisette, in the name of what you hold dearest in the world, teach me what this is about, I beg you.

SILVIA. Teach a man who is leaving?

DORANTE. I will not leave.

SILVIA. If you love me, don't question me. You fear only my indifference and you are very happy when I don't speak. My sentiments do not affect you.

DORANTE. They don't affect me, Lisette? Do you still doubt that I love you?

SILVIA. No, you have repeated it so often that I believe you. But why do you insist? What can I do with this idea? Let me speak frankly. You love me. But your love is not a serious thing for you. There are many ways for you to get rid of it. The distance between us, endless objects which will attract your attention, the desire others will have to move you, the amusements of a man of your position—all that will lessen this love you speak to me about so pitilessly. When you leave this house, you will perhaps laugh at it, and you will be right. But if I remember it, and I fear I will, if it has affected me, what help will I have against it? Who will make up to me for having lost you? Whom can my heart put in your place? Do you know that if I loved you, nothing great in this world would affect me again? Just think of the state I would be in. Be generous enough to hide your love from me. I would hesitate to tell you I loved you in your present state of mind. The confession of my sentiments might endanger your reason, and therefore I have concealed them from you.

DORANTE. Ah! dear Lisette, all that you have said is like a fire burning me. I worship and respect you. All rank and birth and fortune will disappear before a soul such as yours. I would be ashamed if my pride held out against you. My heart and my hand belong to you.

SILVIA. You do deserve that I take your heart and your hand.

THE GAME OF LOVE AND CHANCE

I would have to be too noble-minded to hide from you the pleasure they give me. Do you think it can last?

DORANTE. So you love me?

SILVIA. No, no. If you ask me once again, it will be too bad.

DORANTE. Your threats do not frighten me.

SILVIA. And what about Mario? Have you forgotten him?

DORANTE. No, Lisette. Mario does not alarm me. You do not love him. You can't deceive me any more. Your heart is too honest. You do respond to my love. I know this from the ecstasy that has taken hold of me. You cannot take this assurance away from me.

SILVIA. Oh! I won't try to. Keep it. We shall see what you will do with it.

DORANTE. Do you consent to be mine?

SILVIA. Are you willing to marry me in spite of what you are, in spite of your father's anger and your fortune?

DORANTE. My father will forgive me when he sees you. My fortune is enough for both of us. Personal merit is worth as much as birth. Let us not quarrel. I will never change.

SILVIA. You will never change! Dorante, you please me a great deal.

DORANTE. Stop putting obstacles in the way of your love. Let it respond . . .

SILVIA. Yes, I am over that. You . . . you will never change?

DORANTE. No, dear Lisette.

SILVIA. My love!

SCENE 9. *Orgon, Silvia, Dorante, Lisette, Harlequin, Mario.*

SILVIA. Father, you wanted me to accept Dorante. Come see your daughter obey you with greater joy than there ever has been.

DORANTE. What are you saying? Are you her father, Monsieur?

SILVIA. Yes, Dorante. Each of us had the same idea about our meeting. There is nothing more to say. I do not doubt your love for me. It is your turn to judge my sentiments for you. Judge how much I love you by the way in which I tried to win your love.

ORGON. Do you recognize this letter? That is how I learned of your disguise, but she learned of it only through you.

DORANTE. I can't tell you my happiness, Madame. What delights me most is the proof I gave you of my love.

MARIO. Will Dorante pardon the anger I aroused in Bourguignon?

DORANTE. He doesn't pardon you, he thanks you for it.

HARLEQUIN. Be happy, Madame! You lost your rank, but you are not to be pitied because you still have Harlequin.

LISETTE. A fine consolation! You're the only one to win in that.

HARLEQUIN. I haven't lost. Before I knew who you were, your dowry was worth more than you; now you are worth more than your dowry.

The Barber of Seville
(LE BARBIER DE SÉVILLE)
1775

A COMEDY IN FOUR ACTS
BY
PIERRE-AUGUSTIN CARON DE BEAUMARCHAIS

translated by WALLACE FOWLIE

Pierre-Augustin Caron de Beaumarchais
(1732–1799)

In his life and character Beaumarchais himself was the original, the authentic Figaro. Pierre-Augustin Caron, the son of a clockmaker, was born in Paris, on the rue Saint-Denis. He too became a clockmaker and inventor, as well as a musician and harp teacher to the two daughters of the king. He acquired wealth, purchased two titles in an effort to change his status to that of a noble, adopted the name Beaumarchais which came from land owned by his wife. His enterprises in high finance, lawsuits, duels, and a prison sentence made of his life an exciting dangerous adventure. During the American Revolution he furnished arms to the American colonists.

Beaumarchais' character was made up of many contradictions. He was an intriguer, often impertinent in his dealings with people, and yet he had also generous impulses and enthusiasms. His many acts of kindness offset his buffoonery and knavery.

The greatest popular success in his career of playwright was *Le Mariage de Figaro* in 1784. This comedy, a sequel to *Le Barbier de Séville* in 1775, is more of a satire than the earlier play, more militant in its attack on social abuses. It foreshadows the French Revolution in its parody of the privileged classes and the *ancien régime*.

The Barber of Seville is a comedy of intrigue in which the character Figaro helps his master, Count Almaviva, to win the hand of Rosine. The tutor, Bartholo, plays the part of father and rival suitor. It is an old subject, often treated in early Italian comedies. Molière had used the theme in what became the most successful comedy of his career, *L'École des Femmes*. As Molière had done, Beaumarchais took the side of the young couple against the tyranny and the jealousy of the older man.

Beaumarchais had traveled in Spain, and used his knowledge of the country to provide the background and local color for his farce. Much of the playwright's dramatic skill is concentrated on the character Figaro, who has been compared to

Molière's Mascarille and Lesage's Gil Blas. He actually represents much more, and the very complexity of his gifts and defects makes one realize the degree to which Beaumarchais himself is in his character.

Figaro is a sensitive man who is delighted to bring together two lovers and help make possible their marriage. He is not only a barber, he is a writer and a poet as well. He is on familiar terms with several important Spaniards. Somewhat under their protection, he can afford to demonstrate a certain amount of insolence toward the bourgeois citizens of his town. The situation of the comedy is familiar, and Figaro directs it with tact, swiftness, and explosiveness when necessary.

He is at the heart of the dialogue, which is far more than mere convention. The speeches and the replies are timed with an uncanny sense of precision. The comedy is a game in which each character speaks in turn, at the appropriate moment, in order to help complete the entire pattern and resolve the action. The intrigue of the comedy, the dynamics of Figaro, the alert Bartholo who is not easy to trick, and the ingenuous Rosine, who has traits of malice, restored to the French stage a tone of gaiety which *le drame bourgeois* of Diderot had dissipated in the eighteenth century.

Le Barbier de Séville is the first expression of a theme which is more fully developed in *Le Mariage de Figaro*, and which is nothing less than the belief of the *philosophes* (Voltaire, Diderot, Rousseau) in the need to change or even dissolve the society of their day. It is the desire to live in greater happiness, to enjoy the good things of the world, the determination to attack all existing social abuses and those traditions which impede progress. The boldness of Beaumarchais and his adventurous spirit are incarnated in Figaro. He has a liking for action for its own sake, but also for action that has a purpose. Life itself is the teacher for Figaro (as well as for Beaumarchais) and he loves life deeply in all its aspects of tumult and passion. Both the author and the character have an extraordinary belief in themselves, in the justice of their goals and the means to the goals. The adventurer and the gossip are mingled with the man of generous affection.

In the writing of such a play as *The Barber of Seville*, Beaumarchais probably copied less from other playwrights than Molière did in composing most of his comedies. Yet the plot and the general situation are so familiar that there are few surprises for the spectator. His originality lies in his particular understanding of the theater, and of theatrical devices. He is the kind of playwright who combines several traditions and infuses new life in them. The action of his comedy is not simple, but whatever its complications, it is always close enough to life to be "likely." Whatever trickiness of plot and action exists in *Le Barbier,* it is quickly forgotten or camouflaged by the spirit of wit and comedy which pervades the work and animates the performance. Gestures, attitudes, dialogue, and action move so swiftly toward the denouement that all possible defects are passed over. The impertinences of Figaro ring so true that one easily forgets his many literary ancestors.

The Barber of Seville

CHARACTERS

COUNT ALMAVIVA, a grandee of Spain, the unknown lover of Rosine
BARTHOLO, a physician, guardian of Rosine
ROSINE, a young lady of noble birth, and ward of Bartholo
FIGARO, a barber of Seville
DON BAZILE, organist and singing teacher of Rosine
LA JEUNESSE, an old servant of Bartholo
L'EVEILLÉ, another servant of Bartholo, simple-minded and slothful
A NOTARY
AN ALCADE, a man of the law courts
POLICEMEN and SERVANTS

Scene: Seville. The first act is in the street and under the windows of Rosine. The other acts are in the house of Doctor Bartholo.

ACT I

A street in Seville. All the windows have bars.

SCENE 1. *The Count.* (*He wears a large brown cloak and broad-brimmed hat, and pulls out his watch as he walks.*)

COUNT. It isn't as late as I thought. The time when she usually appears behind the blinds is still far off. No matter. It is better to get here early than to miss the moment when I can see her. If one of the courtiers knew that I am a hundred leagues from Madrid, and stop every morning under the windows of a woman I have never spoken to, he would take me for a Spaniard during the reign of Isabella. But why not? Every man tries to find happiness. For me it is in the heart of Rosine. They will say, why pursue a woman in Seville when

Madrid and the Court offer so many easy rounds of pleasure? That is what I am getting away from. I am tired of those conquests proposed to us by self-interest and suitability or vanity. It is so wonderful to be loved for oneself. If I could be sure that in this disguise . . . The devil take this intruder!

SCENE 2. *Figaro, the Count (hidden).*

FIGARO (*a guitar attached to his back by a scarf. He is singing happily. Paper and pencil in his hand*).

> All sadness I'll expel.
> It feeds upon my life.
> Man needs, to ward off strife,
> The power and the spell
> That wine can give. He'll die
> Without its fire, or strive
> As fools who all day sigh . . .

So far, that's not so bad, is it?

> . . . as fools who all day sigh.
> So, wine and laziness
> Wage war within my heart . . .

No, they don't dispute it; they reign together quite peacefully.

> Dispute . . . within my heart.

Can I say "share"? The writers of comic operas aren't so particular. Nowadays what isn't worth being said is sung. (*Sings.*)

> So, wine and laziness
> Dispute within my heart.

I would like to end with something fine, brilliant, and sparkling which would look like an idea. (*Kneels and writes as he sings.*)

> Dispute within my heart.
> And one holds tenderness . . .
> The other happiness.

THE BARBER OF SEVILLE

Oh! That's flat! It's not right. I need an opposite, an antithesis . . .

> If one . . . is my mistress,
> The other . . .

Ah! I have it!

> The other serves my art.

Very good, Figaro! (*Writes and sings.*)

> So, wine and laziness
> Dispute within my heart.
> If one is my mistress,
> The other serves my art,
> The other serves my art,
> The other serves my art.

When we have the accompaniments, we shall see, gentlemen of the cabal, if I know what I am talking about. (*Sees the* COUNT.) I have seen that priest somewhere. (*Rises.*)

COUNT (*aside*). I am sure I know that man.

FIGARO. No! He is not a priest. That bearing so proud and noble . . .

COUNT. That grotesque figure . . .

FIGARO. I was right. It is Count Almaviva.

COUNT. I think it's that rascal Figaro.

FIGARO. It is, my lord.

COUNT. Knave! If you say one word . . .

FIGARO. Yes, I recognize you. The same familiar kindness with which you have always honored me.

COUNT. I didn't recognize you. You are so fat . . .

FIGARO. How can I help it, my lord, it's hard times.

COUNT. Poor fellow! What are you doing in Seville? Not long ago I recommended you for a position in the government.

FIGARO. I was appointed, my lord, and my gratitude . . .

COUNT. Call me Lindor. Can't you see, by my disguise, that I want to be incognito?

FIGARO. I will leave.

COUNT. No, don't. I am waiting here for something, and two men talking are less suspicious than one man walking back and forth. Let's pretend to be talking. What about that position?

FIGARO. The minister, respectful of your excellency's recommendation, appointed me on the spot apothecary's boy.

COUNT. In the army hospitals?

FIGARO. No! In the studs of Andalusia.

COUNT (*laughs*). A fine beginning!

FIGARO. It wasn't a bad position. Since I had the dressings and the drugs in my charge, I often sold good horse medicines to people.

COUNT. Which killed the King's subjects.

FIGARO. There is no universal remedy which does not sometimes cure Galicians, Catalans, and Auvergnats.

COUNT. Why did you leave it?

FIGARO. Leave it? It left me. Someone maligned me to the powers. "Envy with crooked fingers, with a pale livid face . . ." 1*

COUNT. Spare me, my friend, spare me! Do you write verses too? I saw you scratching away on your knee, and singing early in the morning.

FIGARO. That's just the reason for my misfortune, Excellency. When it was reported to the minister that I had composed some very fine garlands of verses to Cloris, that I had sent riddles to the journals, that madrigals of my composition were circulating—in short, when he learned that I was in print everywhere—he took the matter seriously, and had me dismissed on the pretext that a love of letters is incompatible with the spirit of business.

COUNT. Powerfully reasoned! And you didn't tell him that . . .

FIGARO. I considered myself fortunate to be forgotten. I am persuaded that a grandee is good to us when he does us no harm.

COUNT. You are not telling me everything. I remember that in my service you were something of a rascal.

FIGARO. My lord, people always expect a poor man to be faultless.

COUNT. You were lazy and dissolute . . .

FIGARO. From the virtues demanded of a servant, does your Excellency know many masters worthy of being valets?

COUNT (*laughs*). Not bad. And so you came to this city?

FIGARO. Not right away.

COUNT (*stopping him*). One moment . . . I thought it was she . . . Keep on talking. I can hear you.

---

* Notes are at the end of the play, p. 275.

THE BARBER OF SEVILLE

FIGARO. On my return to Madrid, I tried my literary talents again. The theater seemed to me a field of honor.

COUNT. God keep you there!

FIGARO (*during the reply, the* COUNT *looks attentively at the blind*). I really don't know why I didn't have a great success, for I had filled the pit with the best workers. They had hands like paddles. I had forbidden gloves, canes, and everything else that produces only dull applause. On my honor, before the performance, the café had seemed well disposed toward me. But the efforts of the cabal . . .

COUNT. Oh! The cabal! You were a fallen author!

FIGARO. Like anyone else. Why not? They hissed me, but if I can ever get them together again . . .

COUNT. Through revenge, you would bore them?

FIGARO. I'm laying it up against them, by God!

COUNT. You swear! Do you know that at court you have only twenty-four hours in which to curse your judges?

FIGARO. You have twenty-four years in the theater. Life is too short to wear out such resentment.

COUNT. Your happy anger delights me. But you haven't told me what made you leave Madrid.

FIGARO. It was my good angel, Excellency, since I am fortunate enough to find my old master. Seeing in Madrid that the republic of letters is the republic of wolves, always at each other's throats, and that, delivered up to the scorn to which this ludicrous stubbornness leads them, all the insects, mosquitoes, cousins, critics, journalists, booksellers, censors, and everything that clings to the hide of the poor man of letters, succeeded in lacerating and sucking the little substance that remained to them; tired of writing, weary of myself, disgusted with others, sunken in debts and light of cash; finally convinced that the useful revenue from my razor is preferable to the empty honors of the pen, I left Madrid with my baggage slung over my shoulder, and wandered philosophically through the two Castilles, la Mancha, Estremadura, Sierra-Morena, and Andalusia. I was welcomed in one town, imprisoned in the next, and everywhere I was superior to events. I was praised by some and blamed by others. Making the best of good weather and enduring bad weather, I mocked the foolish, defied the wicked, laughed at my poverty, and shaved everyone. You see me finally established in Seville and ready to serve your Excellency again in anything you may be pleased to order.

Count. Who gave you so merry a philosophy?

Figaro. Everlasting misfortune. I hasten to laugh at everything for fear I may be obliged to weep. What are you looking at over there?

Count. Let's move off.

Figaro. Why?

Count. Come on, you fool! You'll be my downfall. (*They hide.*)

Scene 3. *Bartholo, Rosine.* (*The blind of the second floor opens, and* Bartholo *and* Rosine *appear at the window.*)

Rosine. How pleasant it is to breathe fresh air! This blind is so rarely opened . . .

Bartholo. What is that paper you are holding?

Rosine. These are couplets from *The Useless Precaution* which my singing teacher gave me yesterday.

Bartholo. What is this *Useless Precaution?*

Rosine. A new comedy.

Bartholo. Another play! Another folly of a new type! [2]

Rosine. I don't know much about it.

Bartholo. Well, the journals and the authorities will take our side. It's a barbarous age!

Rosine. You are always attacking our poor century.

Bartholo. Excuse me, but what has it produced that we should praise it? All kinds of silliness: freedom of thought, gravitation, electricity, religious tolerance, inoculation, quinine, the Encyclopedia, plays . . .

Rosine (*drops the paper which falls into the street*). Oh! My song! My song dropped as I was listening to you. Run, run, please! My song! It will be lost!

Bartholo. What the devil! Why didn't you hold on to it? (*Leaves the balcony.*)

Rosine (*looks into the room and signals to the* Count *in the street*). Shh! (*The* Count *appears.*) Pick it up quickly and go hide. (*The* Count *picks up the paper and returns to his hiding place.*)

Bartholo (*comes out from the house and looks for the paper*). Where is it? I can see nothing.

Rosine. Under the balcony, at the foot of the wall.

Bartholo. It's a fine errand you sent me on. Did anyone go by?

Rosine. I have seen no one.

BARTHOLO (*aside*). And I was fool enough to search... Bartholo, you're a simpleton. This should teach you never to open blinds on the street. (*He re-enters the house.*)

ROSINE (*still on the balcony*). My excuse lies in my wretchedness. Alone, locked in, a butt for the persecution of a frightful man. Is it a crime to try to escape from slavery?

BARTHOLO (*appears on the balcony*). Go in, young lady. It is my fault if you have lost your song. But this misfortune will never happen again, I swear it. (*Locks the blinds.*)

SCENE 4. *The Count, Figaro.* (*They enter cautiously.*)

COUNT. Now that they're inside, let's look at this song. There is certainly a mystery hidden in it. It's a note!

FIGARO. He asked what *The Useless Precaution* was.

COUNT (*reads excitedly*). "Your devotion excites my curiosity. As soon as my guardian has left, sing carelessly to the familiar air of these couplets, a few words which will tell me the name, the rank, and the intentions of the one who seems so obstinately attached to the unfortunate Rosine."

FIGARO (*imitates* ROSINE'S *voice*). My song! My song dropped! Run, run. Ha, ha, ha! Oh! These women! If you want to teach cunning to the most innocent girl, just lock her up.

COUNT. Dear Rosine!

FIGARO. My lord, I don't need to look any farther for the motives of your masquerade. You are making love in perspective.

COUNT. Now you know. If you ever talk...

FIGARO. Me, talk? I won't use any high-sounding phrases of honor and devotion, which are always being abused, to reassure you. Just one word. My own interests will answer for me. Weigh everything in that balance, and...

COUNT. Very well. You should know that six months ago, by chance, in the Prado I met a young girl of such beauty ... You have just seen her. I searched for her everywhere in Madrid. Just a few days ago I discovered that her name is Rosine, that she is of noble blood, an orphan, and married to an old physician of this city, called Bartholo.

FIGARO. A pretty bird, but hard to get out of the nest! Who told you she is the doctor's wife?

COUNT. Everyone.

FIGARO. That's a story he made up when he came from

Madrid, in order to trick all suitors and get rid of them. She is only his ward, but soon . . .

Count (*ardently*). Never! What news! I was determined to dare everything to tell her my regrets, and now I learn she is free! There's not a moment to lose. I must make her love me and rescue her from the unworthy marriage they are planning. Do you know this guardian?

Figaro. As well as my mother.

Count. What sort of man is he?

Figaro (*excitedly*). He's a handsome, fat, short, young, old man, dapple gray, crafty, clean-shaven, blasé, peeping, prying, scolding, moaning, all at once.

Count (*impatiently*). I've seen him. What's his character?

Figaro. Brutal, miserly, passionate, and absurdly jealous of his ward who hates him with a terrible hate.

Count. So, his ability to please is . . .

Figaro. Zero.

Count. Good! What about his honesty?

Figaro. Just enough honesty not to be hanged.

Count. Still better. To punish a rascal while finding my happiness . . .

Figaro. Is to do a public and a private good. In truth, a masterpiece of morality, my lord!

Count. You say that fear of suitors makes him keep his door locked?

Figaro. Locked to everyone. If he could stop up the cracks . . .

Count. The devil! That's too bad. Do you have access to the house?

Figaro. Of course I do! The house where I live belongs to the doctor, and he lodges me there free.

Count. I see!

Figaro. And in gratitude, I promise him ten pistoles a year, also free.

Count (*impatient*). Are you his tenant?

Figaro. Much more. His barber, his surgeon, his apothecary. There is not a stroke of the razor, of the lancet, or of the syringe in his house which does not come from the hand of your servant.

Count (*embraces him*). Ah, Figaro, dear friend, you will be my liberator, my guardian angel.

Figaro. Well! My usefulness has shortened the distances between us. Talk to me of men with a passion!

COUNT. Lucky Figaro! You are going to see my Rosine. You will see her! Do you realize your good fortune?

FIGARO. That's the way a lover talks. I'm not in love with her. I wish you could take my place.

COUNT. If we could only get rid of all the guards!

FIGARO. That's what I was thinking of.

COUNT. Just for one day.

FIGARO. By inducing people to look out for their own interests, we'll keep them from interfering with the interests of others.

COUNT. That's right. So?

FIGARO (*reflects*). I am wondering whether the art of pharmacy will not furnish some innocent means . . .

COUNT. Scoundrel!

FIGARO. I don't intend to hurt them. They all need my cane. It's a question of how to treat them all at once.

COUNT. But this doctor may grow suspicious.

FIGARO. We'll have to work so fast that there will be no time for suspicion. I have an idea. The regiment of the heir apparent has just come to the city.

COUNT. The colonel is one of my friends.

FIGARO. Good. Go to the doctor's house in a soldier's uniform, with a billet. He will have to give you lodging. I will take care of the rest.

COUNT. Excellent!

FIGARO. It would be a good idea if you were a bit . . . tipsy . . .

COUNT. Why?

FIGARO. And treat him unceremoniously. A little intoxication would make you unreasonable . . .

COUNT. But why?

FIGARO. So that he will take no offense, and think you more in a hurry to go to bed than to carry on intrigues in his house.

COUNT. A superb plan! But why aren't you in it?

FIGARO. Me? We'll be lucky if he doesn't recognize you whom he has never seen. How could I introduce you afterward?

COUNT. You are right.

FIGARO. But perhaps you won't be able to act out that difficult part. A cavalier—drunk on wine . . .

COUNT. You underestimate me. (*Imitating the speech of a drunkard.*) Isn't this the house of Doctor Bartholo, my friend?

FIGARO. Not bad, really. You should be a little more unsteady on your legs. (*With a more drunken voice.*) Isn't this the house of . . . ?

COUNT. I'm surprised at you. That's the vulgar drunkenness of the people.

FIGARO. It's the best kind. It's the drunkenness of pleasure.

COUNT. The door is opening.

FIGARO. It's our man. Let's get out until he has gone.

SCENE 5. *The Count, Figaro (hidden), Bartholo.*

BARTHOLO (*comes out, as he speaks to someone in the house*). I am coming right back. Let no one in. What a fool I was to have come down! I should have suspected as soon as she asked me. Why doesn't Bazile come? He was to arrange everything for my secret marriage tomorrow. And there's no news. I must go and find out what has delayed him.

SCENE 6. *The Count, Figaro.*

COUNT. What did I hear? Tomorrow he marries Rosine in secret!

FIGARO. My lord, the difficulty of succeeding only adds to the necessity of undertaking.

COUNT. Who is this Bazile who is mixed up with the marriage?

FIGARO. A poor wretch who teaches music to Rosine, something of a rascal infatuated with his art, always in need, on his knees before a crown-piece, and very easy to manage, my lord . . . (*Looks at the blinds.*) There she is! There she is!

COUNT. Who?

FIGARO. Behind her blind. There she is! Don't look! Don't look!

COUNT. Why not?

FIGARO. Didn't she write: "Sing carelessly"? That means, sing as if you were singing . . . only for the sake of singing. Oh! There she is! There she is!

COUNT. Since I have begun to interest her without being known to her, I won't drop the name Lindor which I have assumed. My victory will have greater charm. (*He unfolds the paper which* ROSINE *threw down.*) But how can I sing to this music? I don't know how to write poetry.

FIGARO. Whatever comes into your mind, my lord, will be

excellent. In love, the heart is not demanding on the productions of the mind. Take my guitar.

Count. What can I do with it? I play so badly.

Figaro. A man like you is ignorant of nothing. With the back of the hand: tum, tum, tum ... To sing without a guitar in Seville! You would soon be recognized. You would soon be tracked down. (Figaro *stands close to the wall under the balcony.*)

Count (*sings as he walks back and forth, and accompanies himself on the guitar*).

> You order me to tell my name.
> Unknown, I loved you from afar,
> For with a name, I feared to mar
> My love and speak my lack of fame.

Figaro (*in a low voice*). Why, that's very good. Courage, my lord!

Count.

> I am Lindor, of common birth,
> A student and a youth inspired.
> If I could be a knight of worth,
> I'd offer you my rank admired.

Figaro. The devil! I couldn't do better myself! And I write verses!

Count.

> With tender song, each morning, here,
> I'll say my love so hopeless.
> My joy will be, which has no fear,
> To see you and to sing distress.

Figaro. On my word! Why, this last couplet ... (*Approaches his master and kisses the hem of his cloak.*)

Count. Figaro!

Figaro. Your Excellency!

Count. Do you think she heard me?

Rosine (*inside, singing*).

> All speaks to me of Lindor's grace,
> And I must love with constancy ...

(*A window is closed noisily.*)

Figaro. Now do you think she heard you?

Count. She closed her window. Someone must have come into the room.

Figaro. The poor little thing! She trembled as she sang. She is caught, my lord.

Count. She uses the means she herself pointed out. "All speaks to me of Lindor's charm." What grace! what wit!

Figaro. What cunning! What love!

Count. Do you think she'll be mine, Figaro?

Figaro. If need be, she'll come right through that blind.

Count. The die is cast. I am Rosine's forever.

Figaro. You forget, my lord, that she can't hear you.

Count. Master Figaro, I have but one word to say. She will be my wife. If you serve me by not revealing my name . . . you understand, you know me . . .

Figaro. I agree. Figaro, my son, you will be rich.

Count. Let us leave. We might create suspicion.

Figaro (*vigorously*). I am going into this house, where, by the means of my art, I will, with a single stroke of my wand, put vigilance to sleep, awaken love, banish jealousy, rout intrigue, and overturn all obstacles. You, my lord, go to my house for a soldier's uniform, the billet and gold for your pockets.

Count. Gold for whom?

Figaro (*impatiently*). Gold, my lord, gold is the sinews of intrigue.

Count. Don't be angry, Figaro. I'll take plenty.

Figaro (*leaves*). I'll join you shortly.

Count. Figaro!

Figaro. What is it?

Count. Your guitar!

Figaro (*returns*). I forgot my guitar! I am losing my mind. (*Leaves.*)

Count. And where is your house, my man?

Figaro. Ah! I really am losing control. My shop is a few steps away. It's painted blue, has leaden window frames, three paddles in the air, an eye in a hand, with the motto *consilio manuque*,[3] *Figaro*. (*Exit* Figaro.)

ACT II

The apartment of Rosine. The casement in the back of the stage is closed by a barred shutter.

SCENE 1. *Rosine (alone, a candle in her hand. She takes some paper from the table and sits down to write).*

ROSINE. Marcelline is ill, all the servants are busy, and no one can see me writing. I don't know whether these walls have eyes and ears, or whether my Argus has an evil genie who is always warning him, but I can't say a word or take a step that he doesn't instantly guess its purpose . . . Ah! Lindor! . . . (*She seals the letter.*) I will seal my letter although I don't know when or how I can send it to him. Through the blinds I saw him speak for a long time to the barber Figaro. That good fellow has at times shown some pity for me. I wish I could speak with him for a moment.

SCENE 2. *Rosine, Figaro.*

ROSINE (*surprised*). Ah! Master Figaro! How happy I am to see you!

FIGARO. How is your health, Madame?

ROSINE. Not very good, Master Figaro. I am dying of boredom.

FIGARO. I believe you. Only fools fatten on it.

ROSINE. With whom were you speaking so earnestly down there? I couldn't hear, but . . .

FIGARO. With a young bachelor, a relation of mine, a fellow of great promise and wit, of feeling and talent. And he is good looking.

ROSINE. He is indeed, I assure you! What is his name?

FIGARO. Lindor. He has nothing. But if he hadn't left Madrid in such hurry, he would have found a good position there.

ROSINE. He will find one, Master Figaro, he will find one. Such a young man as you describe cannot remain unknown.

FIGARO (*aside*). Very good. (*Aloud.*) But he has one great fault which will always block his advancement.

ROSINE. A fault, Monsieur Figaro! A fault! Are you quite sure?

FIGARO. He's in love.

ROSINE. He's in love? And you call that a fault?

FIGARO. In truth, it is only a fault in terms of his poor fortune.

ROSINE. Ah! how unfair fate is! Has he told you the name of the one he loves? I am curious . . .

FIGARO. You are the last, Madame, to whom I should confide this secret.

ROSINE (*impetuously*). Why, Master Figaro? I am discreet. This young man is a relative of yours. He interests me greatly . . . Tell me.

FIGARO (*looks at her slyly*). Imagine the prettiest little sweetheart, tender, gentle, and fresh as a rose, provoking a man's appetite with a dainty foot, a lithe slender figure, plump arms, a rosy mouth, and such hands! cheeks! teeth! eyes! . . .

ROSINE. Does she live in this city?

FIGARO. In this neighborhood.

ROSINE. On this street perhaps?

FIGARO. Two feet away from me.

ROSINE. Ah! How charming! . . . for your relative. And this person is?

FIGARO. Haven't I named her?

ROSINE (*excitedly*). That's the one thing you forgot, Master Figaro. Tell me quickly. If someone came in, I might never know . . .

FIGARO. You really wish to know, Madame? Well! this person is . . . the ward of your guardian.

ROSINE. The ward?

FIGARO. Of Doctor Bartholo. Yes, Madame.

ROSINE (*with emotion*). Ah! Master Figaro . . . I really don't believe you.

FIGARO. And that is what he is dying to convince you of himself.

ROSINE. You make me tremble, Master Figaro.

FIGARO. You mustn't say "tremble," Madame! When one yields to the fear of pain, one already suffers from fear. Besides, I have just rid you of all your guards until tomorrow.

ROSINE. If he loves me, he must prove it to me by remaining absolutely quiet.

FIGARO. Madame, can love and quiet dwell in the same heart? Poor young people are so unhappy today that they have only one terrible choice: love without quiet, or quiet without love.

ROSINE (*lowers her eyes*). Quiet without love . . . seems . . .

FIGARO. Very quiet indeed. It seems rather that love without quiet makes a better impression. Now, if I were a woman . . .

ROSINE (*embarrassed*). It is certain that a young lady cannot prevent a gentleman from esteeming her.

FIGARO. And my relative esteems you infinitely.

ROSINE. But if he committed any imprudence, Master Figaro, he would ruin us.

FIGARO (*aside*). He would ruin us! (*Aloud.*) If you forbade him expressly in a little note . . . A note is very powerful.

ROSINE (*gives him the letter she just wrote*). I don't have time to write this over, but when you give it to him, tell him . . . tell him . . . (*Listens.*)

FIGARO. There is no one, Madame.

ROSINE. That all I am doing is out of pure friendship.

FIGARO. That goes without saying. Love is something quite different.

ROSINE. Only out of pure friendship, you understand. All I fear is, that, discouraged by obstacles . . .

FIGARO. Yes, that he might be a will-o'-the-wisp. Remember, Madame, that the wind which blows out a light can kindle a brazier, and that we may be that brazier. Just in speaking of this, he breathes out such a flame that he has made me almost delirious with his passion—and I have nothing to do with it.

ROSINE. Good heavens! I hear my guardian. If he found you here . . . Go through the music room and down the stairs as softly as possible.

FIGARO. Rest assured. (*Aside.*) This is worth more than my observations.
(*Exit* FIGARO.)

SCENE 3. *Rosine.*

ROSINE. I won't be at peace until he's outside . . . How fond I am of Figaro! He's a good man, a good relative. Ah! Here is my tyrant. I must take up my work. (*She blows out the candle, sits down and takes up some embroidery.*)

SCENE 4. *Bartholo, Rosine.*

BARTHOLO (*angry*). Curses on that villain Figaro! He's a rascal and a pirate. I can't leave my house for one moment, and be sure that when I come home . . .

ROSINE. Who has made you so angry?

BARTHOLO. That damned barber who has just crippled my entire household in one stroke. He gave a drug to L'Eveillé, and a powder to La Jeunesse to make him sneeze. He bled Marcelline's foot. He even went to my mule and put a poultice over the eyes of that poor blind beast! Because he owes me a hundred crowns, he's in a hurry to balance his account. Let him bring it! And no one in the anteroom! You can enter this apartment as easily as the parade ground.

ROSINE. Who can get in here except you?

BARTHOLO. I prefer to be afraid with reason than to expose myself without precaution. There are enterprising, bold fellows everywhere . . . Didn't someone pick up your song this morning when I went down to get it? Oh! I . . .

ROSINE. Why do you attach importance to everything? The wind might have carried off that paper, or the first passer-by. How can one tell?

BARTHOLO. The wind, the first passer-by! . . . There is no wind, Madame, and no first passer-by here. There is always someone waiting there on purpose to pick up the papers of a woman who pretends to drop them by mistake.

ROSINE. Who pretends?

BARTHOLO. Yes, Madame, who pretends.

ROSINE (*aside*). Oh! that wicked old man!

BARTHOLO. But it will not happen again. I am going to have the blinds locked.

ROSINE. Don't stop with that! Wall up the windows. There is not much difference between a prison and a cell.

BARTHOLO. That isn't a bad idea for those that open on the street . . . Did that barber come here?

ROSINE. Does he also worry you?

BARTHOLO. As much as any other man.

ROSINE. How straightforward your answers are!

BARTHOLO. Trust everyone and you will soon have in your house a good wife to deceive you, good friends to spirit her off, and good servants to help them do it.

ROSINE. So you don't even grant that I might have principles against the seductions of Master Figaro?

BARTHOLO. Who the devil knows anything about the peculiarities of women? I have seen many lofty virtues . . .

ROSINE (*angry*). But if it is enough just to be a man to please us, why are you so repulsive to me?

BARTHOLO (*amazed*). Why? . . . why? . . . You did not answer my question about the barber.

ROSINE (*beside herself*). Well, yes! He did come into my room. I saw him and I talked to him. I won't conceal the fact that I found him very pleasant; and I hope this makes you die of vexation!

(*Exit* ROSINE.)

SCENE 5. *Bartholo.*

BARTHOLO. Those dogs of servants! La Jeunesse! L'Eveillé! The devil take them!

SCENE 6. *Bartholo, L'Eveillé.*

L'EVEILLÉ (*enters yawning, half asleep*). Aah, aah, ah, ah . . .

BARTHOLO. Where were you, you idiot, when the barber came into the house?

L'EVEILLÉ. Why, sir, I was . . . aah, aah . . .

BARTHOLO. You were planning some trick, I suppose. Didn't you see him?

L'EVEILLÉ. Certainly I saw him, because he found I was sick, that's what he said. It must be true because all my limbs began to pain just hearing him talk . . . Aah, aah . . .

BARTHOLO (*mimics him*). Just hearing him talk . . . Where is that good-for-nothing La Jeunesse? Giving a drug to that fellow without my prescription! There's some dirty business going on.

SCENE 7. *Bartholo, L'Eveillé, La Jeunesse* (*comes in like an old man. He uses a cane as a crutch. He sneezes several times*).

L'EVEILLÉ (*still yawning*). La Jeunesse?

BARTHOLO. You will sneeze on Sunday.

LA JEUNESSE. That makes more than fifty . . . fifty times in a minute. (*Sneezes.*) I am worn out.

BARTHOLO. I asked both of you whether anyone entered Rosine's room, and you didn't tell me that that barber . . .

L'EVEILLÉ (*continues yawning*). Is Master Figaro anyone? Aah, aah . . .

BARTHOLO. I bet the rogue has an understanding with her.

L'Éveillé (*crying like an idiot*). I have an understanding.

La Jeunesse (*sneezing*). But sir, is there ... is there no justice?

Bartholo. Justice! Justice for you, you knaves! I am your master, and I'm always right.

La Jeunesse (*sneezes*). But glory be, when a thing is right ...

Bartholo. When a thing is right! If I don't want it to be right, I will insist that it isn't right. If I allowed all you rogues to be right, you would soon see what would become of authority.

La Jeunesse (*sneezes*). I would rather you dismiss me. It's a terrible job, and there's a row all the time.

L'Éveillé (*cries*). A poor respectable man is treated like a wretch.

Bartholo. Out with you then, poor respectable man. (*Mimics them.*) T'chew! t'chew! One sneezes in my face and the other yawns in my face.

La Jeunesse. Sir, I swear that without Miss Rosine, we could not stay on here. (*Exits sneezing.*)

Bartholo. What a state Figaro has left them all in! I see what it is. The villain wants to pay me my hundred crowns without opening his purse.

Scene 8. *Bartholo, Don Bazile, Figaro.* (*Figaro, hidden in the cabinet, appears from time to time, and listens.*)

Bartholo (*continues*). Ah! Don Bazile, have you come to give Rosine her music lesson?

Bazile. That's the least reason for my haste.

Bartholo. I went to see you and did not find you at home.

Bazile. I was out on business for you. I'm afraid you are in for some very bad news.

Bartholo. Bad for you?

Bazile. No, for you. Count Almaviva is in this city.

Bartholo. Lower your voice. The man who had Rosine sought for throughout Madrid?

Bazile. He is living in a house on the square and appears every day in disguise.

Bartholo. There's no doubt. This does concern me. What can I do?

Bazile. If he were a private citizen, we could get him out of the way.

BARTHOLO. Yes, we could ambush him at night, with sword and buckler . . .

BAZILE. *Bone Deus!* You mean compromise ourselves! Better to start up a nasty affair, and when it is in full swing, slander him to the utmost.

BARTHOLO. That's a strange way to get rid of a man!

BAZILE. By slander? You don't realize what you are scorning. I have seen the best people nearly ruined by it. Believe me there is no vulgar form of evil, no horror, no absurd story that you can't instill in the leisure class of a big city if you go about it in the right way. And we have some very skillful fellows here! . . . First a slight rumor, that grazes the ground like a swallow before the storm. Pianissimo it murmurs and speeds along leaving after it a trail of poison. One person hears it, and piano, piano, slips it adroitly into your ear. The harm is done. It sprouts, begins to crawl, then walks faster, and rinforzando from mouth to mouth speeds along. Suddenly, and I don't know how, you see slander rise up, hissing, swelling, growing before your very eyes. It rushes forward, extends its flight, whirls, envelops, rips, bursts, and thunders, and becomes a general cry, a public crescendo, a universal chorus of hate and denunciation. Who the devil could oppose it?

BARTHOLO. What foolish story are you telling me, Bazile? What connection has this piano-crescendo with my situation?

BAZILE. What connection? What is done everywhere to get rid of one's enemy must be done here to keep yours from approaching.

BARTHOLO. From approaching? I intend to marry Rosine before she even learns this count exists.

BAZILE. In that case, you haven't a minute to lose.

BARTHOLO. How did this come about, Bazile? I entrusted all the details of this affair to you.

BAZILE. Yes, but you skimped on the expenses. In the harmony of our good order, an unequal marriage, a wicked judgment, an obvious injustice, are discords you always have to prepare for and overcome through the perfect harmony of gold.

BARTHOLO (*giving him money*). I see I will have to give in to you. But let's bring it to a close.

BAZILE. Now you're talking! Tomorrow it will all be over. It is your job to keep anyone from telling your ward today.

BARTHOLO. You can trust me. Are you coming this evening, Bazile?

BAZILE. Don't count on it. Your marriage alone will keep me busy all day. Don't count on it.

BARTHOLO (*accompanying him to the door*). Your servant.

BAZILE. Do stay here, Doctor.

BARTHOLO. No, no. I want to close the street door after you.

Scene 9. *Figaro.*

FIGARO (*coming from the cabinet*). A good precaution! You close the street door and I will open it again for the Count when I go out. That Bazile is a great rogue. Fortunately he is a greater fool than a rogue. One needs station, a family, a name, a rank, solidity in a word, to create a sensation in the world by means of slander. But Bazile! If he slandered, he wouldn't be believed.

Scene 10. *Rosine, Figaro.*

ROSINE. Are you still here, Master Figaro?

FIGARO. Luckily for you, Miss Rosine. Your guardian and your music teacher, thinking they were alone, have just spoken openly.

ROSINE. And you listened to them, Master Figaro? Do you know that is very wrong?

FIGARO. To listen? Well, it's the best way to hear. Your guardian is preparing to marry you tomorrow.

ROSINE. Great heavens!

FIGARO. Don't worry. We will give him so much to do that he won't have time to think of it.

ROSINE. He's coming back. Leave by the little staircase. You terrify me.   (*Exit* FIGARO.)

Scene 11. *Rosine, Bartholo.*

ROSINE. Were you here with someone?

BARTHOLO. Don Bazile, whom I took to the door, and with good reason. You would have preferred it to be Figaro?

ROSINE. It makes no difference to me, I assure you.

BARTHOLO. I would like to know what the barber was so impatient to tell you.

ROSINE. Must I really tell you? He gave me an account of Marcelline's condition, and he says she is not very well.

THE BARBER OF SEVILLE

BARTHOLO. He gave you an account, did he? I wager he was instructed to give you a letter.

ROSINE. And from whom, may I ask?

BARTHOLO. From whom? From someone women never name. How should I know? Perhaps the answer to the paper you dropped from the window.

ROSINE (*aside*). He hasn't missed a single detail. (*Aloud.*) It would serve you right if that were true.

BARTHOLO (*looks at* ROSINE'S *hands*). Now I see. You have been writing.

ROSINE (*embarrassed*). Do you intend to make me acknowledge this?

BARTHOLO (*taking her right hand*). Not at all. But your finger is stained with ink. How sly you are!

ROSINE (*aside*). This repulsive man.

BARTHOLO (*still holding her hand*). A woman thinks she is safe when she is alone.

ROSINE. No doubt. Is that a proof? Stop this, you are twisting my arm. I burned myself with the candle, and I was always told you should dip it immediately in ink. That is what I did.

BARTHOLO. So that is what you did? Let's see if a second witness will confirm the deposition of the first. There were six sheets, I know, in this notebook, because I count them every morning, as I did today.

ROSINE (*aside*). Oh! What a fool! The sixth . . .

BARTHOLO (*counts*). Three, four, five. There is no sixth.

ROSINE (*dropping her eyes*). The sixth I used to make a bag for bonbons I sent to Mistress Figaro.[4]

BARTHOLO. To Mistress Figaro? And how did the pen, which was new, become black? When you wrote the address of Mistress Figaro?

ROSINE (*aside*). This man has an instinct for jealousy. (*Aloud.*) I used it to trace a faded flower on the coat I am embroidering for you.

BARTHOLO. How edifying! If you wanted me to believe you, you shouldn't blush when you conceal the truth. But you haven't learned that yet.

ROSINE. Who wouldn't blush to see such wicked consequences drawn from the most innocent of things?

BARTHOLO. Of course, I am wrong. You burn your finger, dip it in the ink, make bags for bonbons, sketch a design for embroidering my coat. What is more innocent? . . . "I am alone, I am not seen, I can lie as much as I please." But the tip of your finger is black, the pen is soiled, the paper is missing. You couldn't think of everything. You can be sure, young lady, when I go to town, a good double lock will answer for you.

SCENE 12. *The Count, Bartholo, Rosine.*

COUNT (*in a cavalry uniform, pretending to be drunk, and singing: "Let's wake her," etc.*).
BARTHOLO. What does this man want? A soldier! Go into your room, Rosine.
COUNT (*sings*). Let's wake her! (*Moves toward* ROSINE.) Which of you ladies is Doctor Balordo? [5] (*Aside to* ROSINE.) I am Lindor.
BARTHOLO. Bartholo!
ROSINE (*aside*). He said Lindor.
COUNT. Balordo, Barque-à-l'eau, it's all the same to me. I have to know which of the two. (*To* ROSINE, *showing her a paper*.) Take this letter.
BARTHOLO. Which of the two! You can surely see it's I you want. Go to your room, Rosine, this man is drunk.
ROSINE. That's why I am staying. You are alone. Sometimes a woman can command respect.
BARTHOLO. Leave us, leave us. I am not afraid.

SCENE 13. *The Count, Bartholo.*

COUNT. I recognized you at once by your description.
BARTHOLO (*to the* COUNT, *who folds the letter*). What are you hiding in your pocket?
COUNT. I am hiding it in my pocket so you won't know what it is.
BARTHOLO. My description! These fellows think they are always speaking to soldiers.
COUNT. Do you think it is hard to describe you?

> With nodding brow and balding head,
> With bleary eyes and glance of dread,
> The fierceness of a savage chief . . .

BARTHOLO. What does all that mean? Are you here to insult me? Clear out now.

Count. Clear out? That's not a nice way to speak. Can you read, Doctor . . . Barbe-à-l'eau?

Bartholo. Another ridiculous question.

Count. It shouldn't upset you, because I am at least as much of a doctor as you are.

Bartholo. How is that?

Count. I am the horse doctor of the regiment. That is why they wanted to put me up with a colleague.

Bartholo. You dare compare me to a veterinarian?

Count.

> No, Doctor, I do not proclaim
> Our art exceeds and makes more claim
> Than that of great Hippocrates.
> Your learning and our colleagues'
> Succeed since they appease.
> And if they don't efface the sickness,
> At least they do efface the sick.

Aren't these words correct?

Bartholo. You ignorant schemer! It becomes you to degrade the first, the greatest, and the most useful of all the arts.

Count. Very useful for those who practice it.

Bartholo. An art whose success the sun is honored to illumine.

Count. And whose blunders the earth hastens to cover up.

Bartholo. I can see by your impudence that you are accustomed to speaking only to horses.

Count. Speaking to horses? Oh, Doctor! For a witty doctor to . . . Isn't it well known that the veterinarian always cures his patients without speaking to them, whereas the doctor speaks a great deal to his?

Bartholo. Without curing them, you say?

Count. *You* said it.

Bartholo. Who the devil sent me this mad drunkard?

Count. I think you are firing epigrams at me.

Bartholo. What do you want? What are you asking?

Count (*pretends anger. He flares up*). What I want? Don't you see?

Scene 14. *Rosine, the Count, Bartholo.*

Rosine. Master soldier, please don't be angry! (*To* Bartholo.) Speak to him gently. A man who is unreasonable . . .

Count. You are right. *He* is unreasonable, but *we* are reasonable. I am polite and you are pretty. That suffices. The truth is that I want to have dealings only with you in this house.

Rosine. How can I serve you?

Count. It's only a trifle. But if there is some obscurity in my words . . .

Rosine. I will understand their meaning.

Count (*shows her the letter*). No, confine yourself to the letter. It is merely a question—and I speak honorably—of giving me a bed tonight.

Bartholo. Only that?

Count. Nothing more. Read this note which our quartermaster has written you.

Bartholo. Let me see it. (*The* Count *hides the letter and gives him another paper.* Bartholo *reads.*) "Doctor Bartholo will receive, feed, lodge, bed . . ."

Count (*underscores*). Bed!

Bartholo. ". . . for one night only, one Lindor called the scholar, a trooper in the regiment."

Rosine. It's he! it's really he!

Bartholo (*quickly, to* Rosine). What's the matter?

Count. Well, am I wrong now, Doctor Bartholo?

Bartholo. One might say that this man takes a malicious pleasure in hurting me in every possible way. The devil with your Barbaro and Barbe-à-l'eau! Tell your impertinent quartermaster that since my trip to Madrid, I am exempt from lodging soldiers.

Count (*aside*). What a terrible trick of fate!

Bartholo. Ah! My friend, that sobers you up a bit. But I still want you to clear out.

Count (*aside*). I almost betrayed myself. (*Aloud.*) Clear out! If you are exempt from soldiers, you are not exempt from politeness. Clear out! Show me your exemption warrant. Although I can't read, I shall soon see . . .

Bartholo. That has nothing to do with it. It is in this desk.

Count (*when* Bartholo *moves, the* Count *says, without moving*). Ah, my beautiful Rosine!

Rosine. What, Lindor, is it really you?

Count. At least take this letter.

Rosine. Take care. His eyes are on us.

Count. Take out your handkerchief. I will drop the letter. (*He approaches* Rosine.)

THE BARBER OF SEVILLE

BARTHOLO. Gently there, my good soldier, I don't like a man looking at my wife so closely.

COUNT. Is she your wife?

BARTHOLO. What about it?

COUNT. I took you for her grandfather, paternal, maternal, eternal. There are at least three generations between her and you.

BARTHOLO (*reads a parchment*). "On the good and faithful considerations which have been given us . . ."

COUNT (*strikes the parchment which falls to the floor*). Do you think I need all that verbiage?

BARTHOLO. Do you know, soldier, that if I call my servants, I'll have you given the treatment you deserve?

COUNT. A fight? With all my heart! A fight! That's my profession. (*Shows the pistol in his belt.*) With this I'll throw powder in their eyes. You have perhaps never seen a fight, miss?

ROSINE. No, and I don't want to!

COUNT. But nothing is gayer than a fight. Imagine (*Pushing the doctor.*) first that the enemy is on one side of the ravine, and the friends on the other. (*To* ROSINE, *showing her the letter.*) Take out your handkerchief. (*He spits on the floor.*) There's the ravine, you understand. (ROSINE *takes out her handkerchief, the* COUNT *drops his letter between her and him.*)

BARTHOLO (*stooping*). Ha, ha!

COUNT (*picks up the letter*). Why! I was going to teach you all the secrets of my trade . . . Truly a very discreet lady! Didn't she drop this note from her pocket?

BARTHOLO. Give it to me.

COUNT. Softly, Papa! no meddling here. What if a rhubarb prescription had fallen from yours?

ROSINE (*extends her hand*). I know what it is, master soldier. (*She takes the letter which she conceals in the small pocket of her apron.*)

BARTHOLO. Are you going to leave?

COUNT. All right, I will go. Good-by, Doctor. No hard feelings. One small compliment, I beg. Ask death to forget me for a few more campaigns. Life has never been so dear to me.

BARTHOLO. Come now! If I had such good credit with death . . .

COUNT. With death! Ah! Doctor! You do so much for death, that she will refuse you nothing. (*Exit the* COUNT.)

Scene 15. *Bartholo, Rosine.*

Bartholo (*watches him leave*). He's gone at last. (*Aside.*) Now I must dissemble.

Rosine. You have to agree that this young soldier is a happy fellow. In spite of his drunkenness, you can see he has wit and some education.

Bartholo. I am glad, my love, that we were able to get rid of him. Aren't you a bit curious to read with me the paper he gave you?

Rosine. What paper?

Bartholo. The one he pretended to pick up to hand to you.

Rosine. Oh! that's the letter from my officer cousin, which had dropped out of my pocket.

Bartholo. I had the impression that he pulled it out of his own pocket.

Rosine. I recognized it easily.

Bartholo. What does it cost to look at it?

Rosine. I don't even know what I did with it.

Bartholo (*pointing to her pocket*). You put it there.

Rosine. Oh! yes! how absent-minded!

Bartholo. Yes! You are going to see that it is something foolish.

Rosine (*aside*). If I don't make him angry, there is no way to refuse him.

Bartholo. Give it to me, my dear.

Rosine. But why do you insist so much? Are you still distrustful?

Bartholo. But what reason can you have not to show it to me?

Rosine. I repeat that this paper is only my cousin's letter which you handed to me yesterday unsealed. And since we're on this subject, I want to say I intensely dislike such liberty.

Bartholo. I don't understand you.

Rosine. Do I examine the papers which come to you? If it is jealousy, I am insulted. If it is the abuse of a usurped power, I am still more disgusted.

Bartholo. What do you mean, disgusted? You have never spoken to me in this way.

Rosine. If I have been restrained until now, it was not to give you the right to insult me with impunity.

Bartholo. What insult are you referring to?

ROSINE. It is unheard of that a man open someone else's letters!

BARTHOLO. Letters to his wife?

ROSINE. I am not yet your wife. But why should she be the object of an indignity you would offer to no one else?

BARTHOLO. You are trying to trick me and divert my attention from the note, which is doubtless from some lover. But I assure you I will see it.

ROSINE. You will not see it. If you approach me, I will run out of this house and ask refuge of the first person I meet.

BARTHOLO. Who will not take you in.

ROSINE. That remains to be seen.

BARTHOLO. This is not France where women are always given their way. But to relieve you of all illusions, I am going to lock the door.

ROSINE (*as he goes to do this*). Heavens! What shall I do? I must exchange it for my cousin's letter, and give him the opportunity to find it. (*She makes the exchange and puts her cousin's letter into her pocket, so that it protrudes a bit.*)

BARTHOLO (*returns*). Now I expect to see it.

ROSINE. By what right, may I ask?

BARTHOLO. By the most universally recognized right, that of the stronger.

ROSINE. You will have to kill me before you get it from me.

BARTHOLO (*stamping*). I say, give it to me.

ROSINE (*falls into an armchair and pretends to be ill*). Oh! What an outrage! . . .

BARTHOLO. Give me that letter or you will feel my anger.

ROSINE (*falls back*). How unhappy I am!

BARTHOLO. What is the matter with you?

ROSINE. What a terrible future!

BARTHOLO. Rosine!

ROSINE. I am choking with anger.

BARTHOLO. She is sick.

ROSINE. I am growing weak. I am dying.

BARTHOLO (*aside*). Now, the letter! I can read it and she won't know. (*He feels her pulse and takes the letter which he tries to read by turning slightly aside.*)

ROSINE (*still reclining*). How unhappy! . . .

BARTHOLO (*drops her arm and says aside*). How mad we are to learn what we are always afraid of knowing!

ROSINE. Poor Rosine!

BARTHOLO. The use of perfumes . . . produces these spasmodic states. (*He reads behind the armchair as he feels her pulse. Rosine begins to rise, looks at him slyly, nods, and falls back without speaking.*)

BARTHOLO (*aside*). My God! It *is* her cousin's letter. This mad anxiety of mine! How can I make amends now! At least she mustn't know I read it. (*He pretends to raise her up and puts the letter back in her pocket.*)

ROSINE (*sighs*). Ah! . . .

BARTHOLO. Well, it's all over, my child. Just a little attack of the vapors, that's all. Your pulse did not change. (*He takes a flask from the table.*)

ROSINE (*aside*). He put back the letter. Fine!

BARTHOLO. Dear Rosine, take a little of these spirits.

ROSINE. I don't want anything from you. Leave me alone.

BARTHOLO. I agree I was too insistent about that letter.

ROSINE. It wasn't just the letter. It's your way of asking for things that is disgusting.

BARTHOLO (*on his knees*). Pardon me. I soon felt how wrong I was. Now I am at your feet, ready to make reparation.

ROSINE. Pardon, indeed! When you believe that this letter does not come from my cousin.

BARTHOLO. Whether it comes from him or from someone else, I want no explanation.

ROSINE (*giving him the letter*). Don't you see, when you behave, I will do anything. Read it.

BARTHOLO. This open gesture would remove my suspicions, if I was wicked enough to have any.

ROSINE. You may read it.

BARTHOLO (*draws back*). God forbid that I should insult you in that way!

ROSINE. I will be displeased if you refuse.

BARTHOLO. Receive as reparation this mark of my absolute confidence. I am going to see poor Marcelline whom Figaro, for some reason or other, bled in the foot. Why don't you come too?

ROSINE. I will go up in a moment.

BARTHOLO. Since we have made peace, my darling, give me your hand. If you could love me, how happy you would be!

ROSINE (*lowering her eyes*). If you could please me, how I should love you!

BARTHOLO. I will please you, I will please you! And when I say that, I will please you! . . . (*Exit* BARTHOLO.)

Scene 16. *Rosine.*

ROSINE (*watches him leave*). Ah! Lindor! He says he will please me. I must read this letter which almost caused me great sorrow. (*She reads and cries out.*) Oh! . . . I am too late. He urges me to keep quarreling with my guardian. I had a good chance and now I have lost it. When I received that letter, I felt I was blushing all over. My guardian is right. I don't yet have those social graces which he says assure the manners of women on every occasion. But an unjust man would succeed in making an intriguer out of innocence itself.

ACT III

SCENE 1. *Bartholo (alone and despairing).*

BARTHOLO. How changeable she is! She seemed calmed down. I'd like to know who put it into her head not to take any more lessons from Don Bazile. She knows that he has something to do with my marriage. (*A knock at the door.*) Try your best to please a woman, and if you forget one single point . . . only one . . . (*Another knock.*) I must see who it is.

SCENE 2. *Bartholo, the Count (as a student).*

COUNT. May peace and joy always dwell in this house!
BARTHOLO (*curtly*). Never was a wish more appropriate! What can I do for you?
COUNT. Sir, I am Alonzo, bachelor and licentiate of arts . . .
BARTHOLO. I don't need a tutor.
COUNT. . . . pupil of Don Bazile, organist in the great convent, who has the honor of teaching music to your . . .
BARTHOLO. Bazile! Organist! Who has the honor . . . Yes, indeed, I know.
COUNT (*aside*). What a man! (*Aloud.*) A sudden illness forces him to stay in bed . . .
BARTHOLO. Stay in bed! Bazile! He was wise to send me word. I will go to see him right away.
COUNT (*aside*). The devil! (*Aloud.*) When I say in bed, sir, I mean in his room.
BARTHOLO. Even if it were a trifling illness . . . You lead the way, I will follow.
COUNT (*embarrassed*). Sir, I was told to . . . Can anyone hear us?
BARTHOLO (*aside*). He must be some rogue. (*Aloud.*) No, mysterious sir. Speak without fear, if you can.
COUNT (*aside*). Confound him! (*Aloud.*) Don Bazile asked me to tell you . . .
BARTHOLO. Speak louder. I am deaf in one ear.
COUNT (*raising his voice*). Of course! That Count Almaviva who lives in a house on the main square . . .
BARTHOLO. Not so loud. Speak lower, please.
COUNT (*louder*). . . . moved out this morning. As it was through me that he knew Count Almaviva . . .

BARTHOLO. Lower, please speak lower.

COUNT (*still loud*). . . . was in this city, and that I had discovered that Miss Rosine had written to him . . .

BARTHOLO. Written to him? My dear friend, let's sit down and have a chat. You say you discovered that Rosine . . .

COUNT (*proudly*). Yes, indeed. Bazile, anxious on your account because of this correspondence, had begged me to show you his letter. But the way in which you take things . . .

BARTHOLO. Why, I take them quite well. But can't you speak in a lower voice?

COUNT. You are deaf in one ear, you say.

BARTHOLO. I am sorry, Master Alonzo, that you found me distrustful and harsh. I am completely surrounded by intriguers and plots. And then, your appearance, your age, your bearing . . . I am truly sorry. Do you have the letter?

COUNT. I am glad you are taking it this way, sir. But I fear someone may be eavesdropping.

BARTHOLO. No, there is no one. All my servants are sick. Rosine is mad and shut up in her room. The devil has entered my house. But I will go to make sure . . . (*He opens* ROSINE's *door softly.*)

COUNT (*aside*). I am in trouble through haste . . . Shall I keep the letter for the moment? I should get out of here. I shouldn't have come . . . Shall I show it to him? Showing it is a master stroke if I can warn Rosine.

BARTHOLO (*returns on tiptoe*). She is seated near her window, with her back to the door, and is reading a letter from her officer cousin which I had unsealed . . . Let me see hers.

COUNT (*gives him* ROSINE's *letter*). Here it is. (*Aside.*) It is my letter she is reading.

BARTHOLO (*reads*). "Since you told me your name and rank." Oh! the wretch! It is her handwriting.

COUNT (*terrified*). It is your turn to speak lower.

BARTHOLO. How much I owe you, dear fellow!

COUNT. When all is over, and you think you owe me something, then you can reward me . . . Don Bazile is now with a lawyer . . .

BARTHOLO. With a lawyer, for my marriage?

COUNT. Of course. He asked me to tell you everything will be ready for tomorrow. Then, if she resists . . .

BARTHOLO. She will resist.

COUNT (*tries to take back the letter, but Bartholo keeps it*). That's the moment when I can serve you. We will show her

her letter, and if necessary (*More mysteriously.*) I will go as far as telling her I have it from a woman to whom the Count gave it. You will see that worry, shame, and anger will drive her immediately . . .

BARTHOLO (*laughs*). Slander! Now I see you really come from Don Bazile. But so this won't seem like a plot, wouldn't it be well for her to know you beforehand?

COUNT (*represses joy*). That was the opinion of Don Bazile. But how can this be done? It is late . . . in the little time that remains . . .

BARTHOLO. I will say you have come in his place. Won't you give her a lesson?

COUNT. There is nothing I wouldn't do to please you. But all those stories of alleged masters are old tricks used in comedies. If she suspects . . .

BARTHOLO. Introduced by me, there will be nothing wrong. You look more like a disguised lover than an obliging friend.

COUNT. Do I? Do you really think my appearance can help in the deceit?

BARTHOLO. No one could really guess the truth. She is in a terrible mood tonight. But if she would only see you . . . Her harpsichord is in this cabinet. Amuse yourself while you wait. I shall do all I can to bring her to you.

COUNT. Take care not to speak of the letter!

BARTHOLO. Before the decisive moment? That would destroy all its effect. You don't need to tell me things twice.

(*Exit* BARTHOLO.)

SCENE 3. *The Count.*

COUNT. Saved! Phew! That man is a devil to handle! Figaro knows him well. I saw myself lying. It made me look awkward and stupid. And he has eyes! Without that sudden inspiration of the letter, I would have fumbled like a fool. They are quarreling in that room. What if she refuses to come! I must listen . . . She refuses to come out of her room, and I have lost the advantage of my trick. (*He listens again.*) She's coming! I shouldn't appear right away. (*He enters the cabinet.*)

SCENE 4. *The Count, Rosine, Bartholo.*

ROSINE (*pretends anger*). Your words will have no effect on me. I've made up my mind. I will hear nothing more about music.

THE BARBER OF SEVILLE

BARTHOLO. Listen, my child. This is Master Alonzo, pupil and friend of Don Bazile, chosen by him to be one of our witnesses. I assure you, music will quiet you down.

ROSINE. You can give up that idea right now. You think I will sing this evening? Where is that teacher you are afraid to dismiss? In two sentences I can tell him what to do and Don Bazile also. (*She sees her lover and utters a cry.*) Ah! . . .

BARTHOLO. What is the matter?

ROSINE (*in great agitation*). Oh! Doctor Bartholo! Oh! Doctor Bartholo!

BARTHOLO. She is sick again, Master Alonzo.

ROSINE. No, I am not sick . . . but as I turned around . . . Ah!

COUNT. Did you turn your ankle, my lady?

ROSINE. Yes! I turned my ankle. I am in terrible pain.

COUNT. I could see that.

ROSINE (*looks at the* COUNT). It seemed to affect my heart.

BARTHOLO. A chair, a chair. Isn't there an armchair here? (*Goes to get one.*)

COUNT. Ah! Rosine!

ROSINE. How imprudent you are!

COUNT. I have a thousand things to tell you.

ROSINE. He won't leave us.

COUNT. Figaro will help us.

BARTHOLO (*brings an armchair*). Here, my sweet, sit down. There is not a chance, master bachelor, that she will take a lesson tonight. It will be for some other day. Good-by.

ROSINE (*to the* COUNT). No, wait. My pain is lessening. (*To* BARTHOLO.) I see that I was wrong, sir. I will follow your example by repairing immediately . . .

BARTHOLO. Ah! the sweet disposition of a woman! But after such pain, my child, I will not allow you to make the slightest effort. Good-by, good-by, master bachelor.

ROSINE (*to the* COUNT). One moment, please! (*To* BARTHOLO.) I will think that you do not like to oblige me if you keep me from showing my regret by taking my lesson.

COUNT (*aside, to* BARTHOLO). If you follow my advice, you will not oppose her.

BARTHOLO. I give in, my love. I am so far from wanting to displease you, that I want to stay here while you take your lesson.

ROSINE. No, no, I am aware that music does not interest you.

BARTHOLO. I assure you that tonight it will give me pleasure.

ROSINE (*to the* COUNT, *aside*). He torments me.

COUNT (*takes a sheet of music from the stand*). Is this what you want to sing?

ROSINE. Yes, it is a very pretty piece from *The Useless Precaution.*

BARTHOLO. *The Useless Precaution* again!

COUNT. It's the latest thing in music. It's a very lively picture of spring. If you wish to try it . . .

ROSINE (*looks at the* COUNT). With pleasure. I love a picture of spring. It is the youth of nature. At the end of winter, it seems that the heart reaches a high degree of sensibility. As a slave who has been confined for a long time enjoys the charm of liberty which has just been offered to him.

BARTHOLO (*in a low voice, to the* COUNT). Her head is always full of romantic ideas.

COUNT (*in a low voice*). Do you see the point of her words?

BARTHOLO. I do indeed. (*He sits in the armchair* ROSINE *has been occupying.*)

ROSINE (*sings*).

> When love brings back
> The spring to fields,
> New life returns
> To flowers, and seals
> The hearts of maids and youth.
> The sight of flocks
> On hillsides soothes
> The passerby
> Who hears the bleat
> Of lambs and sees
> The grazing ewes,
> The faithful dogs,
> The running feet
> Of joyous children everywhere.
> Then too in spring,
> Lindor dreams of love
> And of his shepherdess so fair.
>
> Far from her house
> She goes to meet
> Her love and listen
> To the sweet

THE BARBER OF SEVILLE

Music of pipes,
The song of larks.
She feels the beating
Of her heart
But feigns some anger
When from out
His hiding place
Runs forth Lindor
To kiss away
His lover's pout
And promise her
To love and to adore.

He speaks of sighs
And promises.
By badinage
And tenderness
He coaxes back
The shepherdess
To more loving sentiments.
Most lovers try
To feign offense
And veil their passion
With other names,
But this adds pleasure
To their games.

(*As he listens,* BARTHOLO *falls asleep. During the last stanza, the* COUNT *takes* ROSINE'S *hand and covers it with kisses. In her emotion,* ROSINE'S *singing slows down and grows fainter. Her voice stops in the middle of a cadenza. The orchestra follows the movement of the singer, slows down with her, and stops. The absence of the sound which put* BARTHOLO *to sleep awakes him. The* COUNT *gets up,* ROSINE *and the orchestra continue the song.*)

COUNT. This is truly a charming piece, and you sing it with such understanding . . .

ROSINE. You flatter me, sir. Praise belongs to the teacher.

BARTHOLO (*yawns*). I think I must have slept a bit during the charming piece. I have so many patients. I come and go, and that makes me dizzy. As soon as I sit down, my poor legs . . . (*He rises and pushes back the armchair.*)

ROSINE (*low voice, to the* COUNT). Figaro has not come.

COUNT. We must kill time.

BARTHOLO. Master bachelor, I have already asked old Bazile if there isn't a way to have her study gayer music than those big arias which go up and down, rolling with hi, ho, a, a, a, and which seem to me like funerals. What about those little songs they used to sing when I was young? They were easy to remember. I used to know some of them . . . This one, for example . . . (*He scratches his head and sings, snapping his fingers and dancing with his knees in the manner of old men.*)

> Will you, dear Rosinette,
> Just spread your net
> Over the best of catches?

(*To the* COUNT, *laughing.*) The name Fanchonnette is in the song, but I substituted Rosinette to make it more appealing to her and to fit the circumstances. Pretty good, eh?

COUNT (*laughs*). Ha, ha, ha! Yes, indeed.

SCENE 5. *Figaro* (*in background*), *Rosine, Bartholo, the Count.*

BARTHOLO (*sings*).

> Will you, dear Rosinette,
> Just spread your net
> Over the best of catches?
>
> I'm not the handsomest,
> But in the dark I'm worth my fee,
> And there's no need to see.

(*He repeats the refrain, dancing.* FIGARO, *behind him, imitates his movements.*)

> I'm not the handsomest, etc.

(*Sees* FIGARO.) Come in, master barber! Come in, you are charming!

FIGARO (*bows*). Sir, it is true that my mother used to tell me so. But since then, I am somewhat deformed. (*Aside, to the* COUNT.) Bravo, my lord! (*During this scene, the* COUNT *does what he can to speak to* ROSINE, *but the restless, vigilant eyes of the guardian prevent him. The result is a pantomime between* ROSINE *and the* COUNT, *while the discussion between the doctor and* FIGARO *continues.*)

BARTHOLO. Have you come again to purge, bleed, drug, and prostrate all my household?

FIGARO. Every day is not a feast day, sir. But without counting my daily attentions, you have seen that when needed, my zeal does not wait for orders.

BARTHOLO. Your zeal doesn't wait! What can you say, zealot, to that wretch who yawns and sleeps when awake? And the other fellow who for three hours has been sneezing enough to split his cranium and blow out his brains? What can you say to them?

FIGARO. What can I say to them?

BARTHOLO. Yes!

FIGARO. I will say to them . . . why I will say to the one who is sneezing, "God bless you," and "Go to bed" to the one who yawns. That is nothing, sir, that will increase the bill.

BARTHOLO. In truth, no. It is bleedings and medicines that would increase it, if I would stand it. Is it due to your zeal also that you bandaged the eyes of my mule, and will your bandage give it back its sight?

FIGARO. If it doesn't give it back its sight, it won't prevent it from seeing.

BARTHOLO. Wait until I find it on the bill . . . I don't approve of such extravagance.

FIGARO. Why, sir, there is little to choose between stupidity and madness; where I see no profit, I wish at least to find some pleasure. Long live joy! Who knows whether the world will last three weeks longer?

BARTHOLO. You would do better, master reasoner, to pay me my hundred crowns and interest, without any nonsense, I warn you.

FIGARO. Do you doubt my honesty, sir? Your hundred crowns! I would rather owe them to you for the rest of my life than deny them to you for a single instant.

BARTHOLO. Tell me how Mistress Figaro liked the bonbons you took her.

FIGARO. What bonbons? What do you mean?

BARTHOLO. Yes, those bonbons in the bag which was made out of a sheet of this paper this morning.

FIGARO. The devil take me if . . .

Rosine (*interrupting him*). At least did you take the trouble to give them to her from me, Master Figaro? I had asked you to.

Figaro. Oh! Yes! This morning's bonbons! How stupid of me! I had forgotten about them. They were excellent, Miss Rosine! Admirable!

Bartholo. Excellent! Admirable! Yes, of course! Master barber, retrace your steps. It is quite a business you have.

Figaro. What do you mean, sir?

Bartholo. And which will give you a fine reputation.

Figaro. I will live up to it, sir.

Bartholo. Say that you will live it down.

Figaro. As you please, sir.

Bartholo. You are rather cocky, Figaro. You should know that when I dispute with a fool, I never yield to him.

Figaro (*turns his back on him*). We differ in that, sir, for I always yield to him.

Bartholo. What is he trying to say, master bachelor?

Figaro. You think you are dealing with some village barber, who only knows how to use the razor. You should know, sir, that I have worked with the pen in Madrid, and if it were not for the envious . . .

Bartholo. Why didn't you stay there, instead of coming here and changing your profession?

Figaro. We do what we can. Put yourself in my place.

Bartholo. Put myself in your place! I would say some fine stupidities.

Figaro. Sir, this is not a bad beginning for you. I appeal to your colleague who is dreaming over there . . .

Count. I am not his colleague.

Figaro. No? Seeing you here in consultation, I thought you were pursuing the same objective.

Bartholo (*angry*). Well, what reason brings you here? Is it to bring Miss Rosine another letter this evening? Tell me, should I withdraw?

Figaro. How harshly you treat everyone. Sir, I've come to shave you, that's all. Isn't this your day?

Bartholo. Come back later.

Figaro. Come back! The whole garrison is taking medicine tomorrow morning. I obtained the contract through friends. You can see how little time I have to lose. Will you go into your room, sir?

BARTHOLO. No, I will not go into my room. But what stops you from shaving me here?

ROSINE (*contemptuously*). How polite you are! And why not in my room?

BARTHOLO. You're angry. Excuse me, my child. You take your lesson. It is in order not to lose for a moment the pleasure of hearing you.

FIGARO (*in a low voice, to the* COUNT). We won't get him out of here. Come, L'Eveillé, La Jeunesse, the basin, the water, everything the master needs.

BARTHOLO. Of course, call them! Fatigued, harassed, mistreated by you, didn't they have to go to bed?

FIGARO. Well, I will get everything we need in your room. (*In a low voice, to the* COUNT.) I am going to try to get him outside.

BARTHOLO (*unfastens his bunch of keys, and says reflectively*). No, no, I'll go myself. (*Low voice, to the* COUNT.) Please keep your eyes on them.

SCENE 6. *Figaro, the Count, Rosine.*

FIGARO. We just missed our opportunity! He was going to give me the keys. Isn't the key of the blinds among them?

ROSINE. Yes, it's the newest.

SCENE 7. *Figaro, the Count, Rosine, Bartholo (returning).*

BARTHOLO (*aside*). I don't know why I have this damned barber here. (*To* FIGARO.) Here. (*Gives him the keys.*) In my cabinet, under my desk. But don't touch anything else.

FIGARO. The plague! It would serve you right, with your suspicious nature. (*Aside, as he leaves.*) See how heaven protects innocence.

SCENE 8. *Bartholo, the Count, Rosine.*

BARTHOLO (*in a low voice, to the* COUNT). He is the fellow who took the letter to the Count.

COUNT (*in a low voice*). He looks to me like a rascal.

BARTHOLO. He won't catch me again.

COUNT. As far as that goes, I think the worst is over.

BARTHOLO. Everything considered, I thought it was more

prudent to send him into my room than to leave him with her.

Count. They would not have said one word without my being a third party to it.

Rosine. It is very polite, gentlemen, to whisper all the time. What about my lesson? (*A noise is heard, as of dishes upset.*)

Bartholo (*shouting*). What do I hear? That barber must have dropped everything down the stairs, and the finest pieces in my dressing case! (*Runs out.*)

Scene 9. *The Count, Rosine.*

Count. Let's profit from this moment which the intelligence of Figaro secured for us. Grant me this evening, I beg of you, a moment of conversation. I want to save you from the slavery into which you are falling.

Rosine. Ah! Lindor!

Count. I can climb up to your window. As for the letter I received from you this morning, I find myself forced . . .

Scene 10. *Rosine, Bartholo, Figaro, the Count.*

Bartholo. I was not mistaken. Everything is broken and smashed.

Figaro. It is a great calamity for so much noise. It is impossible to see on the stairs. (*He shows the key to the* Count.) As I was going up, I stumbled on a key . . .

Bartholo. You should be more careful. Stumbling over a key! What a clever man!

Figaro. Sir, try to find a cleverer one.

Scene 11. *The preceding, Don Bazile.*

Rosine (*aside, terrified*). Don Bazile!

Count (*aside*). Good heavens!

Figaro (*aside*). It's the devil!

Bartholo (*going to greet him*). Ah! Bazile, my friend, you are feeling better! Did your accident have any bad consequences? Truly, Master Alonzo had frightened me about your condition. You can ask him—I was leaving in order to see you. If he hadn't held me back . . .

Bazile (*surprised*). Master Alonzo?

Figaro (*stamps his foot*). Is this another delay? Two hours for one miserable beard . . . What a loathsome profession!

BAZILE (*looking at everyone*). Gentlemen, will you please tell me . . . ?

FIGARO. You can speak to him when I'm gone.

BAZILE. But I insist that I . . .

COUNT. You will have to be silent, Bazile. Do you think you can teach him something he doesn't know? I told him that you had asked me to give a music lesson in your place.

BAZILE (*more amazed*). A music lesson! . . . Alonzo! . . .

ROSINE (*aside to* BAZILE). Please be still.

BAZILE. She too!

COUNT (*in a low voice, to* BARTHOLO). Whisper to him that we are in agreement.

BARTHOLO (*aside to* BAZILE). Don't give us the lie, Bazile, by saying he is not your pupil. You would spoil everything.

BAZILE. Ha, ha!

BARTHOLO (*aloud*). It is a fact, Bazile, your pupil is very talented.

BAZILE (*astonished*). My pupil! (*Low voice.*) I came to tell you that the Count has moved away.

BARTHOLO (*quietly*). I know. Be quiet.

BAZILE (*quietly*). Who told you?

BARTHOLO (*quietly*). He, of course!

COUNT (*quietly*). I did. If you would only listen.

ROSINE (*aside, to* BAZILE). Is it that difficult to be quiet?

FIGARO (*aside, to* BAZILE). Hum! You big hippogriff! He is deaf!

BAZILE (*aside*). Who is being fooled around here? Everyone is in the secret.

BARTHOLO (*aloud*). Well, Bazile, your lawyer? . . .

FIGARO. You have the whole evening to talk about the lawyer.

BARTHOLO (*to* BAZILE). Just one word. Tell me if you are satisfied with the lawyer.

BAZILE (*terrified*). With the lawyer?

COUNT (*smiles*). Didn't you see the lawyer?

BAZILE (*impatient*). No, I did not see the lawyer.

COUNT (*aside, to* BARTHOLO). You don't want him to explain before her, do you? Send him off.

BARTHOLO (*low, to the* COUNT). You are right. (*To* BAZILE.) But what made you ill so suddenly?

BAZILE (*angry*). I don't understand you.

COUNT (*aside, puts a purse into his hand*). Yes, the doctor asks why you came here in your present state of illness.

FIGARO. He is as pale as death.

BAZILE. Ah! I understand . . .

COUNT. Go to bed, my dear Bazile. You are not well, and you have given us a terrible fright. Go to bed!

FIGARO. He looks upset. Go to bed.

BARTHOLO. Upon my word, you could tell a league away that he has fever. Go to bed.

ROSINE. Why did you come out? They say it is contagious. Go to bed.

BAZILE (*completely astonished*). I, go to bed?

ALL. Go to bed!

BAZILE (*looking at them all*). Well, gentlemen, I think it would be wise for me to withdraw. I feel that here I am not quite myself.

BARTHOLO. We will see you tomorrow if you are better.

COUNT. Bazile, I will be at your house very early.

FIGARO. Follow my advice. Keep yourself warm in your bed.

ROSINE. Good night, Master Bazile.

BAZILE (*aside*). The devil take me if I can understand anything here. If it were not for this purse . . .

ALL. Good night, Master Bazile!

BAZILE (*going*). Good night, then, good night! (*They accompany him, with laughter.*)

SCENE 12. *The preceding, except Bazile.*

BARTHOLO (*pompously*). That man is not at all well.

ROSINE. His eyes look wild.

COUNT. I think he caught a chill.

FIGARO. Did you see how he talked to himself? The same thing could happen to us. (*To* BARTHOLO.) Are you going to decide this time? (*He pushes an armchair some distance from the count and hands him the linen.*)

COUNT. Before we finish, I must tell you one thing very essential to the progress of the art I have the honor of teaching you. (*He approaches and whispers in her ear.*)

BARTHOLO (*to* FIGARO). Say, it might seem that you're standing in front of me on purpose to keep me from seeing . . .

COUNT (*in a low voice to* ROSINE). We have the key to the window and we'll be here at midnight.

FIGARO (*puts the towel around* BARTHOLO's *neck*). See what? If it were a dancing lesson we would let you look at it. But a singing lesson! Ahi! Ahi!

BARTHOLO. What is the matter?

FIGARO. Something has gotten into my eye. (*He brings his head nearer.*)

BARTHOLO. Don't rub it.

FIGARO. It's the left eye. Would you try to breathe a little harder for me? (BARTHOLO *takes* FIGARO's *head, looks over it, pushes him away violently, and goes behind the lovers to listen to their conversation.*)

COUNT (*in a low voice, to* ROSINE). And as for your letter, I soon found it so hard to stay here . . .

FIGARO (*at a distance, warning them*). Hem! . . . Hem!

BARTHOLO (*slips between them*). Your disguise useless!

BARTHOLO (*slips between them*). Your disguise useless!

ROSINE (*terrified*). Oh!

BARTHOLO. You don't need to be dismayed! Why, under my very eyes, in my presence, you dare to insult me in this way!

COUNT. What is the matter, sir?

BARTHOLO. Perfidious Alonzo!

COUNT. Master Bartholo, if you often have whims like that of which chance has made me a witness, I am not surprised at the disgust which the young lady feels at the prospect of becoming your wife.

ROSINE. His wife? Me? Spend my days with an old jealous husband who in place of happiness, offers my youth an abominable slavery!

BARTHOLO. Ah! What are you saying?

ROSINE. Yes, I will say it in public. I will give my heart and my hand to the one who will rescue me from this horrible prison, where my person and my fortune are held in defiance of all laws.

(*Exit* ROSINE.)

SCENE 13. *Bartholo, Figaro, the Count.*

BARTHOLO. I am choking with anger.

COUNT. But, sir, it is difficult for a young woman . . .

FIGARO. Yes, a young woman and old age. That is what disturbs the minds of old men.

BARTHOLO. What! When I have caught them in the act! Infernal barber! I have a mind to . . .

FIGARO. I am leaving. He is mad.

COUNT. And I too. Upon my word, he is mad.

FIGARO. He is mad, he is mad. (*They both leave.*)

Scene 14. *Bartholo (alone, runs after them).*

BARTHOLO. I am mad! Infamous bribers! Emissaries of the devil whose work you are doing here. May he carry you all off! I am mad! ... I saw them as clearly as I see this music stand ... and they brazened it out before me! Only Bazile can explain this to me. Yes, I must send for him. Holloa, somebody! Oh! I forgot. No one is here ... A neighbor, the first comer, no matter who. This is enough to make me lose my mind.

(During the entr'acte, the stage is darkened. The noise of a storm is heard.)

ACT IV

The stage is dark.

SCENE 1. *Bartholo; Don Bazile, a paper lantern in his hand.*

BARTHOLO. What, Bazile, you don't even know him? Is what you say possible?

BAZILE. If you asked me a hundred times, I'd give you the same answer. If he gave you Rosine's letter, he is doubtless one of the Count's emissaries. But from the generosity of the present he made me, he could easily be the Count himself.

BARTHOLO. Speaking of that present, why did you take it?

BAZILE. You two seemed to be in agreement. I understand nothing, and in all cases that are hard to judge, a purse of gold always seems to me an argument not to be opposed. And then, as the proverb says, what is good to take . . .

BARTHOLO. I know, is good . . .

BAZILE. To keep.

BARTHOLO (*surprised*). Ha! ha!

BAZILE. Yes, I have arranged in that form several little proverbs with variations. But let us come to the point. What are your plans?

BARTHOLO. In my place, Bazile, wouldn't you make a great effort to keep her in your power?

BAZILE. No, Doctor, I wouldn't. In every kind of property, possession amounts to very little. It is the enjoyment which makes one happy. My opinion is that marrying a woman who does not love you, is exposing yourself . . .

BARTHOLO. You'd be afraid of accidents?

BAZILE. Ha, ha, sir! There have been a great many this year. I would not do violence to her heart.

BARTHOLO. I am your servant, Bazile. It is better for her to weep at having me, than for me to die at not having her.

BAZILE. So, it is life or death! Marry her, Doctor, marry her.

BARTHOLO. I will, and this very night.

BAZILE. Good-by, then. Remember, when you speak to your ward, to paint them all blacker than hell.

BARTHOLO. You are right.

BAZILE. Slander, Doctor, slander. We must always use it.

BARTHOLO. Here is Rosine's letter which Alonzo gave me,

and he showed me, unwittingly, the use I should make of it in dealing with her.

BAZILE. Good-by. We shall all be here at four o'clock.
BARTHOLO. Why not sooner?
BAZILE. Impossible! The notary is engaged.
BARTHOLO. For a marriage?
BAZILE. Yes, at Figaro's house. His niece is being married.
BARTHOLO. His niece? He has no niece.
BAZILE. That's what they told the notary.
BARTHOLO. The devil take it! That fellow is in the plot.
BAZILE. Would you think . . . ?
BARTHOLO. Rogues like him are quite alert. My friend, this troubles me. Go to the notary's. Tell him to come here immediately with you.
BAZILE. It's raining and foul weather. But nothing will stop me from helping you. What are you going to do?
BARTHOLO. I will take you to the door. Figaro has crippled every servant in this house. I am alone here.
BAZILE. I have my lantern.
BARTHOLO. Here, Bazile, here is my passkey. I'll wait. I'll watch for you. Come who will, none but you and the notary will get in here tonight.
BAZILE. With such precautions as these, you are sure of your case.

SCENE 2. *Rosine (alone, coming out of her room).*

ROSINE. It seems to me I heard someone talking. It has just struck midnight. Lindor has not come. This bad weather must have helped him. He was sure not to meet a soul . . . Ah, Lindor! if you have deceived me! What is that noise? Heavens! it is my guardian. I must go back.

SCENE 3. *Rosine, Bartholo.*

BARTHOLO (*holding the lamp*). Ah, Rosine! since you have not yet gone back into your room . . .
ROSINE. I am going to retire.
BARTHOLO. In this terrible weather, you won't get any rest. And I have very important things to say.
ROSINE. What do you want from me? Isn't it enough to be tormented by day?
BARTHOLO. Rosine, listen to me.

THE BARBER OF SEVILLE

ROSINE. I will listen to you tomorrow.

BARTHOLO. One moment, I beg you!

ROSINE (*aside*). What if he should come!

BARTHOLO (*shows her the letter*). Do you recognize this letter?

ROSINE (*recognizes it*). Good heavens!

BARTHOLO. Rosine, my intention is not to reproach you. At your age, one can make mistakes. But I am your friend. Listen to me.

ROSINE. I can stand no more.

BARTHOLO. This letter that you wrote to Count Almaviva . . .

ROSINE (*astonished*). To Count Almaviva!

BARTHOLO. Now hear what a terrible man this Count is. As soon as he received it, he made a trophy out of it. I learned this from a woman to whom he gave it.

ROSINE. Count Almaviva!

BARTHOLO. I see it is hard for you to realize this horror. Inexperience, Rosine, makes your sex confiding and credulous. You should know the trap you were being drawn into. That woman told me the whole story, apparently in order to get rid of a rival as dangerous as you are. I tremble when I think of it! The most abominable plot between Almaviva, Figaro, and Alonzo, that imaginary pupil of Bazile, who bears another name and who is only a vile agent of the Count, was going to drag you down into an abyss from which nothing could have drawn you out.

ROSINE (*overwhelmed*). How horrible! . . . Why, Lindor! . . . why, that young man! . . .

BARTHOLO (*aside*). So! it is Lindor.

ROSINE. It is for Count Almaviva . . . It is for another . . .

BARTHOLO. That is what I was told when they gave me your letter.

ROSINE (*angry*). What a low trick! He will be punished for it. Sir, do you wish to marry me?

BARTHOLO. You know the ardor of my feelings.

ROSINE. If you still feel this way, I am yours.

BARTHOLO. Good! The notary is coming this very night.

ROSINE. That is not all. Oh, heaven! How humiliated I am! You should know that in a little while the traitor will enter through this window. They were skillful enough to steal the key from you.

BARTHOLO (*looks at his bunch of keys*). Oh! the rascals! My child, I will not leave you alone.

ROSINE (*in terror*). But what if they are armed?

BARTHOLO. You are right! I would lose my revenge. Go upstairs to Marcelline. Lock yourself in her room with a double bolt. I am going to get the police, and wait for him outside near the house. If he's arrested as a thief, we'll have the pleasure of being both avenged and delivered from him. You will see that my love will repay you . . .

ROSINE (*in despair*). You must forget my mistakes. (*Aside.*) I am surely punished for them.

BARTHOLO (*leaving*). Now, to set our trap! At last I have her. (*Exit* BARTHOLO.)

SCENE 4. *Rosine.*

ROSINE. His love will repay me! . . . How miserable I am! (*She takes her handkerchief and weeps.*) What can I do? He will come. I will stay, and pretend with him, so that I can see him for a moment in all his corruption. The baseness of his action will protect my feelings. I will need this. What a noble face, what gentleness, what a tender voice! . . . Yet he is the vile agent of a seducer! Oh! how wretched I am! Heaven! Someone is opening the blind. (*Runs out.*)

SCENE 5. *The Count, Figaro* (*wrapped in a cloak, appears at the window*).

FIGARO (*speaks from outside*). Someone ran off. Shall I go in?

COUNT (*outside*). A man?

FIGARO. No.

COUNT. It's Rosine. Your ugly face put her to flight.

FIGARO (*leaps into the room*). Yes, I think it did . . . Here we are at last in spite of the rain, the thunder, and the lightning.

COUNT (*wrapped in long cloak*). Give me your hand. (*Leaps in.*) Victory!

FIGARO (*throws off his cloak*). We're drenched. What charming weather to go looking for our fortune! My lord, how do you like this night?

COUNT. It is superb for a lover.

FIGARO. Yes, but what about the confidant? . . . And what if someone surprised us here?

COUNT. Aren't you with me? I have another worry: to persuade her to leave her guardian's house immediately.

FIGARO. You have on your side three passions that are very powerful over the fair sex: love, hate, and fear.

COUNT (*looking into the dark*). How can I tell her abruptly that the notary is waiting for her at your house to unite us? She will think this plan too bold. She will call me audacious.

FIGARO. If she calls you audacious, you call her cruel. Women like to be called cruel. Moreover, if your love is as strong as you think it, you will tell her who you are. You will not doubt your sentiments.

SCENE 6. *The Count, Rosine, Figaro.* (*Figaro lights all the candles on the table.*)

COUNT. Here she is! My lovely Rosine!

ROSINE (*calmly*). I was beginning to fear you would not come.

COUNT. Charming anxiety! . . . I must not take advantage of circumstances to propose that you share the lot of an unfortunate man. But whatever place of refuge you choose, I swear on my honor . . .

ROSINE. Sir, if the gift of my hand had not instantly followed the gift of my heart, you would not be here. I hope that necessity will justify for you the irregular aspects of this interview.

COUNT. You, Rosine, the companion of a poor wretch without fortune and birth!

ROSINE. Fortune and birth! Let us forget those games of chance. If you assure me that your intentions are pure . . .

COUNT (*at her feet*). Oh, Rosine! I love you!

ROSINE (*indignant*). Stop! You are a profaner. So you love me! Now you are no longer dangerous. I was waiting for that word in order to detest you. But before giving you over to the remorse which will be yours (*cries*) you should know that I loved you. My happiness was to be in sharing your unfortunate lot. Wicked Lindor! I was going to give up everything to follow you. But the cowardly abuse you made of my kindness, the indignity of the terrible Count Almaviva, to whom you sold me, caused this testimony of my weakness to come back to me. Do you recognize this letter?

COUNT (*excited*). Which your guardian gave you?

ROSINE (*proudly*). Yes, I am obliged to him for it.

COUNT. This makes me happy. I gave it to him. In my embarrassment yesterday, I used it to draw him out, and I could find no moment in which to tell you. Ah! Rosine, it is true, then, that you really loved me?

Figaro. My lord, you were looking for a woman who would love you for yourself . . .

Rosine. My lord! What is he saying?

Count (*throws off cloak, appears in rich clothes*). O beloved, I must not deceive you any longer. The happy man you see at your feet is not Lindor. I am Count Almaviva. I am desperately in love with you and have been vainly seeking you for six months.

Rosine (*falls into his arms*). Ah! . . .

Count (*frightened*). Figaro!

Figaro. Don't worry, my lord. The sweet emotion of joy never has any bad consequences. Now she is recovering her senses. My! She is beautiful!

Rosine. Ah, Lindor! Ah, my lord! How guilty I am! Tonight I was going to give myself to my guardian.

Count. You, Rosine!

Rosine. It was to be my punishment. I would have spent my life hating you. Ah, Lindor! The greatest torture is hating when one feels the desire to love.

Figaro (*looks out of window*). My lord, the return is blocked. The ladder has been removed.

Count. Removed!

Rosine (*anxious*). Yes, it is my fault. It was the doctor. This is the result of my credulity. He deceived me. I confessed all, betrayed all. He knows you are here and will come back with the police.

Figaro (*looks again*). My lord, they are opening the street gate.

Rosine (*fearfully runs into the* Count's *arms*). Ah, Lindor! . . .

Count (*firmly*). Rosine, you love me. I fear no one. You will be my wife. I will have the pleasure of punishing, as he deserves it, this hateful old man.

Rosine. No, no, you must pity him, Lindor. My heart is so full that there is no place for vengeance.

Scene 7. *Notary, Don Bazile, the preceding.*

Figaro. My lord, it is your notary.
Count. And friend Bazile with him.
Bazile. Ah! what do I see?

THE BARBER OF SEVILLE

FIGARO. By what chance, my friend . . .

BAZILE. By what accident, gentlemen . . .

NOTARY. Are these the betrothed?

COUNT. Yes, sir. You were to marry Miss Rosine and myself tonight at the barber Figaro's house, but we preferred this house for reasons I will tell you. Do you have our contract?

NOTARY. Have I the honor of speaking to his Excellency Count Almaviva?

FIGARO. Yes, it is he.

BAZILE (*aside*). So this is the reason he gave me the passkey.

NOTARY. You see, I have two marriage contracts, my lord. We must not confuse them. Here is yours. And here is the contract of Lord Bartholo and Miss . . . Rosine also. These young ladies are apparently two sisters who bear the same name.

COUNT. Let us sign the contract. Don Bazile will be good enough to serve as a second witness. (*They sign.*)

BAZILE. But, your Excellency . . . I don't understand . . .

COUNT. Master Bazile, a trifle embarrasses you and everything confuses you.

BAZILE. My lord! . . . But if the doctor . . .

COUNT (*throwing him a purse*). You're behaving like a child! Sign quickly.

BAZILE (*astonished*). Ah! Ah! . . .

FIGARO. Why is it so hard to sign?

BAZILE (*weighing the purse*). It isn't hard any more. You see, when I have once given my word, I need reasons of a great weight . . . (*He signs.*)

SCENE 8. *Bartholo, a justice of the peace, policemen, servants with torches, and the preceding.*

BARTHOLO (*sees the* COUNT *kiss* ROSINE'S *hand, and* FIGARO *grotesquely embrace* DON BAZILE. *He seizes the* NOTARY *by the throat and yells*). Rosine with these rogues! Arrest everyone. I have one by the collar.

NOTARY. It is your notary.

BAZILE. It is your notary. Is this a joke?

BARTHOLO. Ah! Don Bazile. How do you happen to be here?

BAZILE. And why weren't you here?

JUSTICE (*pointing to* FIGARO). One moment. I know this man. What are you doing in this house, at this late hour?

FIGARO. Late hour? You can see it is as close to morning as

to night. Moreover, I am in the company of his Excellency Count Almaviva.

BARTHOLO. Almaviva?

LA JEUNESSE. They are not thieves then?

BARTHOLO. Let us skip that. Everywhere else, my lord, I am the servant of your Excellency. But you understand that the superiority of rank here has no effect. I beg you to leave.

COUNT. Yes, rank is not important here, but what is important is the preference which Miss Rosine has granted me over you, by willingly giving herself to me.

BARTHOLO. What is he saying, Rosine?

ROSINE. He speaks the truth. Why are you surprised? Wasn't I to be avenged of a deceiver this very night? I am.

BAZILE. Didn't I tell you it was the Count himself, Doctor?

BARTHOLO. That is of no importance. This is a joke of a marriage. Where are the witnesses?

NOTARY. Nothing is lacking. These two gentlemen assisted me.

BARTHOLO. What! Bazile! Did you sign?

BAZILE. What could I do? The pockets of this gentleman are always full of irresistible arguments.

BARTHOLO. I scorn his arguments. I shall use my authority.

COUNT. You lost it when you misused it.

BARTHOLO. The young lady is a minor.

FIGARO. She has just come of age.

BARTHOLO. Who is speaking to you, you rascal?

COUNT. This lady is noble and beautiful. I am a man of rank, young and rich. She is my wife. Do you intend to dispute her with me over that title which honors us equally?

BARTHOLO. You will never take her from me.

COUNT. She is no longer in your power. I place her under the authority of the law. And this gentleman, whom you brought here yourself, will protect her against the violence you may wish to use. The real magistrates are the protectors of all those who are oppressed.

LA JEUNESSE. Most certainly. And this useless resistance to the most honorable marriage indicates clearly his terror over the bad administration of the property of his ward, of which he will have to render account.

COUNT. If he gives his consent, I will ask for nothing.

FIGARO. Except the receipt for my hundred crowns. Let's not lose our heads.

BARTHOLO (*irritated*). They were all against me. I stuck my head into a wasp's nest.

BAZILE. What wasp's nest? If you can't have the woman, Doctor, remember that you can have the money, and . . .

BARTHOLO. Eh! let me alone, Bazile. All you think of is money. I pay no attention to money. So I will keep it. But do you think that is the motive which has made up my mind? (*Signs*.)

FIGARO (*laughing*). Ha, ha, ha! my lord. They belong to the same family.

NOTARY. But gentlemen, I make nothing out of this. Aren't there two ladies who have the same name?

FIGARO. No, sir, there is only one.

BARTHOLO (*sadly*). And it was I who took away the ladder, so that the marriage would be more certain. Ah! I was defeated for lack of precautions.

FIGARO. For lack of good sense. Let's be fair, Doctor. When youth and love are agreed to deceive an old man, all that he does in order to prevent it can justly be called *The Useless Precaution*.

NOTES

1. A parody of a line from Voltaire's poem, *La Henriade* (IX, 45).
2. "Bartholo does not like plays. Perhaps he had composed a tragedy in his youth." (Note by Beaumarchais.) Bartholo preferred the old *tragédie* which was beginning to give way to the new *drame*.
3. *Consilio manuque:* by deliberation and by force.
4. There is no indication in the play who Mistress Figaro is.
5. *Balordo:* Italian for "booby."

SELECTED BIBLIOGRAPHY

FRENCH CLASSICISM

Borgerhoff, E. B. O., *The Freedom of French Classicism*. Princeton University Press, 1950.

Peyre, Henri, *Le Classicisme Français*. Maison Française, New York, 1942.

Turnell, Martin, *The Classical Moment: Studies of Corneille, Molière, Racine*. New Directions, 1947.

CORNEILLE

Œuvres de Corneille. Edition Marty-Laveaux. Grands Ecrivains de France. Hachette. 12 vols.

Brasillach, Robert, *Corneille*. Fayard, 1938.

Dorchain, A., *Pierre Corneille*. Paris, 1918.

Lanson, Gustave, *Pierre Corneille*. Paris, 1913.

May, Georges, *Tragédie corneillienne, tragédie racinienne*. University of Illinois Press, 1948.

RACINE

Œuvres Complètes de Racine. Edition Raymond Picard. Paris, 1951–52.

Brereton, Geoffrey, *Jean Racine, a critical biography*. London, 1951.

Lapp, John C., *Aspects of Racinian Tragedy*. Toronto, 1955.

Maulnier, Thierry, *Racine*. Gallimard, 1936.

Mauriac, François, *La Vie de Racine*. Paris, 1928.

MOLIÈRE

Œuvres Complètes de Molière. Edition Despois et Mesnard. Grands Ecrivains de France. Hachette, 1873–1893. 13 vols.

Brisson, Pierre, *Molière, sa vie dans ses œuvres*. Gallimard, 1942.

Fernandez, Ramon, *Molière: the man seen through the plays*. Hill and Wang, 1958.

Fowlie, Wallace, *Dionysus in Paris*. (chapter: *Molière Today*.) Meridian Books, 1960.

Simon, Alfred, *Molière par lui-même*. Editions du Seuil, 1957.

SELECTED BIBLIOGRAPHY

MARIVAUX

Théâtre Complet de Marivaux. Edition de la Pléiade, Gallimard, 1955.

Arland, M., *Marivaux*, 1950.

Larroumet, G., *Marivaux, sa vie et ses œuvres*. Hachette, 1882.

McKee, Kenneth, *Theater of Marivaux*. New York University Press, 1958.

BEAUMARCHAIS

Théâtre de Beaumarchais. Edition de la Pléiade, Gallimard, 1949.

Bailly, A., *Beaumarchais*. Paris, 1945.

Hallays, A., *Beaumarchais*. Hachette, 1897.

BANTAM WORLD DRAMA

Introducing a new library of living theater—from Euripides to Osborne. This series contains authoritative editions as well as fresh modern translations of the classics and important contemporary plays including the latest experiments of the avant-garde. Many of the plays contain introductions and commentaries by leading critics and scholars.

☐ THREE PLAYS Thornton Wilder	ST7	75¢
☐ CYRANO DE BERGERAC Edmond Rostand	HT5	60¢
☐ FOUR GREAT PLAYS Ibsen	HT6	60¢
☐ PLAYS William Saroyan	NT10	95¢
☐ TEN PLAYS Euripides	NT11	95¢
☐ COMPLETE PLAYS OF SOPHOCLES	NT4021	95¢
☐ ELIZABETHAN DRAMA	QT4031	1.25
☐ RESTORATION DRAMA	QT4041	1.25
☐ EIGHTEENTH-CENTURY ENGLISH DRAMA	QT4032	1.25
☐ MAN AND SUPERMAN George Bernard Shaw	NT20	95¢
☐ CLASSICAL FRENCH DRAMA	NT4096	95¢

PLAYS BY ARTHUR MILLER

☐ THE CRUCIBLE	NT2	95¢
☐ INCIDENT AT VICHY	NT3	95¢
☐ AFTER THE FALL	NT4	95¢
☐ A VIEW FROM THE BRIDGE	NT1	95¢

PLAYS BY JOHN OSBORNE

☐ LOOK BACK IN ANGER	NT17	95¢
☐ THE ENTERTAINER	NT8	95¢
☐ EPITAPTH FOR GEORGE DILLON	NT9	95¢

AVAILABLE WHEREVER PAPERBACKS ARE SOLD

Bantam Books, Inc., Dept. NWD, Room 607, 271 Madison Ave., New York, N. Y. 10016

Please send me the Bantam Books which I have checked. I am enclosing $_____ (check or money order—no currency please). Sorry, no C.O.D.'s. Note: Please include 10¢ per book for postage and handling.

Name_____

Address_____

City_____ State_____ Zip Code_____

Allow two to three weeks for delivery   NWD-11-67

Bantam Modern Classics

- [ ] SY4018 APE AND ESSENCE Aldous Huxley 75¢
- [ ] SY4014 MADELEINE André Gide 75¢
- [ ] SY4012 DESERT OF LOVE François Mauriac 75¢
- [ ] NY4058 THE TIME OF THE ASSASSINS Godfrey Blunden 95¢
- [ ] NY4010 GOODBYE, COLUMBUS Philip Roth 95¢
- [ ] NY4054 DEMIAN Hermann Hesse 95¢
- [ ] NY4009 ALL THE KING'S MEN Robert Penn Warren 95¢
- [ ] QY4013 MAN'S HOPE André Malraux $1.25
- [ ] QY4006 THE LAST TEMPTATION OF CHRIST Nikos Kazantzakis $1.25
- [ ] NY4089 LADY CHATTERLEY'S LOVER D. H. Lawrence 95¢
- [ ] SY4074 ZAZIE Raymond Queneau 75¢
- [ ] NY4090 EYELESS IN GAZA Aldous Huxley 95¢
- [ ] NY4008 DARKNESS AT NOON Arthur Koestler 95¢

Available wherever paperbacks are sold

BANTAM BOOKS, INC., Dept. BMODC, Room 300, 271 Madison Ave., New York, N. Y. 10016

Please send me the Bantam Books which I have checked. I am enclosing $_____(check or money order—no currency please). Sorry, no C.O.D.'s. Note: Please include 10¢ per book for postage and handling on orders of less than 5 books. Allow two to three weeks for delivery.

Name_____

Address_____

City_____ State_____ Zip Code_____

BMODC 1/68

RUSSIAN LITERATURE

☐ **NC283 TEN EARLY PLAYS / CHEKHOV......95¢**
The only complete collection of Chekhov's short plays, this edition includes Ivanov, Uncle Vanya, The Wood Demon, plus eight one-act plays. Edited and translated by Alexander Szogyi.

☐ **HC190 FOUR GREAT PLAYS / CHEKHOV....60¢**
The Sea Gull, Uncle Vanya, Three Sisters, The Cherry Orchard. Translated by Constance Garnett.

☐ **HC140 CRIME AND PUNISHMENT / DOSTOEVSKY......60¢**
Translated from the Russian by Constance Garnett.

☐ **SC231 THE GAMBLER / DOSTOEVSKY......75¢**
The first new translation of this work in 50 years, by Andrew R. MacAndrew.

☐ **NC279 THE IDIOT / DOSTOEVSKY.........95¢**
Translated by Constance Garnett.

☐ **NC293 THREE SHORT NOVELS / DOSTOEVSKY......95¢**
Poor Folk, The Double, The Eternal Husband. Translated by Andrew R. MacAndrew.

☐ **SC168 NINETEENTH CENTURY RUSSIAN DRAMA......75¢**
John Gassner, general editor. The Stone Guest, by Pushkin; The Inspector General, by Gogol; A Month in the Country, by Turgenev; The Thunderstorm, by Ostrovsky; The Power of Darkness, by Tolstoy. Translated and edited by Andrew R. MacAndrew.

CRL 1/68

☐ **H2669 ONE DAY IN THE LIFE OF
IVAN DENISOVICH / SOLZHENITSYN**...60¢
The brutal portrayal of life in a Siberian prison camp. Translated by Ronald Hingley and Max Hayward.

☐ **QD1014 RUSSIAN STORIES**................$1.25
Gleb Struve, editor. Twelve original works presented with facing-page translations, special vocabulary, notes on unusual phrases and expressions, and a history of the development of Russian literature. A Dual-Language Edition.

☐ **NC180 ANNA KARENINA / TOLSTOY**.......95¢
Translated by Joel Carmichael.

☐ **NC291 WAR AND PEACE / TOLSTOY**.......95¢
An abridged edition, translated by Constance Garnett.

☐ **HC214 FATHERS AND SONS / TURGENEV**..60¢
Translated by Barbara Makanowitzky.

☐ **SC92 FIVE SHORT NOVELS / TURGENEV**....75¢
The Diary of a Superfluous Man, Rudin, First Love, A King Lear of the Steppe, Spring Torrents. Translated by Franklin Reeve.

BANTAM BOOKS ARE AVAILABLE AT NEWSSTANDS EVERYWHERE

BANTAM BOOKS, INC., Dept. CRL, 271 Madison Ave., New York, N. Y. 10016
Please send me the Bantam Books which I have checked. I am enclosing $.........
(Check or Money Order—No Currency Please.) Sorry, no C.O.D.'s. Note: Please include 10¢ per book for postage and handling on orders of less than 5 books.

Name_____

Address_____

City_____State_____Zip_____
Allow two to three weeks for delivery   CRL 1/68